Boston Cocktails: Drunk & Told

The Follow-up to 2012's

Drink & Tell: A Boston Cocktail Book

With Over 850 New Recipes!

Frederic Yarm

Copyright

֍֍֍

Table of Contents

"Are you a Mixologist?"

"No. I water down spirits and babysit adults.
And sometimes, we do arts and crafts..."

Acknowledgements

A lot of my major thanks were covered in the first book's acknowledgements; however, many of these bear repeating. First, I am thankful to the Boston bartenders who gave their time, recipes, and hospitality to make this second edition possible. It has been a great adventure for me starting as an enthusiast and learning the art from our city's bartenders before writing the first book to becoming a professional bartender and enjoying the other bartenders' comradery and sharing of information before writing the second. Again, I am grateful for my wife Andrea for being the impetus to start mixing drinks, for being the best drinking companion I could ask for, and for putting up with cocktails taking over my life. Thanks again to Jessica Marcus who was inspired by my drink journaling to take things to the next level by starting a blog and later inviting me along on the ride.

In my development from writer to bartender, I would like to thank John Gertsen for his drink mentorship and words of support from my early visits at No. 9 Park to my early years as a bartender. I am ever thankful to Matthew Schrage for providing me the opportunity to get behind the stick for a night and planting a seed of what my next career path should be. And to Sam Gabrielli who hired me at Russell House Tavern, as well as to the bartenders and barbacks there who helped guide me through my first bar job. There are plenty of others along the way such as Dave Cagle who saw something in me and frequently told me before the first book was ever published that I should consider bartending as a profession.

As for writing this book, I am thankful for the folk who guided me through the first one such that the second one almost wrote itself. A few of these characters include Camper English, Cecilia Tan, Stephanie Schorow, and Ed Walter's mom. Sadly, Ed's mom passed away in January of 2015. After the funeral service, we gathered at the Walter house and Ed showed me the book that I had signed. It read, "Mother Helen, thank you for convincing me to do this! Cheers, Frederic Yarm." Ed then reminded me that his mom was quite proud of how her words of encouragement had such a profound effect on me. Sláinte!

And thank you to the blog readers and book purchasers who have kept in contact over the years and have sat at either of my bars. The words of encouragement and thanks have helped to keep my motivation for drink writing high.

Thanks to the following bars and restaurants for their recipes, knowledge, and guidance:

A4cade
Abigail's
Alden & Harlow
Ames Street
Area Four Boston
Armsby Abbey
Art Bar
Audubon
Automatic
Backbar
Bancroft
Bar Mezzana
Barrel House Beverly
Belly
Benedetto
Bergamot
Blue Dragon
Blue Room
Boston College Club
Brick & Mortar
Bronwyn
Casa B
Catalyst
Central Kitchen
Citizen Public House
Citizen (Worcester)
Clio
Craigie on Main
Dante
Deep Ellum
Drink
East Coast Grill
Eastern Standard
Estragon

Fairsted Kitchen
Felipe's
Firebrand Saints
Franklin Café
Franklin Southie
Frogmore
Gallows
GrandTen Distillery Bar
Green Street
Hawthorne
Highball Lounge
Highland Kitchen
Hojoko
Hungry Mother
Independent
Island Creek Oyster Bar
J.M. Curley
Kirkland Tap & Trotter
La Brasa
Lincoln
Lineage
Little Donkey
Local 149
Loyal Nine
Merrill & Co.
Mooo
Myers & Chang
No. 9 Park
Park Cambridge
Pomodoro
Puritan & Co.
Regal Beagle
Rendezvous
Rialto

Ribelle
Russell House Tavern
Saloon
Sarma
Scholars
Shojo
Short & Main
Sichuan Garden II
Silvertone
Sinclair
Spoke
State Park
Steel & Rye
Stoddard's
Straight Law
Sunday Salon
Sycamore
Tavern Road
Temple Bar
Think Tank
Tiger Mama
Toro
Townshend
Townsman
Trade
Tremont 647
Trina's Starlite Lounge
Upstairs on the Square
Viale
Ward 8
West Bridge
Wink & Nod
Yvonne's
Zocalo

Finally, I would like to acknowledge the help in naming both of my books. The name for the first book was one that took a little mulling over until I decided to read over all of the clues that Jessica left on the blog when she set it up as well as updated it for the additional writers a few months later. In the "Who? What?" description in the upper right was the answer in, "The euphemisms are getting a bit stale, suffice to say: four people in Boston -- two of whom are much more prolific writers than the other two (including the originator of this blog, who has no excuse apart from laziness) -- who drink and tell."

For the second book, I read through all of the text driven parts of the blog to uncover the next name. Unfortunately, that was not so successful. Instead of giving up, I utilized a lifeline on Facebook and asked for suggestions. The winner "Drunk & Told" came first from my father of all people followed by two people who said the same thing without reading through the replies first. I was hoping for a different name so that I could refer to the first book as D&T and this one as another set of initials. To avoid confusion or having to refer to this as D&T2, I decided to swap things around and call it "Boston Cocktails: Drunk & Told" instead of "Drunk & Told: Yet Another Boston Cocktail Book."

I was indeed amused by the other responses, and here are a smattering of them:

Truth or Drink
Love on the Rocks
Drink & Tell II: The Yarmening
Drink & Tell II: Electric Bugaloo
Drink & Tell II: Drink Harder, Tell Harder
I Still Know What You Drank & Told
A Good Day to Drink & Tell Hard
Drink & Tellnado
I Came, I Drank, I Told
I Make Drinks to Make Other People More Interesting
A Guy Walks into a Boston Cocktail Bahh
Guns, Germs, & Genever
The Origins of Consciousness in the Breakdown of the
    Undershaken Fernet Flip
Do Androids Dream of Electric Blenders?

Ryan McGrale

(No. 9 Park, Hawthorne, Storyville, and Tavern Road)

December 18, 1978 – November 14, 2015

Last call came too soon.
I'll buy the first round the next time I see you.

Introduction

My cocktail journey began in 2006 when my wife suggested that we make drinks on Sunday nights to enjoy on our second floor deck overlooking scenic Winter Hill, and I began collecting recipes on my LiveJournal. What was the first drink I made? The Cosmopolitan! It was easy given our small bar at home. Over time, the drinks got more advanced between seeking out better cocktail books and seeking out better liquor bottles. I tried to build the bottle collection slowly by obeying the "two hand rule" where I restricted myself to purchasing two bottles per trip to the liquor store. Within a few months, I had stumbled upon the Pegu Club that not only gave me an appreciation for gin but was the first cocktail I made at home that I still proudly suggest and make for guests. While my first drink book purchase was Mittie Hellmich's *The Ultimate Bar Book*, my drink making took off with the purchase of an old Trader Vic cocktail book as well as Patrick Duffy's *The Official Mixer's Manual*.

About a year later in June 2007, my wife commented that we ought to go out to this bar in town that was making drinks like we were making at home. I replied that no one was making drinks like we were making at home. Boy was I wrong, for that trip to Eastern Standard opened our eyes, and our first craft bartender, Tommy Schlessinger-Guidelli, shaped our view of what hospitality and what a bartender could be. We soon started exploring other bars including Green Street, Deep Ellum, and No. 9 Park to name but a few.

My journaling continued, and it inspired my friend Jessica Marcus to start the *Cocktail Virgin* blog in September of 2007. The title described how she was entering into the world of cocktails and exploring. Her start was a lot more dignified than my early cocktail journal entries; for example, her fourth drink recipe posted was the Lucien Gaudin and her tenth was the Last Word. By May of 2008, she felt that the name was inappropriate, and she felt experienced enough to change the name to *Cocktail ~~Virgin~~ Slut*. It was unrelated to her opening the blog up a month later to my wife Andrea, our mutual friend Rishi, and myself to join in on the fun. And luckily, Jess did not change the name to *Cocktail Orgy*. Although perhaps *Cocktail Swingers* has enough class and intrigue to have worked.

The first major change in my seriousness about cocktailing was in Spring of 2009 when I submitted my celery bitters recipe to a competition searching for the first offerings of Barkeep Bitters. It was only open to bartenders, but I asked John Gertsen if I could claim that I was a barback at Drink. John agreed and let me bus a few glasses for which I was paid a quarter. A few weeks later, I was surprised that I had made the finalist cut in that bitters challenge. Andrea was excited and declared that we should go to Tales of the Cocktail that year so that I could compete. That was 6 weeks out and by 4 or 5 weeks out, we decided that we would elope in New Orleans as well. That trip brought me in contact with greats like Ted Haigh, Wayne Curtis, Paul Clarke, Chuck Taggart, and others, and it brought me to great bars like The Cure. Unfortunately, my bitters did not win the spot despite being one of the owners' favorites. But it did advance me into the next level of thinking about the world of cocktails.

While my excitement kept growing, the other writers on the blog seemed to fizzle out with the last post being from Andrea around 2010. During that time, I was working at a biotech company where my boss supported my blogging on company time as long as everything he asked for got done when he needed it. That job continued until the final week of 2011 when I had completed my last project. I remember applying to more biochemistry jobs in the first few months of 2012 with good spirits and a positive outlook. After four months or so, my mood began to darken. One of my friends needed some help with his Mac, and I stopped over to lend expertise. As the files were transferring, I went downstairs where Ed's mom was sitting. Ed's mom Helen gestured that I should sit down and have some coffee with her. She fondly remembered having coffee with Henry at this table. Knowing that Ed used to manage punk bands, I asked "Henry Rollins?" Why yes, and she continued on as to how I reminded her of Milo. "Milo of the Descendents?" Yes again, and I found this curious for Milo Aukerman was a biochemist too, and he switched between that and punk rock throughout the years. Then she told me that I should write a book.

9

I mulled over the idea for a few weeks until Camper English of *Al-cademics* was in town, and I took him on an epic five-stop bar crawl. Somewhere early on in the libation process, I asked Camper for his opinion on the book concept. He declared that he had thought about doing a similar concept for San Francisco, but he ended up not doing so; however, he did give me some solid advice and great motivation to start this project. When I say start this project, I had already been sitting on years of recipes and drink photos that desperately needed to be organized and curated. People were surprised to hear that I wrote a book in 3 months (with a 4th month spent with logistics), but it was certainly not just a few months in the making.

Once the ball got rolling, I began getting up at 8 am every morning, powering myself up with coffee, and beginning to work at or before 9 am. My attitude soured by months of unemployment brightened for I had a project to do. I think that the layout of all 505 drinks into the book happened in a 3 day highly caffeinated binge that was in excess of 40 hours of computer time.

In September 2012, my book *Drink & Tell: A Boston Cocktail Book* was released. The announcement that my book was about to come out generated a lot of surprise since I had not started posting about things on social media until August when my first galley proof had showed up on my doorstep. The publication of the book was a catalyst for the local press to take my efforts seriously in ways that they had not really done before when I was merely a blogger. Soon, I was interviewed by *Boston Magazine*, the *Boston Globe*, the *Metro*, and *Eater-Boston*, and then I was invited to speak at Portland Cocktail Week in a session on writing a book and to teach a class with John Gertsen at Barbara Lynch's Stir on the history of Boston cocktails. The biggest change was when Matt Schrage invited me to get behind the bar at the Blue Room during their Whiskey-Amari night series. Each week in February of 2013 (plus a fifth bonus night in March), there were two bartenders who put together a menu, and it turned out that I was the only one of the ten who was not a professional bartender. My partner in crime for the night was Katie Emmerson then of the Hawthorne, and we put together a nine drink list of novel cocktails in tribute to the "Women of the Wild West." The night went well – perhaps too well. I semi-jokingly commented to my wife that I should become a bartender to which she replied that I should. I was surprised by her seriousness and questioned when I would see her since much of bartending is on the opposite schedule of the day walkers. She supported the idea with something along the lines of "we'll figure it out."

I still was applying to biotech jobs after the book project was over, and I remember being at an interview dressed in a suit and tie and realizing that I was more excited about my barback stage at Drink the following week than I was about this company. What I learned in this phase of job seeking was that pretty much no one wanted to hire me in the bar world. I parsed together that I was too old and knowledgeable to be a barback and I was too inexperienced in restaurants to be a bartender. It was an odd concept, but I would not take no and the undertone of "just go away" for an answer in my quest. Finally, Sam Gabrielli on Facebook put up a post looking for a barback, and alas, I had my start in the business. I attribute a lot of my future success to Sam for first giving me a chance when the rest of Boston had seemingly turned their back on me, and for second teaching me how to be a good barman from the basics of stocking a bar to the minutia of hospitality. For that, I will always be raising a Valkyrie cocktail in your honor, sir. Moreover, I would like to raise a Fernet to Adam Hockman, James Miranda, John McElroy, Victor Pelegrin, and Ashish Mitra at Russell House Tavern for their tutelage along the way.

Over the course of two years, I worked my way up from barback to daytime bartender to a mix of days and nights. I remember blogger Erik Ellestad and others warning me that my writing would trail off once I started bartending professionally. It did slightly in 2014 as I dedicated a lot more time learning about the world of beer, but my post count soon rebounded. In early 2015, I decided that I needed to change my surroundings and applied for and accepted a job at Loyal Nine as a bartender. Soon, I was running the weekly menu at the rather successful Yacht Rock Sundays. And with the opening head bartender's departure, I soon took over that role and its responsibilities.

As I wrote in the acknowledgements for *Drink & Tell*, people would always ask if I was ever planning on writing a first book, and I always shrugged away the concept. After the book was released, people wondered if there was going to be a second. I explained that the book never made me a lot of money, but perhaps one day I would do it all again. About 4 years after my working on the first book, I found myself on an airplane flying off to Tales of the Cocktail in July 2016. I was trying to figure out what to do with myself and with the restaurant's bar program to elevate things. In that list of drink ideas and other concepts was the note "Book by September 2017: 5 year anniversary."

Since the publication of the first book, I had been keeping a Microsoft Word file of all of the Boston drinks just in case I decided to write another book. The list making process by going through all of the blog entries was enormously time consuming the first time, but doing it piecemeal was not as trying. Unlike the first time, I was not unemployed though, and I wondered if I could get the job done in my 3 days off each week (which also included my sleep recovery, errands, and adventures on the town). I then decided at the end of August 2016 that if I put one foot in front of the other, eventually the journey would find itself at the finish line. I slowly began collecting material, and I started ramping up as the colder weather set in.

Like the first book, I tried to stick to the philosophies of *Beta Cocktails* in terms of how the majority of their recipes were easy to make without infusions or difficult to source spirits. For the syrups and shrubs, I included only those that were easy to make or available commercially. I do understand the frustration that many of these drinks cannot be made with the average home bar inventory, but hopefully, there are enough here to make this collection worthwhile. Likewise, may these recipes inspire you to figure out what to buy next to expand your home drinking experiences. Do not feel obligated to match the brands listed; use your best judgment to determine which spirit would match the flavor profile. Often, individual drink recipes were made with a variety of brands over the years depending on what was available at the bar. Moreover, in this book's technique section, I recommended some substitutions to make in a pinch and attempted to rate these suggestions by their degree of interchangeability.

This book like the previous one is not meant to be a collection of classics or even your first or second book; it is meant to be a supplement to a basic library. I do not see my role as recreating the wheel by making a better basic bar guide with recipes that have been published countless times through the years. For those, I would recommend Robert Hess' *The Essential Bartender's Guide*, Dale DeGroff's *The Craft of the Cocktail*, and Gary Regan's *The Joy of Mixology* which do it with panache. Moreover, neither of my books were meant to be a beginner's guide with extensive sections on technique. I did include a small technique section here as well as in my last book, but please do yourself a favor and read Jeffrey Morgenthaler's *The Bar Book* and Dave Stolte's *Home Bar Basics* or any of the three books by Hess, DeGroff, and Regan mentioned above. Use those books as a guide to select the right tools from shaker tins to jiggers and to learn the proper techniques.

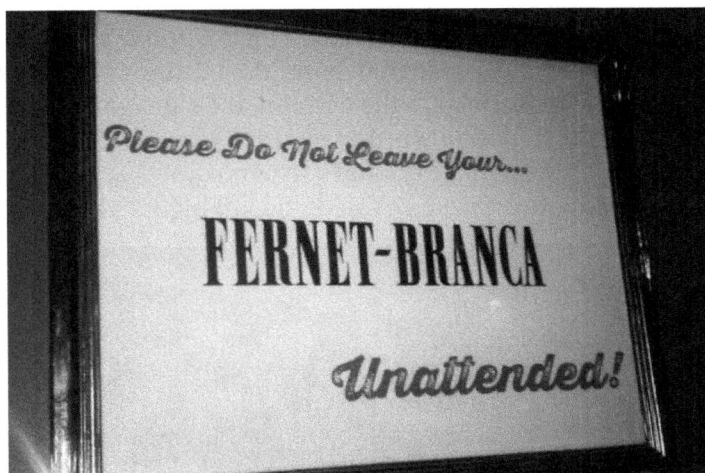

Please use this book to supplement the classics as well as a way to learn about Boston cocktail culture. The drink recipes in both of these books span a decade-plus of time, and a good number of these establishments have either closed or undergone significant changes, so think of these collections as a time capsule of what Boston was. And consider these drinks as the roots the city uses to base its new growth upon. If you have experienced these bars and their cocktails first hand, hopefully the recipes inside will be of some of your favorite drinks and will bring back fond memories of great friends and great hospitality. While Boston is definitely more than a collection of recipes, one has to start somewhere. And a drink is often a great place to start one's adventure. Cheers!

Speakeasies in Boston

Some of the best cocktail dens in Boston follow the Speakeasy-aesthetic popularized by Manhattan bars such as Milk & Honey and P.D.T. No, not something akin to the illicit bars that popped up during Prohibition and that still exist according to hearsay across town, but ones hidden in plain sight. Drink perhaps started the movement by picking a then somewhat desolate stretch of Fort Point and putting up a miniscule sign to indicate that it existed; however, the windows at foot level did give passers-by a gander into the ice block chipping and cocktail making that was occurring within. John Gertsen and Ben Sandrof worked with their No. 9 Park owner Barbara Lynch to open this world-class cocktail Mecca in the latter end of 2008. To perhaps mirror the bygone days of alcohol bans, the bottles at Drink are all hidden from view. Despite the acclaim, the signage has still remained minimal; however, word of mouth has made a doorman at the bottom of the stairs necessary to control the occupancy of the room that is often packed even on the off nights of the week.

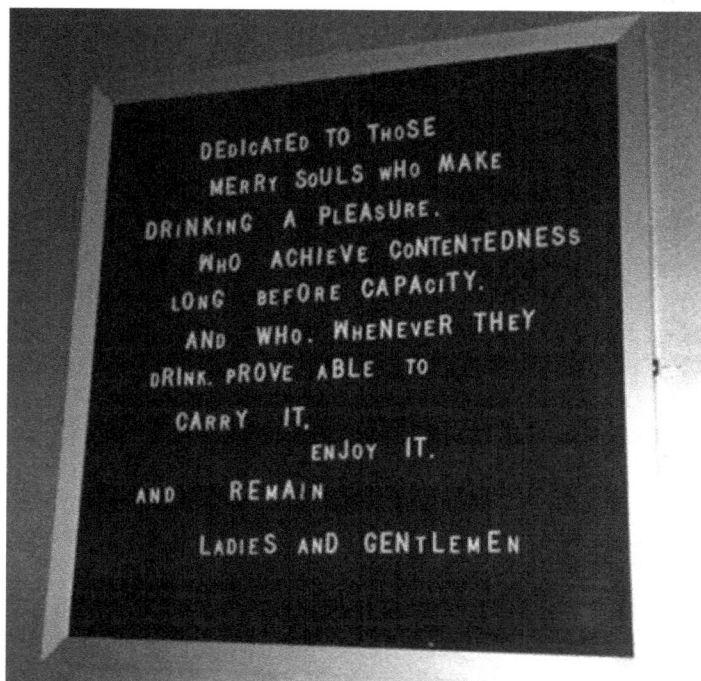

DEDICATED TO THOSE MERRY SOULS WHO MAKE DRINKING A PLEASURE. WHO ACHIEVE CONTENTEDNESS LONG BEFORE CAPACITY. AND WHO, WHENEVER THEY DRINK, PROVE ABLE TO CARRY IT. ENJOY IT. AND REMAIN LADIES AND GENTLEMEN

Three rather notable Speakeasy establishments were all spawned by or initially headed by Drink alum all around the 2010-2011 timeframe. First, Brick & Mortar maintains this aesthetic by having absolutely no signage whatsoever. They are simply the unlabeled door next to Central Kitchen's labeled one, and the steps lead up to what used to be the Enormous Room and before that, when I first got to town, a rather good Indian restaurant. Central Kitchen's ownership collaborated with Patrick Sullivan, best known for founding the legendary B-Side Lounge before moving on to develop the cocktail program for the Legal Sea Food chain, to work on this project. Patrick's ace in the hole was bringing on Drink-alumni Misty Kalkofen to lead the program. There, Misty and the other starting staff assembled an edgy cocktail menu featuring mezcal, amari, sherry, and grappa all served from the copper horseshoe bar. A variety of bartending superstars have shared the stage there including Evan Harrison, Matt Schrage, Will Thompson, and Patrick Gaggiano, and the bar is still going strong today.

The second is Backbar that is hidden down an alley in Union Square, Somerville. Though there is a small sign next to the door, that door was less prominent than the entry to Journeyman restaurant. The bar idea began when the owners of Journeyman wanted to renew their lease after the first year, and the landlords forced them to take on the space behind the restaurant that previously housed offices with a separate entrance. The idea for the space was to open an adjoining bar that matched the same level of quality and presentation as the restaurant. The owners hired Sam Treadway and brought him back from Hawaii where he was the opening manager of a hotel bar, and Sam brought with him fellow Drink alumni Bryn Tattan. The bar still holds their creative initial concept by offering drink of the day and week as well as a frequently changing seasonal menu. To even add a bonus Speakeasy element to Backbar, the staff assembled a 5 seat bar in a large closet that they dubbed "7 Minutes in Heaven." This bar within a bar (technically, it is off the hallway just before entering the main bar's space) holds theme nights with both house and guest bartenders and sells seats by a reservation system.

The third one spawned by Drink bartenders pre-dated the other two and actually ran its course before the other two opened. Not too long after Ben Sandrof left Drink to become a liquor rep, he began to miss bartending. He soon found an outlet by collaborating with Trina's Starlite Lounge in Spring of 2010; Trina's had two bars that were connected by a hallway near the bathrooms, but they soon found it not worth opening the second bar except on Friday and Saturday nights. Ben was able to secure the bar on Sunday evenings to make recipes that he enjoyed back in his days of No. 9 Park and Drink as well as newer ones. Instead of using the front door at Trina's, the back door that led into this second bar area was left unlocked that night, and people who found their way in by word of mouth were treated to a special menu for the "Sunday Salon" that varied week to week. Most nights, it was a small collection of regulars both cocktail enthusiasts and bartenders, although on a few nights it was a bit more rowdy as the unofficial after-event gathering spot. Luckily, most nights were delightfully sedate and cocktail-centric with Ben showcasing drinks like the Silent Order and Cuban Anole. Ben did give me permission on writing about the drinks, but we agreed to keep the venue identity under wraps. Sadly, what we had cheekily dubbed "Ben's Backdoor" had to end after a little over a year's run as Trina's Starlite Lounge decided to use the space to open their version of a sports bar, Parlor Sports, in Fall of 2011.

Other bars have taken on the aesthetic. For example, Saloon in Davis Square has a small sign affixed on the light globe above the door that leads to the steps down to their establishment. Hawthorne, despite the windows, has no signage and the entrance is within the Commonwealth Hotel on a door solely marked "500A." Hawthorne, Saloon, and Brick & Mortar actually all opened about the same time. Wink & Nod in the South End has also adopted the ideals especially given their name; the biggest tell of their location is probably their doorman. And more recently, the A4cade's entrance in Central Square is hidden within a Roxy's Grilled Cheese via a swinging kitchen door followed by a faux-walk in refrigerator door. Indeed, sometimes getting there is half the fun.

The Daiquiri Time Out

The combination of rum, lime, and sugar is a beautiful triangular thing when all the forces are in balance. While the combination had probably been done countless times before the drink was named the Daiquiri, it is often associated with 1898 Cuba. Charles H. Baker Jr. in *The Gentleman's Companion* described how malaria and other germ fears made people very careful of what they drank on the island, and the alcohol and the acid helped to purify liquids, and the sugar and ice helped to make the medicine go down easier. Baker cites Harry Stout, his friend, and Jennings Cox, a mining engineer associate for Bethlehem Steel, as the two main conspirators that summer of 1898. They came up with the drink in the village of Daiquiri near Santiago, and the drink took the name; also supporting the story is the fact that this was in close proximity to the original Bacardi rum distillery. On drink balance, Baker insisted, "And remember please, that a too-sweet Daiquiri is like a lovely lady with too much perfume."

The Daiquiri has also been tied to Boston with its role in rum production up until Prohibition as well as during the last few years with craft distilleries popping up across the map. The Massachusetts-based Kennedy clan were big fans of the drink whether on Martha's Vineyard or on the mainland. And the drink started a phenomenon in 2010 when M.S. Walker sales rep Andrew Dietz and friends came together on Martha's Vineyard to discuss the historical and sociological importance of this epic Rum Sour. His efforts amounting to countless Daiquiris and Daiquiri-drinking converts being made across town was celebrated in Boston in 2013 at the Thing gala for the Thirst Boston cocktail summit. I will always remember the moment when a hidden room opened late in the night and we were surprised with the opportunity to take a moment. For this bonus room had some of the city's best bartenders including John Gertsen, Misty Kalkofen, and Sam Treadway armed with tins and ready to shake and strain Daiquiris for all.

The Daiquiri Time Out movement hit a bigger stage when Dietz teamed up with Ann Tuennerman of Tales of the Cocktail in 2015 to bring the #DTO to the world with a ballroom filled with a few dozen rum and cachaça brands from large international companies down to small upstart distilleries. Each brand was supported by a bar crew who mixed up Daiquiris or variations to highlight the individual spirit and their home bar that they represented.

I found that there was no better way to capture the Daiquiri Time Out phenomenon than to interview the biggest DTO advocate out there – namely, Andrew Dietz:

What year did the DTO start for you? What were the circumstances?

The DTO started in the summer of 2010. A group of like-minded friends and myself were out on Martha's Vineyard (specifically Chappaquiddick) discussing some historical situations and how they may have played out differently had the people involved stopped, taken a moment, and had a well-made Daiquiri to pontificate upon. We didn't make a decision for the following week without a Daiquiri in hand.

Are DTOs full sized drinks? Are they split?

A DTO is a celebration of the act of taking a moment through one of the most simple and versatile cocktails of all time. Everyone's DTO is different. It can be a shot or large format. It can be classic, blended, or an obscure rift – just as long as time slows down.

Describe how the momentum behind the DTO built up to the room at Boston's The Thing 2013 and Tales of the Cocktail 2015?

The Daiquiri has a tremendous amount of history here in Massachusetts. Starting with the storied history of rum production, to the favoring of the cocktail by the Kennedys, to the modern resurgence of classic cocktails, this was bound to be a cocktail we aligned with here. I got back from Martha's Vineyard that summer and grabbed all of Boston's best bartending talent including Jackson Cannon, John Gertsen, Pat Sullivan, and many others, and lobbied that this is the way we should greet one another and celebrate our industry, and it took hold. The Thing was an event to celebrate Boston's best bartending talent, so it was only fitting that we stopped in the middle to take a collective time out. As for Tales, the DTO has spread across the country and even the globe, so given that Tales of the Cocktail is our national/global cocktail festival, Ann figured this was a good way for everyone to take a moment and celebrate what it is we all do.

Where does the Daiquiri fit into the cocktail craze?

The Daiquiri fits in beautifully for a couple of reasons. It is one of the simplest cocktails to make well while providing an incredible canvas for improvisation. I think the Daiquiri will be an important cocktail for many years to come.

Can you judge how good a bartender is by their balance and ingredient choices?

As for judgment, I'm biased... of course I do!

What have you learned about bars from their Daiquiri theory and quality?

Watching the different variants of the DTO has taught me a lot because the DTO is as much about hospitality as it is about quality. I have seen bars create DTO-only cocktail lists, mail DTOs via FedEx, make frozen DTO popsicles, dehydrate DTO into powder, [use] DTO-filled squirt guns, and many more. It has taught me all of the different ways that we can celebrate and collaborate in this industry and have a great deal of enjoyment doing it. As for the Daiquiris themselves I have seen an endless amount of variations at this point so honestly it has only challenged my understanding of just how incredibly versatile a drink like this can be.

Do you have any favorite rums or combinations for a DTO? Or any favorite Daiquiri riffs?

Tough to say. As I've said I have probably had a few thousand combinations at this point. My favorite DTO is usually the last one I had. With that said, it's January in Boston right now and the last Plantation 5 Year Barbados DTO I had tasted pretty damn good.

Have you embraced or separated from the Kennedy history?

Haha, can I say no comment? I'll say this, the Kennedys were Massachusetts royalty and seemed to love life and Daiquiris as much as I do. We happened to come up with this concept while hanging on Chappaquiddick. If there were Daiquiris consumed on that night in 1969, let's just call it a coincidence.

Who else would you credit for building up the DTO as we now know it?

The list goes on and on and there are too many shout outs to mention. I will say it truly calls home here in Boston, so I would have to give particular love to Patrick Sullivan, Ted Kilpatrick, John Gertsen, Jackson Cannon, Kevin Martin, and Tom Schlesinger-Guidelli. That is barely even scratching the surface just for Boston, but it's a start.

Outside of Boston, the satellite offices of DTO seem to be in Denver as a result of Sean Kenyon, Seattle because of Jim Romdall, and Nantucket because of Clinton Terry. I've heard of DTOs being taken in Montréal, Vancouver, Taipei, Munich, London, and Paris, but I'm not totally sure whom to credit.

Is the DTO the same as the NYC Snaquiri? Any thoughts on that trend?

I love the Snaquiri! And the two seem to be brothers in arms albeit with slightly different motivation. From my understanding, the Snaquiri is essentially an aperitif Daiquiri whereas the DTO (although it often serves that purpose) is a little more geared towards the celebration of the individuals and that moment.

A few notable DTO's published here and in *Drink & Tell*:
- Chappaquiddick & Archipelago (Eastern Standard)
- Maritime Out (Steel & Rye)
- Mytoi Gardens & Césaire Daiquiri (Russell House Tavern)
- Vielle Daiquiri (No. 9 Park)
- Navy Dock Daiquiri (Drink)
- Black Arrow (Brick & Mortar)
- Crimson Daiquiri (Sinclair)
- Daq in Black (Backbar)
- Haitian Monk (Lineage)
- Figawi (Citizen Public House)
- Periodista (Across Town)

Tom Schlesinger-Guidelli

Over the years, I have been discussing various Boston bartenders and their contributions to the Boston cocktail scene that still hold weight in the modern day mixology world. One name that kept popping up was Tom Schlesinger-Guidelli who has graced the bars of Eastern Standard, Craigie on Main, and to some degree Island Creek Oyster Bar. Since Tom was my first craft bartender back in June 2007, he has set the bar for what hospitality and drink craftsmanship can be, and it seemed like a good place to start this series. And I figured that a 5 drink retrospective might be a fitting tribute to these Boston Cocktail Allstars.

1. Jaguar (Drink & Tell: 92)
Very few people were mixing with tequila in Boston back in 2007 save for various Margarita variations and the like. Everything was shaken and laden with citrus juice to dull the edge of the spirit. A stirred tequila drink? Unheard of. Balancing it with bitter and herbal liqueurs? Sure, if it's 2012, but 5 years prior to that? The

secret of this drink was how well the edges of tequila and Green Chartreuse were soothed over by the caramel-dark orange richness of Amer Picon. This drink opened my eyes to what agave spirits could offer, and how blessed Boston was back then with our unearthed stash of Amer Picon that Eastern Standard luckily did not buy up the whole of (and I still have half of my one liter bottle from that discovery).

2. Prospect Park (Drink & Tell: 131)
I remember drinking many of these in Eastern Standard's gorgeous coupe glasses (as well as Hoskins which were invented by then New Orleans blogger Chuck Taggart). The recipe might have been one of the first famous Manhattan variations to come out of our city, and it showcases our inexplicable love of Maraschino liqueur. I have heard the drink described once as an Aperol-stretched (or -softened) Red Hook which could explain why the balance works so wonderfully. Moreover, I have recently had good luck switching the rye here to either brandy or aged rum with great success showing how timeless and versatile the base structure is.

3. Northern Lights
(Drink & Tell: 119)
In late 2008, Tom crossed the river and helped Tony Maws transition across town from Craigie Bistro to Craigie on Main. I recall how difficult it was to score a seat in the bar or lounge back then, for this level of craftsmanship was novel on that side of the Charles River. The Northern Lights was what Tom created on his brief hiatus from the stick, and was inspired by drinking with friends in Wesport, MA, under the stars. One of the Northern Lights' secret weapons was the hot new St. Germain, but it was balanced by smoke and pine notes from Scotch and an-

other new ingredient, Douglas Fir eau de vie, respectively. The third hot ingredient in the mix was the Bittermens Tiki Bitters. Seven ingredients in all that tie together gracefully.

4. Jerez Flip (Drink & Tell: 93)
My first egg drink was served to me by Tommy, which he was eager to do because I told him that I was a little scared of egg drinks. That was back at Eastern Standard, and I do remember that the recipe was based off of a Vieux Carré with different pro-portions. At Craigie on Main, there was no shortage of Flips ei-ther. While the **Florentine Flip** (Drink & Tell: 76) almost got the spot here, the Jerez Flip won out for it focused on sherry which was rather novel and hip back then. While I will have to give the nod to Misty Kalkofen for bringing sherry to the forefront of Boston mixology, the ingredients in this drink complemented the sherry rather elegantly.

5. Pirate's Revenge (Page 236)
After Craigie on Main, Tom stepped back from the bar to assume a more managerial position at Island Creek Oyster Bar. Yet, he was not able to stay away from tinkering with recipes though. The Pirate's Revenge was something that he and Vikram Hedge came up with -- a four equal part number with a few dashes of

something extra that has the feel of something Sam Ross would come up with.

These recipes do show but one side of Tom with the other being the hospi-tality side. While I do re-member the first conversations we had with him back in 2007 about pastis brands and how he took the time to talk to us throughout the night despite the full bar on an early Saturday evening, one story stands out in my head about what TSG hospitality was about. It involved the Espresso Martini... and two incredulous women doubting that Eastern Standard could make a good one. Tom handled their attack with grace and explained lovingly how the house Espresso Martini was made with such poetry that I was even tempted to get one. I recall how the two women looked at each other and nodded, and then ordered probably the best Espresso Martini they have ever tasted. Perhaps due to the ingredients and thought behind it, but most definitely because someone took the time to treat their inquiry as seriously as a discussion of Islay Single Malt Scotches or the rare amari on the shelves. And that is what has helped define what Boston hospitality is all about. And personally, thinking back to when I was making drinks at home and doubted my wife (then girlfriend) that there were bars out there making drinks like I was doing at home, Tom was the one that guided me across that threshold. Tom has since moved on to consulting and setting up bar programs, but he can still be found a night or two each week tending bar at Green Street. So cheers to TSG!

Boston Cocktail Allstars #2:

Misty Kalkofen

In continuing my tribute of Boston bartenders and their long
lasting contributions to the Boston cocktail scene, I would like to
honor Misty Kalkofen who temporally might have been our next
craft bartender in Boston after Tom Schlesinger-Guidelli. I know
that we were drinking at Green Street back in mid-2007, about a
year after Misty started there; we followed her to Drink in late
2008 and then Brick & Mortar in the vapors of 2011. I am not
sure whether her infectious laugh or her recipes travel further,
but for now, I will deal more with the recipes. And with great difficulty like last time, I will narrow this down to five drinks that
define my version of her Boston legacy.

1. Fort Washington Flip (Drink & Tell: 77)
While Misty is frequently known for her early adopter status
with St. Germain, mezcal, and sherry (more on that in the next
few drinks), one thing that she brings to the table, er... bar is a
love of egg drinks. In fact, for Easter 2007, she assembled an egg-

forward cocktail menu, and *DrinkBoston* quoted her as saying "You hard boil your Easter eggs. We separate and shake ours." This is not to say that she was the first, for No. 9 Park was definitely doing their share and Eastern Standard had already started their "oeuf" section on their menu. As one of her best egg drinks during this time period, Misty brought a bunch of Fall flavors to-

gether and named it after a Revolutionary War-era fortification, Fort Washington, which still exists as remnants several blocks away from Green Street. While my first egg drink was at Eastern Standard, my love of the style blossomed at Misty's bar. Though not her drink, her choice to put Angus Winchester's Peanut Malt Flip on the menu made my nightcap drink choice easy -- I would just ask then Green Street bartender Derric Crothers for a "PMF."

2. Maximillian Affair (Drink & Tell: 108)

Before her love of sherry reared itself, it was St. Germain and mezcal. One of the first drinks that had both was the Maximilian Affair which she symbolically named after a French intervention in Mexico during the mid-19th century. When I asked Misty about the drink later, she explained how she created the drink at Green Street for Ron Cooper of Del Maguey after he pulled a bottle of mezcal out for her to try. The Del Maguey products were not available here at that time, so luckily she still had enough of a sample to use it in a St. Germain recipe competition. Until quality mezcals became available, she was often forced to use blanco tequila in its place. Floral and fruit notes from the St. Germain intervene with the heat and smoke of the Mexican spirit, and the combination is magically bound with Punt e Mes and lemon. Perhaps her **Bohemian** (Drink & Tell: 43) is a better introduction to St. Germain, but I personally return to the Maximilian Affair for personal and guest consumption more often.

3. Armada (Drink & Tell: 33)

During the Drink era, Misty did not have the benefit of getting cocktails on a menu for that bar lacks a written one. New ideas were more fleeting and often required them to be made by the creator. Luckily, we had quite a few of these during the time period. Originally, I was going to go with the **Dunaway** (Drink & Tell: 65) that showcases Misty's finesse with sherry. However, I spotted the Armada which included sherries as well as Genever -- a spirit that Misty also produced great recipes with including the **1820** (Drink & Tell: 25). Genever is less forgiving of a spirit than gin or whiskey that lay on either side of it on the flavor spectrum, yet Misty was able to craft gems like the Armada.

4. Teardrop (Drink & Tell: 152)

Once Misty moved on to Brick & Mortar, she created some of the most intriguing combinations on paper that turned out to be delicious medleys in the glass. The first that I tried at Brick that December of 2011 was the Teardrop which Misty described as one the first successes for the opening menu. It also showcased a new

tool in her cocktail arsenal -- having a person who could generate names. Bar co-owner Patrick Sullivan had a notebook of names that he wanted to find homes for, and Misty had a bunch of cocktail ideas that needed names. Here in the Teardrop, Cardamaro takes center stage to balance the gin; while Averna donates a bit of richness, it is the light touch of absinthe that makes things work by brightening up the drink. Overall, it was not overpowering in any direction or proof. The latter part was not so true on the **A Bullet for Fredo** (Drink & Tell: 28) that I had that night. No, it was balanced, but this chilled but undiluted number packed a punch especially given the serving size (see the photo above)! It also displayed how aged grappa could be utilized elegantly as a based spirit. Apparently, during Brick & Mortar training, the staff greatly enjoyed drinking Nardini Aquavite Bassano Riserva Aged Grappa over other spirits, perhaps due to its vanilla, spice, chocolate, and tobacco notes, and various grappas ended up in their recipes as a result.

5. Streets of Gettysburg (Drink & Tell: 149)

For a second drink to sum up Misty's time at Brick & Mortar, I was torn between two cocktails that featured sherry and Benedictine. The one that I did not choose is the amusingly named **Honky and the Donkey** (Drink & Tell: 88). Perhaps it should have gotten the nod, but Misty's love of mezcal has been mentioned a few times above. Instead, here is a rye whiskey one, but what does it have to do with the name? Legend has it that Patrick Sullivan had spotted it as the caption to a friend's photo on Facebook and put it his drink name notebook, and it later called out to Misty. The trio of sherry, Benedictine, and coffee liqueur is just magic in this drink.

Currently, Misty has taken her love of agave spirits to the next level and the next stage in her career, that of being an educator as well as working for Del Maguey Mezcal. I remember the first time that Misty visited me at Russell House Tavern shortly after making that move. I had to figure out what drink would match her tastes, and the one I chose was my **Downtown at Dawn** (Page 129) which features mezcal, apple brandy, and Benedictine that she has utilized in many of her drinks over the years. If I could have fit sherry, Lillet, Drambuie, and egg in there as well, the world might have exploded. So let us all raise a stigi of mezcal to Misty. Cheers!

29

John Gertsen

In continuing on in the series of bartenders, past and present, who have helped to shape the Boston cocktail scene, I feel that it would be a serious omission if I left out John Gertsen. In one part for what he has done for Boston and in another part for what he has done for me. I dis-
tinctly remember meeting Gertsen in August 2007 at a LUPEC Boston-spon-sored Chartreuse event at Green Street in Cambridge. A man dressed up as a Carthusian monk was ei-ther introduced to me or started talking to me -- namely, John Gertsen in a costume. I later learned that there was not a cos-tume that John would not don for a cocktail event (including a Colonial fop for Boston Thirst). John gestured that we should sit down and we continued our conversation partially
cloaked to the rest of the world by the robe-hood about cocktails, life, and how veering from what one went to higher education for was not a bad thing. From there, I soon made Tuesdays and Sat-urdays, John's nights on the No. 9 Park bar, part of my haunts. And shortly thereafter, I met his loyal followers who also flocked to the bar on those nights such as Monica and Tyrone.

Like the other Allstars, I will cover 5 drinks that span the bars that I knew the bartender at. However, there are many classic cocktails that I associate with him. First, there is the Sazerac. John's enthusiasm made the ritual of building and serving the regular rye whiskey Sazerac a joy to behold, but he utilized it as a platform to make simple tweaks into new gems including my first Gin or Scotch Sazerac. It also felt special because you could sense the lineage in this drink as he spoke of the bartenders and their bars in New Orleans who made this drink a special one for him. The second is the Tom & Jerry. No, he did not create the Tom & Jerry, nor as Dave Wondrich explained, neither did Jerry Thomas. But Gertsen helped to define the drink as the appropriate beverage to have when it snows in town. And perhaps only when it is snowing. People would later seek out his approval if he did not send it out on social media that it was Tom & Jerry weather. Indeed, No. 9 Park was one of the few bars to have a Tom & Jerry bowl set on display during the winter season. The third was the **Knickebein** (Page 300) -- that crazy layered pousse-café drink with an unbroken egg yolk in the middle and beaten-stiff egg whites on top that is taken in a four step ceremony. No, he never served one to me, but my witnessing him serving it to one of his groupies to see how far he could take things, was enough to have me try it at home. And that transference of enthusiasm for the drink led to me recently being asked to write an article in the upcoming *Oxford Companion to Spirits and Cocktails* about the drink. With those three classics out of the way, here are 5 drinks or so crafted by John that help define how he helped to shape my view of Boston cocktails, and perhaps how he helped to shape the Boston drinking scene overall.

1. Flight of Heraldry: The Negroni, Contessa (Drink & Tell: 57), and **Patrician** (Drink & Tell: 124)
One thing that John was involved in at No. 9 Park was making up cocktail flights. The first I remember was the Flight of Aviation that traced the drink through the decades as different ingredients became less available and as tastes changed. However, one that preceded it, the Negroni-inspired Flight of Heraldry, was one that he had a hand in creating and includes two drinks that are still made around town to this day. Perhaps tack on the Negroni as one of the other classics that John helped to inspire me to love (and I have to include Ben Sandrof in on this for serving me at No. 9 Park a Negroni made with xanthum gum-infused Campari for a richer mouthfeel). With the Negroni being so hot these days, it is good that John's contributions were captured in Gaz Regan's *The Negroni* book. And as a show of his influence, my Negroni Knickebein appeared in that book as well!

31

2. Helsingor (Drink & Tell: 86)

The Helsingor is a transitional cocktail of sorts. It was created once John opened up Drink, but was based off of a No. 9 Park cocktail the Copenhagen. Unlike No. 9 Park, Drink lacked the necessary Gamel Dansk; therefore, John generated this Angostura-

heavy riff back in 2009 for one of his old No. 9 regulars Tyrone. A half ounce of Angostura Bitters may or may not seem like a lot of bitters now, but back then, it definitely was. True, the Trinidad Sour was kicking around as well as some classics from the literature. That level of absurdity carried on in drinks like the **Mission of Burma** (Drink & Tell: 134, photo to left), the inverse proportioned Pegu Club riff that John created for a Grand Marnier event. I am also thankful for John (and Jeff Grdinich) inviting Andrea and me to have a drink on that Grand Marnier event menu, namely the **Lioness of Brittany** (Drink & Tell: 105).

3. Means of Preservation (Drink & Tell: 112)

Of course, not everything memorable that John created at Drink was over the top, and the Means of Preservation is a fine example. Paul Clarke writing about the Ephemeral Cocktail back in 2009 inspired John to make his own riff. One of the key ingredients in both is celery bitters; however, they were not commercially available in Boston at that time. Luckily, I had been supplying Drink with my celery bitters since 2008 to make up that lack. In thanks, John let me "work" at Drink so I could compete at Tales of the Cocktail in 2009 in a bitters competition (there, I used the royal "we" a lot in describing how "we" used those celery bitters at Drink). Technically, I did bus our cocktail and water glasses once the night that he agreed to let me claim to be a barback. And perhaps, I should have sought out back then to have actually gotten a job as a barback for real...

4. Double Plus Good (Drink & Tell: 65)
In preparing for a guest shift at Los Angeles' Edison, John created a cross between a Mai Tai and a Pisco Sour by taking the former and adding an egg white and including Angostura Bitters as a garnish. John always enjoyed describing how Mai Tai was called that for being the Tahitian translation of "out of this world," and he took that one step further with his *1984* Newspeak name for this riff. He also opted for white rum to give this drink a purity of color (save for the two Angostura Bitters plus-signs as garnish).

5. Krakatoa (Page 191)
Nothing is as stunning as fire when it comes to garnishes or drink preparation. True, John and the rest of Drink helped to bring back the Blue Blazer, but I never took to the concept of hot, booze-depleted Scotch. The Krakatoa was a colder drink that utilized a Batavia Arrack Toronto to extinguish flaming Green Chartreuse in the glass to generate an awesome flavor explosion. John did similarly in expanding the 1895 Star Cocktail into the **Super Nova** (Drink & Tell: 149) that night, but somehow the Krakatoa got left out of the first book.

August 2014 saw Boston saying goodbye to John as he left Drink for the West Coast to work at %ABV in San Francisco via a Gertstravaganza celebration at the Hawthorne. Indeed, John also introduced me to Scott Holliday as Scott returned back from Canada in 2008 right before he took over Rendezvous' bar program, so the picture on the next page is quite fitting. The drink that Scott presented that night in John's honor was something the two of them created post-shift, late at night, when they were roommates, namely the **Negrimlet** (Page 219) -- a Negroni-Gimlet mash up. While John is in San Francisco, our paths will surely cross again. I did have the honor in 2015 of having him and David

Wondrich sitting at my bar at Loyal Nine before they moved on to a table to have dinner. I think that was the first time I actually served him a drink, and it was an honor to switch sides of the game that night. Cheers, Mr. Gertsen!

Ryan Lotz

For the fourth installment of the Boston Cocktail Allstars series, I figured that I would change gears for a moment. The first three, Tommy, Misty, and John, have all gotten a lot of press around Boston and across the country to varying degrees. However, often there are gems that fly under the radar a bit. In this instance, bartender Ryan Lotz has shown a great deal of creativity, hospitality, and scholarship in the 7 years that I have known him. Early in 2010, Ryan called both Lauren Clark of *DrinkBoston* and me out on Twitter to come visit him at Lineage in Brookline. Being a ways off the beaten path, Lineage's drink program was not getting that much notice back then. One of the first things that Ryan was doing that caught my attention was working his way through Ted Haigh's *Vintage Spirits and Forgotten Cocktails*. Each weekend, he was featuring a pair of drinks, and he progressed through the book over the next several months until completion. We rather enjoyed visiting Ryan at Lineage from March 2010 on for we could go at the tail end of the crowds and catch dinner without a wait; and after the throngs had left, we had plenty of undivided attention from the barstaff to talk about cocktails. Ryan later departed Lineage to become one of the opening bartenders of the Hawthorne, the bar manager at No. 9 Park, and finally a manager and beverage director at Bar Mezzana.

1. The Fritz (Drink & Tell: 80)

One of the first intriguing cocktail recipes of his that Ryan offered me was the Fritz -- a drink that was inspired by one of my recipes, **The Gerty** (Drink & Tell: 81). Here, he balanced a four equal part drink where one quarter was Peychaud's Bitters in an inverse Martinez-like formulation. He dubbed this one after Fritz Bultman, an abstract expressionist from New Orleans. Also on the absurd tip was the **Monk's Thistle** (Drink & Tell: 115) that was his riff on Ben Sandrof's Green Chartreuse-laden **Silent Order** (Drink & Tell: 142).

2. Final Voyage (Drink & Tell: 74)

Ryan's drink making prowess was not just freakish and ex-treme, as he ranged from clas-sical to Tiki as well. For a proto-Tiki-inspired one, the Final Voyage, a Jamaican rum riff on the Last Word that fell somewhere between a Peri-odista and the Culross given the apricot liqueur, was de-lightful. **The Exhibition Swiz-zle** (Drink & Tell: 72, photo to right) also had a tropical feel despite being a tribute to Aperol's launch for Haitian rum, faler-num, and lime helped to set that stage.

3. Black Cadillac (Drink & Tell: 41)

One of the drink styles that Ryan enjoyed tinkering with were egg drinks, and the egg drink that I featured in the *Drink and Tell: A Boston Cocktail Book* technique section was this one, the Black Cadillac. This stout ale Flip bolstered by demerara syrup, Scotch, and Jamaican rum had all the makings of early 19th century liba-tions but with a flavor profile that fit in quite nicely with modern mixology.

4. Andorra (Drink & Tell: 31)

At the Hawthorne, Ryan had less control over the cocktail menu than he did as bar manager of Lineage, but he still was able to offer guests some excellent libations. One that sums up this era was the Andorra. Comparing it to a Negroni would sell it short, but Cognac as the spirit, sherry as the wine element, and Amaro Nardini as the bittering agent in equal parts gave way for a complex tipple. Add in a little salted rooibos syrup to mollify the amaro's bitterness, and the flavor profile offered chocolate, toffee, and nuttiness that complemented the brandy.

5. Riviera de Ponente (Page 246)

I think that the Hawthorne's refined elegance prepared him well for the next stage of his career at No. 9 Park. Strangely, he had been churning out some of the most interesting Tiki drinks in town using inspiration from Italian ingredients and classic cocktails. The Riviera de Ponente mixes in amaro and other liqueurs in something akin to a Zombie. And his Negroni Week 2015 offering, the **Amaro di Cocco** (Page 71) beautifully merged a Rum Negroni with a Piña Colada into what could have been dubbed the Piña Negrada. Also, his Tiki prowess has led him to teach classes with Beachbum Berry where Ryan offered up the **Benny & the Jets** (Page 84). He has recently moved on to manage Bar Mezzana where the menu has plenty of examples of this sort of amaro Tiki tinkering.

For these reasons, I am adding Ryan to this small but growing list of Boston Cocktail Allstars. It is a bit harder to catch Ryan at the bar at Bar Mezzana for he is also working the floor as a manager for part of the time, but it is still a joy when our schedules match up. So cheers to Ryan!

37

Matthew Schrage

For the fifth installment of the Boston Cocktail Allstars, I am paying tribute to a gentleman that falls somewhere between amaro master and social dadaist, namely Matthew Schrage. I was first introduced to Matt towards the latter half of 2008 as John Gertsen and Ben Sandrof were departing No. 9 Park to open up Drink,  and Matt was moving from serving on the floor to fill in the void behind the bar. I believe that I was the first person to take a picture of Matt's hands while bartending in Boston when he made for me the Henry V Flip; alas, that recipe was never fully recorded and later attempts to sort that one out as I wrote *Drink & Tell: A Boston Cocktail Book* never prospered. Matt has spent the years since doing some combination of bartending, managing, and consulting on bar programs. Besides all of the delicious cocktails that he served me of which I will feature five below, I owe Matt two major thanks. The first was inviting me to participate in the Whiskey & Amari Night series in 2013 that he organized while bar managing the Blue Room; there, I had my first swing at being a professional bartender, albeit for a single night along side industry starlet Katie Emmerson. Those four hours behind the stick changed my career direction then and there. Second, he introduced me to my current chef, Marc Sheehan, back in 2011 at No. 9 Park -- actually, this should be first temporally although the end result came later. I stopped in for a drink as they had dinner and plotted their next Brass Tacks pop-up dinner party event, and I ended up getting kidnapped to Brick & Mortar to continue hanging out with them. When Marc was opening up

Loyal Nine, I applied to help open his bar program. Eventually, Matt's proclivity to Brick & Mortar would lead him to join the program and help to take it over and cement its spot as one of the nationally recognized cocktail party centers of Boston (in *Esquire* and *Playboy* magazines).

1. Soekarno (Drink & Tell: 145)

One of the most influential cocktails that Matt had a hand in creating at No. 9 Park was the Soekarno that I tasted in September of 2009. That drink was the Indonesian take on the Haitian Petion; instead of Clairin from Haiti, this utilized Batavia Arrack. The drink taught me how well Benedictine pairs with funky rums, and I modified this recipe into the **Danger Zone Swizzle** (Page 119) for Loyal Nine's Yacht Rock Sundays after having made the No. 9 Park classic several times that month for various guests.

2. Nebbia Di Garda (Page 218)

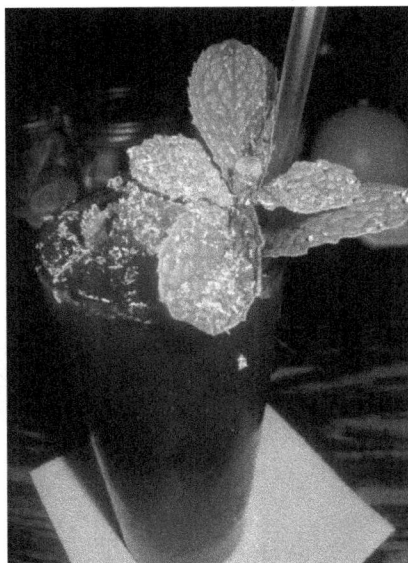

After Matt's stint at the bar at No. 9 Park, he slid over to Menton (which lacked a bar until 2015), and then over to manage the Hawthorne. After the Hawthorne spot ended in late 2012, Matt return to a life behind the stick starting with rebuilding the Blue Room's bar program. One of the things he focused on was bolstering the amaro program, and the Nebbia di Garda named after a foggy alpine lake in Northern Italy featured two of these to great effect. Even in winter, the two amari along with citrus helped to conjure up springtime in my mind.

3. From the Hip (Page 151)

One of the wider effects Matt has had on the Boston cocktail scene has been by consulting and setting up a variety of bar programs across town. One of my favorites from this aspect is the From the Hip that he created for Ribelle. In fact, I once had two bar guests that were discussing an amazing mezcal over crushed ice drink that one of them had but could not recall the name. When I butted in and inquired where they had it, my guess of "From the Hip" was indeed the proper answer-response to "Ribelle" (and yes, they looked at me like I was a wizard). Lime, falernum, and mint along with the mezcal, Angostura Bitters garnish, and Campari drizzled over the top sealed the deal. He later brought this drink to the Highball Lounge menu after he departed Brick & Mortar.

4. Red Duster Swizzle (Page 243)

In spring of 2013, Matt moved over to Brick & Mortar where he ran not only the cocktail program but also planned theme nights as well. One of my favorite creations from Matt during this stage

of his career is the Red Duster Swizzle, a Royal British Merchant Navy-themed Negroni-inspired Swizzle using formulas from Death & Co. that he learned during his time at the Hawthorne. Merging one of the favorite cocktails of bartenders, the Negroni, with a Swizzle was a thing of beauty.

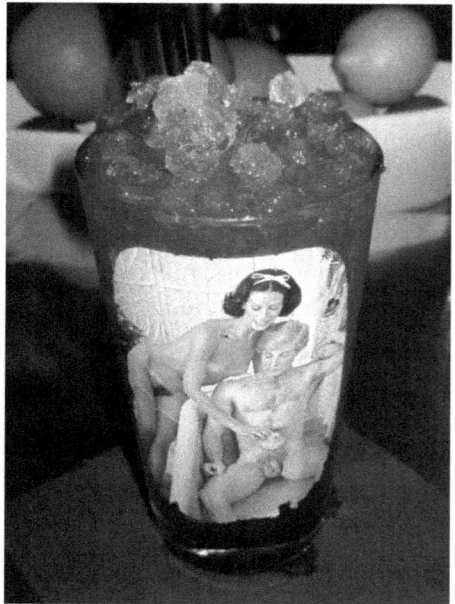

5. I Know You Know (Page 172)

One of the elegant drinks that Matt came up with at Brick & Mortar was the I Know You Know that won him the Lustau Brandy competition held at the Hawthorne in 2014. Back when I was at Russell House, I was trying to find the final piece for a menu item that turned into the **Endicott Cobbler** (Page 137), and I stopped into Brick & Mortar for guidance. Matt collaborated with me to try a few combinations out and make my idea sing. He later took his part of the idea and converted it into the championship drink, the I Know You Know named after a song from a jazz singer he used to listen to at Wally's. Indeed, I have actually learned a lot about obscure music through Matt's drink names such as learning about Jens Lekman via **A Postcard to Nina** (Page 239).

Here, Matt was teaching a class at Boston Thirst 2014 about some of the forgotten ways to enjoy fifty-fifty Dry Martinis, and my turn at the lesson followed soon after. Matt has since moved on to manage the Highball Lounge where he can frequently be found at the stick. Overall, Matt's contribution to the Boston cocktail scene has been rather solid whether building bar programs or building 8 or more drinks at once while working Friday night service bar at Brick & Mortar. So to Matt Schrage, let us all raise a shot glass of Amaro Braulio with a Budweiser chaser in hand and say cheers to this Boston Cocktail Allstar!

John Mayer

For the sixth installment in the series of bartenders, past and present, who have helped to shape the Boston cocktail scene, I chose another bartender who we followed to three establishments, namely John Mayer. We met John at Craigie on Main in the summer of 2010, and followed him to Loyal 149 and Citizen Public House before he recently retired from the stick (save for guest appearances) to work for a liquor company. John's combination of hospitality, cocktail creativity, and curious drink names always led to a great bar experience. As for the cocktail names, he did live up to his *OnTheBar* profile quote of "If the drink is named after Texas, firearms, or sex toys, there's a good chance I created it." He also surprised and impressed me with his movie, literature, and music references. Without further ado, here is a five drink retrospective (with a few bonus allusions thrown in) to reflect on his Boston bartending contributions.

1. Libretto (Drink & Tell: 105)
One of the things that John did at Craigie on Main was strengthen my interest in tequila and mezcal drinks, and it was hard to pick one of them to represent with the **Wilhelm Scream** (Drink & Tell: 166) and the **Degüello** (Drink & Tell: 64) both worthy of this spot. In terms of drink names, John apparently was not great at translating into Italian though for he picked the wrong word to name this libation for a librarian guest, yet he proudly kept his mistake. But flavor-wise, it was no mistake; this combination of aged tequila, sweet vermouth, and chocolate bitters also had the interplay of the highs of elderflower liqueur balancing the lows of Cynar.

2. Throw the Gun #2 (Drink & Tell: 155)
Besides agave spirits, John also showed off his mastery of gin while at Craigie on Main. Getting the nod over the spiced and spicy (for being named after a sex toy issue) **Magic Wand Malfunction** (Drink & Tell: 107) (note: his wife is a sex-ed teacher) was a cinematic Flip called Throw the Gun #2 after the moment the bad guy runs out of bullets and discards his weapon and flees. Perhaps not a Flip since it contains a touch of citrus, and this citrus, creaminess, and gin did remind me of a Ramos until the nutty sherry and herbal amaro notes entered the swallow.

3. 2011 (Acquired Taste) (Page 65)
After Craigie on Main, John took a position closer to his home in South Boston, namely as the bar manager for Local 149. One of my favorites that he created in 2013 was a commentary on popular trends in mixology that he called an Acquired Taste before he changed it to a tribute to the year 2011. Hints of mezcal smoke accented the pinch of salt-dampened combination of Campari and Bonal that were supported by nutty sherry. Overall, disparate ingredients lacking a base spirit came together to play off of each other in a Negroni sort of fashion.

4. Face for Radio (Page 140)
Sometimes delicious drinks can look rather ugly, and John Mayer's submission to the Bacardi Competition in 2013 was definitely in that category. Therefore, he ran with it and gave this one an amusing name, a Face for Radio. Orgeat will often do that, and this is why opaque and colorful mugs are often used to serve Tiki drinks. With Becherovka, lime, and cinnamon honey syrup rounding out this drink, it came across like a cinnamon and clove-spiced Mai Tai variation.

5. 11 + 2 / 12 + 1 (Page 63)
With a good few years of tenure at Local 149, John moved on to the Citizen Public House. The curiously named 11 + 2 / 12 + 1 was the last drink that he made for me back in early 2014; I later

asked John to explain the riddle, and he noted that both sides have the same 13 letters in them in different orders. The drink got even more curious as it was equal parts Green Chartreuse and Zucca that were accented by grapefruit bitters and twist oils. Overall, there was a lot of elegance and complexity in this seeming simplicity.

One of the drinks that I wanted to feature was part of a duo that John served to me called the **Love in an Elevator** (Page 202). This combination of dark rum, oloroso sherry, Benedictine, and Punt e Mes was rather delightful; however, it was created by his coworker at the time Matt Whitney. While I was sipping this cold libation towards the end of June, John took out a pair of Blue Blazer mugs and started to work on the drink across the bar. I commented to my wife that someone was silly enough to order a Blue Blazer on a hot, almost summer evening. After putting on the show pouring the flaming drink back and forth including igniting a pair of lemon oil puffs from twists, he then set the drink in front of me. At that moment, I realized that I was the silly fool getting a hot drink on a warm evening. John's companion piece, the **Death in a Doublewide** (Cocktail Virgin blog: July 2013; photo above), was inspired by the Diamondback, but he could not get it to work chilled, so it was suggested that he go warm. I think that this moment captures the cinematic absurdity that made sitting at John's bar such a treat. John has since guest bartending at the Hawthorne for their Swizzle Sundays albeit on a night I was also working, so chances are that I have not had the last drink from this Boston Cocktail Allstar.

Technique

This section was not designed to be a basic primer on drink making, but it is meant to clarify some of the directions in the recipes as well as to impart some of the wisdom I have gained personally as both a home and a professional bartender as well as by watching the masters at work. For the basics, see my suggestions for books by Jeffrey Morgenthaler, Dave Stolte, Robert Hess, Dale De-Groff, and Gary Regan in the introduction.

Measure: I am a big proponent of measuring everything that goes into a drink to get the desired effect of the recipe as written as well as to achieve consistency between drinks. While there are a handful of bartenders across town that I trust to free pour accurately with speed pourers, I never recommend it since it inserts a lot of new variables into drink making precision and reproducibility. And besides, most home bars do not have speed pourers. I recommend either a set of jiggers or a graduated mixing cup such as from the OXO brand. There are also jiggers made by OXO and Cocktail Kingdom that have handy internal markings to do other volumes. The only other measuring tools needed for these recipes would be a standard barspoon that is perfect for 1/8 oz volumes (confirm your tools by filling and pouring into a jigger) and perhaps a teaspoon set.

Stir: The common rule is that straight spirits drinks (drinks lacking juice, dairy, or eggs) are always stirred, not shaken. The converse is not always true, for there are drinks when the bartender will stir a drink containing a tart citrus juice like lemon or lime as a balance for sweetness in the drink. When these drinks are stirred, the bartender desires a smoother, silkier texture and not a brighter, livelier tone. To stir a drink, add ice to the ingredients in a mixing glass then stir with a spoon for 30-40 seconds. Do not add the ice first for the clock for melting and diluting starts once the first ingredients hits the ice. In a bar setting, if one ingredient is short and needs to be fetched in the stockroom, the spirits, syrups, and bitters already added will probably end up in the sink. The minimum amount of ice that will achieve a decent amount of cooling seems to be three one-inch cubes if they are cracked into smaller pieces; if not cracked, either more ice or more stirring time will needed to acquire the proper chilling and dilution. Of course, filling the mixing glass removes these worries. The stirring should be moderate in speed – not fast or violent enough to add air into the drink or splash ice or liquid out of the mixing vessel. The end result will be a drink that is almost a third larger in volume, such that a three ounce pre-melt volume becomes close to a four ounce chilled one. Remember, there is no chilling without dilution since the cooling energy released from ice stems from it melting from solid to liquid. To strain, a Julep strainer is often used to hold back the ice during straining, but for some mixing vessels a Hawthorne strainer will work better. A secondary fine strain step to catch ice and other particulates is not as important in a stirred drink as it is in a shaken drink, but some bartenders include it anyways especially if the ice is prone to chipping.

Build: Certain drinks are constructed in the serving glass itself. These include some Highballs, Old Fashioneds, and room temperature cocktails such as Scaffas. Often a quick, gentle stir is necessary for Highballs to disperse the spirits into the mixer (see the section below on Fizzes, Collins, and Champagne Cocktails). With Old Fashioned-styled drinks containing ice, stirring for 15 seconds or so with the ice will get the ingredients integrated and the chill and dilution started. Lastly, room temperature drinks require only enough stirring to make the mixture homogeneous throughout.

Swizzle: Swizzling is a Caribbean style of mixing drinks that is more violent than stirring but more gentle than shaking. It is also often an extension of the built drink mentioned above as the ingredients and crushed ice are added to a tall glass such as a Collins glass or Tiki mug. The traditional mixing implement is a wooden 5-pronged swizzle stick called a Bois Lélé that is prepared from a tree found in the Caribbean; these are available through Cocktail Kingdom's webstore but are otherwise hard to come by. As a substitute, use a barspoon or a spoon straw; the stereotypical ornamental swizzle sticks will not fit the bill here. To mix the drink, spin the swizzle stick or spoon back and forth between the palms of the hand until the drink is chilled; changing height of the swizzle stick's blades or spoon's bowl will quickly chill all parts of the drink. With Collins glasses, the appearance of a frost on the outside of the glass is generally the stopping point although that is harder to achieve in the low humidity Winter months.

Shake: Drinks with egg, dairy, muddled fruit, and juices are almost always shaken. Since egg drinks are more complex, there is more about them in the next section. For shaking vessels, the options include the Boston, Parisian, and Cobbler shakers. After adding ice to the ingredients in the shaker of choice, shaking vigorously for 20 seconds or so is sufficient to reach the desired chilling and dilution. Some bartenders choose to do this by feel and stop when the shaker feels rather cold, but counting seems to be a preferred method for many. With the Boston or Parisian shaker, the drink is strained out with a Hawthorne strainer; with a Cobbler shaker, the strainer of course is built in. Often a secondary straining step is added to catch ice shards, citrus pulp and pips, muddled fruit and herbs, and coarse egg material. For ice shards, a Julep strainer between the shaker and the glass will work in a pinch; however, a mesh tea strainer is necessary to catch all smaller debris. Some people do not mind or actually prefer the ice shards or citrus pulp, so act accordingly with the choice to add a secondary straining step.

Fizzes, Collins, and Champagne Cocktails: All of the instructions in the recipe section are written to add a prescribed amount of sparkling wine or soda water to the glass first and then strain the shaken or stirred drink over the top. The reasons are two fold. First, individual bars' recipes are standardized to their glassware and average ice cube size, so "topping" with a sparkling ingredient is somewhat regular in volume there; how-ever, here in this book, there are over a hundred bars' recipes that need to work with everyone's random assortment of glass-ware types. Therefore, measurements for this carbonated ingre-dient were included with the recipes as a baseline. Second, since most shaken or stirred drinks containing syrup or liqueurs are denser than sparkling wine or soda water, topping with the car-bonated liquid does not allow for very good mixing and will re-sult in layered drinks where the carbonation is on top and much of the spirituous flavor is on the bottom (and close to the straw if present). In reverse, the denser shaken or stirred component when strained will sink and mix with the carbonated component that was added first. After this, ice can be added to the top of the glass (if required), and this formula will work regardless of what your ice and glass sizes are. With sugared sodas such as ginger ale and cola, the shaken or stirred drink may be lighter. Two ap-proaches can be utilized here with the first being to put the soda in afterwards and then give a quick stir. The second will work even with sparkling wine and soda; here, add the carbonated in-gredient to the shaker tin or mixing glass after shaking or stirring and then strain the combination into the glass. The goal of all of these approaches is to mix the components as well as retain as much of the carbonation as possible.

Egg Drinks: There are forty-something drinks containing egg white, yolk, or both in this collection. The instructions included with these recipes are written "Shake once without ice and then once with ice." For the first or "dry" shake, the rationale is to emulsify the egg proteins into solution. Some bartenders will do this with just the citrus and liquor components with the egg and add the rest of the ingredients before the second or "wet" shake. The reason is that acids such as citrus juice promote the unfold-ing of egg proteins which will cause the egg white proteins to later foam up. Sugar from syrups and liqueurs will inhibit this initial unfolding and prevent a good foam from forming, but once the foam has formed, sugar will help stabilize it. The recipes here skip this segregation of ingredients for simplicity's sake. The sec-ond or wet shake will contain the rest of the ingredients and ice; this shake is for chilling and dilution purposes similar to all other shaken drinks. The dry shake is often shorter than the wet shake and 10 seconds or so should be sufficient for this first shake. I do not recommend dry shaking egg drinks in Parisian shakers because they require a vacuum derived from chilled ingredients to seal properly.

Egg Fizz Drinks: One of the bars in town that has Ramos and other Fizzes down to a science is Drink in Fort Point. While the lore of Ramos Gin Fizzes needing to be shaken for many minutes exists, this does not seem to be necessary to get the desired light, fluffy consistency. Drink in its high volume moments cannot afford that amount of time, so they figured out a solution. Instead of straining the shaken drink into the glass and topping off with soda water, they add the soda water to the glass and strain into it. This way, the soda water's air bubbles integrate into the drink immediately and less gas is wasted. Next, they add extra soda water to the ice inside the strained-out shaker, swirl, and strain or spoon out this light foam on top to add a glorious head to the drink.

Rinse: About two dozen of the recipes in this book include the rinsed glass technique, so I will share my thoughts about it. There are two purposes to rinsing a glass with a spirit. The first is to add a small amount of the ingredient into the flavor profile in a showier way than adding it to the mixing glass. The second and more important reason is to coat the exposed sides of a glass with an aromatic ingredient so it adds to the drink's nose. For rocks glasses and other glasses where the drink does not come up to the top, the technique has the most value. There are two ways of accomplishing a rinse. The most common way is to add a small amount, often around a quarter ounce, to the glass; the glass is tilted and slowly rolled so the insides are completely covered. Often times, the excess is dumped out, but sometimes the bartender chooses to leave the small excess in the glass to either add to the flavor more or to not be wasteful. The second way is to use a mister and spritz the sides. This technique is certainly faster but it requires a dedicated piece of barware. I could definitely see the home bartender making good use out of an absinthe-filled one especially if Sazeracs were a common occurrence. From there, the shaken or stirred drink is soon after strained into this rinsed glass.

Twist Garnish: A citrus twist garnish is meant to add aromatic oils to the top of the drink, and there are a few variations on this technique. One method is to use a channel knife close to the surface of the drink, and the mere act of making that ribbon of peel will cast off a lot of oils. The other is to use a vegetable peeler or knife to make a wide twist or a coin that is squeezed over the drink. From there, the twist can be dropped, floated, or discarded; in the text, the phrase "garnish with lemon oils from a twist" implies that the bartender who made the drink opted for discarding the peel, whereas the phrase "garnish with a lemon twist" implies that the peel was added to the glass in some fashion after expressing the oils over the surface of the drink. If the peel is discarded, the twist technique utilized has less relevance save for the amount of aromatic oil donated. If it is added, the size, shape, and curling will affect the aesthetics of the cocktail. Why add the twist? Two reasons. First, it makes a cocktail appear different from the next, which will break up the monotony especially if you frequently tend towards brown cocktails or other. Second, it can infuse citrus flavors into the drink over time especially in higher proof straight spirits drinks. Finally, a handful of recipes in the book call for a flamed twist. By using a lighter or match as a flame source, squeeze the peel through the flame to express the oils on the surface of the drink; some bartenders will often heat the peel before squeezing. While I have heard lore of the oils being caramelized, side-by-side experiments have made me skeptical that there is much difference. One difference is that flaming can add a charred, sulfurous component to the drink if done incorrectly with a match. The match should be allowed to burn for a bit so that the sulfurous head is burned away. This can be avoided by using the less glamorous cigarette lighter. The heating of the peel can also deposit carbon onto the twist; if it is dropped into the drink, a ring of soot can sometimes be released onto the surface. To avoid some of these issues, I have seen some bartenders opt to garnish with a second un-flamed peel. The only good argument that I have heard for the flamed twist is from Dale DeGroff who speaks highly about the visual appeal of the burst of fire from igniting the citrus oils; it will make the cocktail the envy of drinkers down the bar by catching their attention. I cannot deny this effect for it works in similar ways for flaming drinks and fancy drink vessels as well, but otherwise, you have my blessing to ignore the directions to flame a twist and to just use a regular one.

Bitters Garnish: Another popular garnish in the collection is the bitters or liqueur garnish to add both aromatic and visual appeal. The two drinks types that call for it here are egg drinks where the froth will support the bitters and crushed ice drinks where the ice will hold the garnish in place; other drinks that can garner that egg white-like level of supportive froth are heavy bitters, pineapple juice, and espresso containing cocktails. Carefully dribbling out of a dasher bottle, using an eyedropper, or spritzing with a mister are all viable options. One popular technique with the garnishes for egg or egg white drinks is to carefully deposit the drops on the surface and using a toothpick or thin straw to draw designs through the drops or dashes. At work, I have also cut out stencils using plastic lids to paint on designs using spritzed bitters as paint.

Chilled Glassware: To spare the repetition, I left out the instruction to strain into chilled glassware. Clearly, a cold glass will help the drink remain colder for a longer time. The two general methods for chilling glassware are placing the glasses in the freezer or filling the glasses with ice water, with the former being more effective. From experiments that I have done, the difference between using a glass from the freezer and one at room temperature is that the cocktail poured into the freezer-chilled glass will remain colder for 5-10 minutes longer than one poured into a room temperature glass. The downside of the freezer technique is that it requires freezer space to include glasses of each type needed. It also requires forethought for full chilling of the glassware requires about a half hour. An equivalent amount of chilling as the ice water technique can be reached in 6-8 minutes in the freezer. Filling with ice water is a great compromise for it is immediate. In about 4-5 minutes, the glass will come into equilibrium with the ice water; it will not be as effective as freezer-stored glasses but it is rather a good compromise on time and space concerns. Storing glassware in the refrigerator is also a decent compromise but it still comes with space constraint issues. I will say that it is not a major deal if you opt not to chill the glassware especially for drinks that are more robust and do not require ice-coldness to make them palatable.

Pinch of Salt: Generally the intent of adding salt to a cocktail is not to make things taste salty but to cut bitterness, make drinks brighter, and increase sweetness. Therefore, if the drink begins to taste salty, this pinch was overdone. Perhaps a dozen grains of table salt will achieve this cocktail effect. Several bars utilize eye-droppers containing a concentrated saline solution to achieve this delivery more consistently, but for the sporadic user, I find that a fine touch with a pinch of salt will work rather well. To make that salt solution to add dropwise, combine 1 weight of table salt with 4 weights of hot water (such as 20 grams to 80 grams). Around 3 drops of this solution should be equivalent to a pinch of salt. Do not substitute this solution for salt grains when garnishing an ice cube though.

Lemon or Lime Wedge: Whether for garnishing or muddling, I generally process medium lemons or limes into 6 wedges cut down the long access. Perhaps a large lemon could be cut into 8 wedges. The volumes that are extractable by full muddling or squeezing would be around 1/6 oz and 1/4 oz for lime and lemon wedges, respectively. Muddling not only extracts juice but peel oils as well.

Substitutions:

I included this section as a start of a conversation, not as a definitive answer as to whether these ingredients are indeed interchangeable or moderately so. I am sure this section will be a pleasant list of suggestions for some and a source of aggravation to others especially perfectionists. The reality is that not every home or restaurant's bar can have every bottle out there, and substitutions may have to occur. I hope that the list inspires an author in the future to expand and edit the comparisons below.

Interchangeable
Suze, Avèze, and Salers Gentian Liqueurs
Lillet Blanc, Cocchi Americano, Kina l'Aero d'Or, Dubonnet Blanc
Dubonnet Rouge, Lillet Rouge
Herbsaint, Pastis
Crema de Mezcal, 9 parts Mezcal to 1 part Agave Nectar
Curaçao, Triple Sec, Cointreau
Zucca, Amaro Sfumato

Moderately Interchangeable (especially in a pinch)
Averna, Amaro Nonino
Campari, Gran Classico
Absinthe, Pastis, Herbsaint (depends on use and amount
    especially due to sugar content in pastis and Herbsaint)
Dubonnet, Bonal
Green Chartreuse, Dolin Genepy des Alpes
Yellow Chartreuse, Strega
Fino Sherry, Manzanilla Sherry
Amontillado Sherry, Oloroso Sherry, Palo Cortado Sherry
Lustau East India Solera Sherry, 3 parts Amontillado to 1 part
    Pedro Ximenez
Sercial Madeira, Verdelho Madeira
Bual Madeira, Malmsey Madeira
Curaçao, Dry Curaçao, Grand Marnier
Tawny Port, Ruby Port

Syrup Recipes

The following are instructions on how to make every syrup and shrub in this book. If kitchen work is not your thing, do not fret for at the end of the section are a list of commercial syrup producers that offer many of these syrup as well.

Simple, Demerara, Brown Sugar Syrups

Note: all syrups here are presented as 1:1 simple syrups and no rich 2:1 syrups are used. For simple syrup, I prefer dehydrated sugar cane juice crystals over white sugar, but both will work. Demerara and other dark sugars will add more flavor and mouthfeel although they are slightly less sweet than pure white sugar.

>1 cup Sugar (of the proper type)
>1 cup Water

Heat and stir until the sugar has dissolved. Let cool.

Grenadine

>1 cup Pomegranate Juice
>1 cup Sugar
>1 tsp Orange Blossom Water (optional)

Heat juice and sugar, and stir until the sugar has dissolved. Let cool and then add orange blossom water if desired. Many bars such as Eastern Standard opt for the orange blossom water for greater aromatics.

Honey Syrup
        1/2 cup Honey
        1/2 cup Water
Boil the water, add to the honey, and stir until the honey is integrated.
Note: not all bars utilize 1:1 honey syrups and instead use stronger ones, but all recipes in the book have been standardized to this recipe.

Agave Syrup
        1/2 cup Agave Nectar
        1/2 cup Water
Boil the water, add to the agave nectar, and stir until the nectar is integrated.
Note: not all bars utilize 1:1 agave syrups and instead use stronger ones, but all recipes in the book have been standardized to this recipe.

Mint Syrup
        1 cup White Sugar
        1 cup Boiling Water
        Leaves from 12 or more sprigs of Mint
Stir sugar into boiling water until dissolved. Add mint leaves and muddle. Allow mint leaves to steep an hour or more, up to overnight. Strain the leaves from syrup and discard. In a pinch, muddling the leaves of a mint sprig in 1 oz simple syrup will work.

Lavender Syrup
        1/2 cup Water
        1/2 cup Sugar
        4 Tbsp Lavender
Heat until the sugar is dissolved. Let cool and fine strain. Recipe from Misty Kalkofen.

Rosemary Syrup
        1/2 cup Water
        1/2 cup Sugar
        Leaves from 4 sprigs of Rosemary
Bring the water and sugar to a boil, add rosemary leaves, and simmer for five minutes. Cover, let cool, and strain after an hour or more of steeping.

Spiced Syrup

>1 cup Water
>1 cup Sugar
>12 Cloves
>1-2 Star Anise
>1/8 tsp Ground Cinnamon

Bring water and spices to a gentle boil and then simmer for 2 minutes. Add sugar, stir to dissolve, and simmer 2 minutes more. Let cool and then fine strain. Recipe is from Eastern Standard.

Five Spice Syrup

>1 cup Water
>1 cup Sugar
>1 Tbsp Five Spice Powder

Bring to a boil and simmer for 15 minutes. Let cool and strain. Five spice powder is common in Chinese cooking, and the blend can be purchased or made from a mix of Sichuan pepper corns, star anise, clove, cinnamon, and fennel seed.

Tea Syrup

(Includes teas like black, Earl Grey, green, blossom oolong, lapsang souchong, and chai, and tisanes like rooibos, hibiscus, peppermint, and chamomile)

>1 cup Water
>1 cup Sugar
>1 Tbsp Tea (or use ~2 tea bags)

Boil water and steep with the tea leaves for 5 minutes. Strain out the tea leaves (or remove tea bags) and stir in the sugar until dissolved.

Cinnamon Syrup

>1 cup Water
>1 cup Sugar
>3 Cinnamon Sticks

Crush the cinnamon sticks into small pieces. Add water and sugar and bring to a boil. Let simmer for 5 minutes. Let cool and steep for an hour (or overnight), and then strain.

Ginger Syrup
    1 cup Water
    1 cup Sugar
    2 oz Ginger, approx. 2 inches (peeled and sliced)
Heat sugar and water until dissolved. Add ginger and bring to a boil. Let simmer for 10 minutes, cool and steep for at least 30 minutes, and then strain.

Pineapple Syrup
    1 small Pineapple (peeled and cubed)
    Just enough simple syrup to cover the pineapple cubes
Place pineapple cubes (approximately 1 inch cubes) in a bowl. Add enough simple syrup to cover all the pineapple, and let the syrup infuse in a covered bowl for 24 hours. Strain syrup away from pineapple cubes. Squeezing some of the cubes to add some pineapple juice is recommended by some.

Pineapple Shrub
Shrubs are like syrups in that they are sweetened but differ for they also add vinegar to balance the sweetness akin to a sour mix and to help in preservation. While I removed all of the shrubs from the first book and many of the shrubs from this one, there were plenty of Boston drinks that included pineapple shrub as an ingredient that I felt I would branch out. That, and the number of commercial shrub offerings has skyrocketed in the last 5 years.

The process for making a pineapple shrub is similar to making the syrup above:
    1 small Pineapple (peeled and cubed)
    1 cup Sugar
    1 cup Vinegar (such as Apple Cider)
Place pineapple cubes (approximately 1 inch cubes) in a bowl; scale up the recipe for larger pineapples. Cover with sugar, lightly crush the pineapple, and let sit overnight covered with Saran wrap. Add vinegar and let sit for 24 hours (covered) while stirring throughout to dissolve the sugar. Strain out the fruit. I refrigerate my shrubs to preserve flavor, but our Colonial ancestors did this all without such technology.

Passion Fruit, Guava Syrups

    200 gram (3/4 cup) Frozen Passion Fruit or Guava Pulp
    2 cup Simple Syrup (see recipe on page 54)

I thaw my frozen passion fruit or guava in warm freshly made simple syrup, and the IceFruit brand available at my local Brazilian markets requires no straining. Shake or stir to incorporate.

Berry Syrup

(Recipe works for Blackberry, Strawberry, and Raspberry)
    1 cup Blackberries, Raspberries, or sliced Strawberries
    1 cup Water
    1 cup Sugar

Bring the ingredients to a boil and simmer for 10 minutes. Mashing the berries slightly with a spoon during this process would not hurt. Strain when cooled.

In berry syrups, I have found that frozen fruit works just as well as store-bought fresh. During the growing season, fresh is often cheaper, while during the off-season, frozen is the more affordable option. Moreover, in a pinch, muddling fruit in simple syrup and fine straining will work well too.

Vanilla Syrup

    1 cup Water
    1 cup Sugar
    1 Vanilla Bean split lengthwise

Bring to a boil while stirring to dissolve sugar. Let simmer for 5 minutes and cool for 1 hour. Remove the vanilla bean.

Cardamom Syrup

    1 cup Water
    1 cup Sugar
    1 Tbsp Black Cardamom Pods

Coarsely grind cardamom pods in a spice grinder or use a muddler or mortar and pestle to crack the cardamom seeds. Combine with water and sugar and bring the ingredients to a boil while stirring to dissolve sugar. Cover, let cool for 20 minutes, and strain.

Eastern Standard uses 2 parts black cardamom to 1 part green cardamom in their syrup, but most other places use solely black cardamom.

Clove Syrup
        1 cup Water
        1 cup Sugar
        2 tsp Cloves
Coarsely grind cloves in a spice grinder; alternatively, use a muddler or mortar and pestle for the same effect. Combine with water and sugar, and bring the ingredients to a boil while stirring to dissolve sugar. Cover, let cool for 20 minutes, and strain.

Molasses Syrup
        1 cup Water
        1 cup Sugar
        2 oz Grade A Molasses
Boil water and add to sugar and molasses. Stir to dissolve sugar and integrate the molasses.

Coffee Syrup
        1 cup Water
        1 cup Sugar
        3 Tbsp Ground Coffee Beans
Boil the water and sugar, stir to dissolve the sugar, add coffee grounds, and let cool. Strain.

Orgeat
There are many orgeat recipes there ranging from using a presoak to just using almond milk. This is the one that I use at home that streamlines the process without resorting to the nut milk trick. I also eschew orgeat recipes that include large amounts of almond extract for the end result begins to taste more almond than almonds.
        1 cup Water
        1 cup Sugar
        1 cup Sliced Almonds
        1/2 tsp Orange Blossom Water
Blend almonds in a food processor. Heat sugar and water, and stir until the sugar is dissolved. Add blended almonds, bring to a boil, cover, and let cool. Let sit overnight and then strain (I usually squeeze through a tea towel to extract every last drop). Add the orange blossom water.

Lime Cordial

> 1 cup Lime Juice
> 1 cup Sugar
> Zest of 8 Limes

Heat lime juice and sugar and stir until dissolved; do not boil. Add lime zest, let sit covered for 30 minutes, and strain.

Maple Syrup

Use directly from the bottle. Maple syrup does not need to be diluted before use.

Commercial Sources for Syrups

While I recommend making many of these syrups your self, there are commercial options out there. There is no shame in purchasing craft made syrups instead of making them yourself. Below are some syrup manufacturers with high marks going to BG Reynolds, Small Hands Foods, Royal Rose, Liber & Co., and Ginger People. Note that these companies make other syrups that are not used in this book and thus not listed here.

For shopping, I recommend **The Boston Shaker Store** in Davis Square, Somerville, MA, in person if you are local to Boston or on the web (http://www.thebostonshaker.com) if not. They carry BG Reynolds, Liber & Co., Royal Rose, and Stirrings syrups in addition to shrub offerings and other syrup brands. The photos in this section were taken at the store.

BG Reynolds (http://bgreynolds.com)
Cinnamon syrup, falernum, ginger syrup, hibiscus grenadine, orgeat, passion fruit syrup, and vanilla syrup.

Small Hands Foods (http://smallhandfoods.com)
Gomme simple syrup, orgeat, pineapple gum syrup, raspberry gum syrup, and grenadine.

Liber & Co. (https://www.liberandcompany.com)
Grenadine, orgeat, passion fruit syrup, ginger syrup, and pineapple gum syrup.

Royal Rose (http://royalrosesyrups.com)
Demerara syrup, cardamom clove syrup, lavender-lemon syrup, and raspberry syrup.

Ginger People
Ginger syrup.

Stirrings
Simple syrup and grenadine.

Fee Brothers
Blackberry syrup, raspberry syrup, strawberry syrup, pineapple syrup, passion fruit syrup, cinnamon syrup, falernum, orgeat, and grenadine.

Monin
Pure cane simple syrup, raspberry syrup, strawberry syrup, blackberry syrup, pineapple syrup, vanilla syrup, cinnamon syrup, ginger syrup, mint syrup, lavender syrup, passion fruit syrup, almond syrup (orgeat), blackberry syrup, and grenadine.

Torani
Almond syrup (orgeat), blackberry syrup, strawberry syrup, raspberry syrup, cinnamon syrup, ginger syrup, passion fruit syrup, pineapple syrup, and vanilla syrup.

The Recipes

❧

854 Drinks from in and around Boston

4 Devils

Wink & Nod's 2015 tribute to the 1929 movie about a trapeze artist at a circus.

1 1/2 oz Bulleit Rye
1 oz Lustau Oloroso Sherry
1/2 oz Benedictine
1/4 oz Fernet Branca
Stir with ice and strain into a cocktail glass.

4–5–6

Kenny Belanger's smoky and bitter cocktail at Brick & Mortar circa 2013.

2 oz Douglas XO Scotch
1/2 oz Luxardo Amaro Abano
1/2 oz Simple Syrup
2 dash Fee's Whiskey Barrel Bitters
Stir with ice, strain into a rocks glass, and garnish with orange oil from a twist.

10 Cent Loosie

At Brick & Mortar, Kenny Belanger paid tribute to solo cigarette sales back in the day with this smoky libation in 2013.

2 oz Del Maguey Mezcal Vida
1/2 oz Cardamaro
1/2 oz Cardamom Syrup
2 dash Bittermens Mole Bitters
Stir with ice, strain into a cocktail coupe, and garnish with lemon oil from a twist.

11 + 2 / 12 + 1

At the Citizen Public House in 2014, John Mayer named this simple but elegant drink after a 13-lettered word wonder.

1 1/2 oz Zucca Rabarbaro Amaro
1 1/2 oz Green Chartreuse
2 dash Bitter Truth Grapefruit
  Bitters
Stir with ice, strain into a rocks glass, and garnish with grapefruit oil from a twist.

#13

Hungry Mother's Rob Roy-Whiskey Sour mash-up from their early menu circa 2008; it is very reminiscent of drink recipes by James Maloney circa 1900.

2 oz Famous Grouse Scotch
1/2 oz Ferreira Tawny Port
1/4 oz Lemon Juice
1/4 oz Simple Syrup
Shake with ice, strain into a rocks glass, fill with ice, garnish with a cherry, and add straws.

# #

(The) 47%.

An adaptation of a drink served at T.J. the DJ's "Re-elect Senator John"-themed Spin the Bottle event in 2012 at Brick & Mortar.

1 1/4 oz Del Maguey Crema de Mezcal
1 oz Cocchi Americano
1/2 oz Combier Orange Liqueur
1/2 oz Zucca Rabarbaro Amaro
Stir with ice and strain into a rocks glass. Substitute a 9 part mezcal to 1 part agave nectar blend for the crema de mezcal.

#64

Hungry Mother's mezcal Bijou variation circa 2009-2010.

1 oz Del Maguey Mezcal Vida
1 oz Carpano Sweet Vermouth
1/2 oz Green Chartreuse
2 dash Orange Bitters
Stir with ice, strain into a rocks glass, and garnish with lemon oil from a twist.

3:20 in the Morning

Fred Yarm at Russell House Tavern in 2013 riffed on Jason Schiffer's Michigander and named this in tribute to the 320 Main bar in Seal Beach, California.

3/4 oz Great King Street Scotch
3/4 oz Laird's Bonded Apple Brandy
3/4 oz Drambuie
3/4 oz Cynar
3/4 oz Lemon Juice
1/4 oz Honey Syrup
Shake with ice, strain into a single Old Fashioned glass, and garnish with lemon oil from a twist.

1491

Ryan Lotz and Jenna Rycroft created this pre-Columbian tribute for the opening menu of Bar Mezzana in 2016.

1 1/2 oz Macchu Pisco
1/2 oz Del Maguey Mezcal
1/2 oz Blanco Vermouth
1/2 oz Elderflower Liqueur
3/4 oz Lemon Juice
1 Egg White
Shake once without ice and once with ice, strain into a cocktail coupe, and garnish with 5 drops of Angostura Bitters.

1788 Buck

A spiced and funked out Highball created by Chad Arnholt in 2012 at the Citizen Public House in honor of the year that Smith & Cross' distillery was founded.

1 3/4 oz Smith & Cross Rum
3/4 oz Five Spice Syrup
3/4 oz Lime Juice
Shake with ice, strain into a Collins glass containing 2 oz ginger beer, fill with ice, garnish with a lime wedge, and add a straw.

1818 Cocktail

At Spoke Wine Bar in 2013, Lena Webb riffed on Drink's 1919 to make a sherry-driven variation.

1 oz El Maestro Oloroso Sherry
1 oz Old Monk Rum
3/4 oz Punt e Mes
1/4 oz Benedictine
1 dash Mole Bitters
Stir with ice, strain into a rocks glass, and garnish with orange oil from a twist.

1919'36

Audobon Boston's 2015 riff on Drink's 1919 utilizing Kahlua which was first produced in 1936.

1 1/2 oz Old Monk Rum
1/2 oz Kahlua Coffee Liqueur
1 oz Punt e Mes
1 bsp Allspice Dram
1 dash Bittermens Mole Bitters
Stir with ice, strain into a cocktail coupe, and garnish with flamed orange oil from a twist.

2011

John Mayer at Local 149 in 2013 paid tribute to the hot trends in Mixology two years before with a drink that was originally dubbed "Acquired Taste."

1 oz Campari
1 oz Lustau Oloroso Sherry
1 oz Bonal Gentiane-Quina
1 dash Angostura Orange Bitters
1 pinch Salt
Stir with ice, strain into a rocks glass pre-rinsed with Fidencio Mezcal, and garnish with orange oil from a twist.

Abricot Chevalier

Sahil Mehta was inspired at Estragon in 2016 to create a Sidecar variation with more funk, and it was named after a Salvador Dali painting translating into "Apricot Knight."

1 1/2 oz Fernando de Castilla Spanish Brandy
1/2 oz Luxardo Apricot Liqueur
1/2 oz Cynar
1/2 oz Lemon Juice
1 dash Angostura Bitters
Shake with ice and strain into a cocktail coupe.

Absinthe Buck

The Baldwin Bar at Sichuan Garden II's spicy delight created circa 2015.

1 oz Absinthe Ordinaire
1 oz Lime Juice
1/2 oz Orgeat
Shake with ice and strain into a Collins glass containing 3 oz ginger beer. Fill with ice, garnish with 3 dashes Angostura Bitters, mint sprigs, and a lime wedge, and add a straw.

Act of Union

Citizen Public House's 2012 creation to celebrate the union of England and Scotland back in 1707.

1 1/2 oz VDC's Scotch Malt Whisky
1/2 oz Aperol
1/4 oz Orgeat
1/2 oz Simple Syrup
1/2 oz Lemon Juice
Shake with ice, strain into a cocktail coupe, and garnish with a grapefruit twist.

Adams

Sahil Mehta's spiced riff on a Boulevardier that he created at Estragon in 2013.

1 1/2 oz Diabolique Bourbon
3/4 oz Campari
3/4 oz Lacuesta Sweet Vermouth
1/4 oz Combier Kümmel
1 dash Angostura Bitters
Stir with ice and strain into a cocktail glass.

CRINCRONDRINCRONDRINCRONDRINCRONDRINCRONDRINCRIN

Adriatic Yacht Club

Brandon Rucker's Italian riff on the Royal Bermuda Yacht Club circa 2015 at Sarma using Amaro Montenegro instead of triple sec.

1 oz Dark Rum
1 oz Amaro Montenegro
3/4 oz Falernum
3/4 oz Lime Juice
3 dash Angostura Bitters
Shake with ice and strain into a Collins glass. Fill with crushed ice, garnish with mint sprigs and grated nutmeg, and add a straw.

Adventures of Peat & Peat

Patrick Andrew and Vannaluck Hongthong started with the challenge of a stash of Scotch at the Baldwin Bar at Sichuan Garden II in 2016 and ended up crafting this Tiki tribute to a children's television series.

1 1/2 oz A.D. Rattray Cask Islay Scotch
1/2 oz Campari
1/2 oz Orgeat
3/4 oz Pineapple Juice
1 oz Lime Juice
Shake with ice, strain into a Collins glass, garnish with a pineapple slice and an orchid, and add a straw.

Adventures of Peat & Peat, Sichuan Garden II

Aftermath

Backbar crafted this collision of a Lion's Tail, Bobby Burns, Toronto, and Junior in 2012.

1 oz Dewar's Scotch
1 oz Applejack
1/2 oz Benedictine
1/4 oz Fernet Branca
1 bsp Allspice Dram
1 dash Peychaud's Bitters
Stir with ice and strain into a cocktail coupe pre-rinsed with Laphroaig Scotch.

Afterword

A sparkling Last Word riff crafted by Sam Karachi at Spoke Wine Bar in 2013.

1/2 oz Mezcal
1/2 oz Yellow Chartreuse
1/2 oz Amaro Montenegro
1/2 oz Lime Juice
Shake with ice and strain into a cocktail coupe containing 1 oz Nino Franco Prosecco.

Against the Strain

Sean Maher crafted this equal parter at Barrel House in Beverly in 2014 and named it after one of Cynar's old ad slogans.

3/4 oz St. George Dry Rye Gin
3/4 oz Cynar
3/4 oz Campari
3/4 oz Lemon Juice
Shake with ice and strain into a cocktail glass.

Agave Snake

A drink created at Backbar for the Chinese New Year in 2013, the year of the Water Snake.

1 oz El Buho Mezcal
1 oz Lustau Amontillado Sherry
1/2 oz Lime Juice
1/2 oz Agave Syrup
1 dash Soy Sauce
1 dash Brooklyn Hemispherical's Sriracha Bitters
1 slice Cucumber
Muddle cucumber in agave syrup, add rest of the ingredients, shake with ice, and strain into a cocktail glass.

Albariza

At Straight Law, Sean Sullivan crafted this subtle and elegant sparkler for the 2015 Vino de Jerez competition; he named it after the chalky soil that makes sherry great.

1 oz Lustau Manzanilla Sherry
1/2 oz Dolin Blanc Vermouth
1/2 oz Lemon Juice
1/4 oz Salers Gentian Liqueur
1 dash Orange Bitters
Shake with ice, strain into a flute glass containing 2 oz cava, and garnish with a long lemon twist.

A Lesser Man

Barrel House in Beverly's tribute to one of their mezcal-loving regulars, Michael Lesser, circa 2016.

1 1/2 oz Peloton de la Muerte Mezcal
3/4 oz Grapefruit Juice
1/2 oz Yellow Chartreuse
1/2 oz Falernum
Shake with ice and strain into a cocktail glass.

Ali–Frazier

Fred Yarm in 2012 adapted the Alcazer from Pioneers of Mixing at Elite Bars and altered its name to one of the most famous pugilistic match ups.

1 1/2 oz Rye Whiskey
1/2 oz Cointreau
1/2 oz Fernet Branca
1/2 oz Lemon Juice
Shake with ice, strain into a cocktail glass, and garnish with lemon and orange oil from twists.

All Seeing Eye

Steve Bookman created this riff on a Mary Pickford as part of Highball Lounge's secret Tiki menu circa 2015.

1 oz Leblon Cachaça
1 oz Plantation Barbados Rum
1/2 oz Luxardo Maraschino
1/2 oz Grenadine
1/2 oz Pineapple Juice
1/2 oz Lime Juice
Shake with ice and strain into a Pilsner glass containing 1 oz soda water. Fill with crushed ice, garnish with pineapple fruit leaves and a lime wheel-cherry flag, and add a straw.

Almost Famous

The Franklin Café in 2015 seemingly crossed the Naked and Famous with the Culross.

3/4 oz Del Maguey Mezcal Vida
3/4 oz Rothman & Winter Apricot Liqueur
3/4 oz Cocchi Americano
3/4 oz Lemon Juice
1 dash Angostura Orange Bitters
Shake with ice and strain into a rocks glass.

Always Sunny

A classic styled Buck with a pop culture name created at Russell House Tavern circa 2011, and it was originally crafted with strawberry syrup before it switched over to a raspberry one a year or two later.

2 oz Privateer Silver Rum
3/4 oz Lime Juice
3/4 oz Raspberry Syrup
2 dash Orange Bitters
Build in a rocks glass, add 2 oz ginger beer, fill with crushed ice, and add straws.

Andean Flamingo,
The Hawthorne

Amaro di Cocco

Ryan Lotz merged a Kingston Negroni with a Piña Colada at No. 9 Park for this Campari Week 2015 offering that almost got named the Piña Negrada.

1 oz Appleton 12 Year Rum
3/4 oz Pineapple Juice
3/4 oz Campari
3/4 oz Cinzano Sweet Vermouth
3/4 oz Coconut Cream
Shake with ice and strain into a white wine or snifter glass. Fill with crushed ice, float 1/4 oz Hamilton's Jamaican Black Strap Rum, and add straws.

Americano Squeeze

Kirstin Amann and Jay Cool served these Americano-Italian Greyhound hybrids at a Fernet Branca-sponsored breakfast themed night at the Franklin Café in 2015.

2 oz Punt e Mes
1 oz Aperol
4 oz Pink Grapefruit Juice
Build in a Collins glass, fill with ice, garnish with a grapefruit twist, and add a straw.

Anchor Of Light

Keith Corbett crafted this Pisco Punch variation at Stoddard's in 2016 and named it after one of his video game addictions.

2 oz La Caravedo Pisco
1/2 oz Pineapple Juice
1/2 oz Lime Juice
1/2 oz Yellow Chartreuse
1/2 oz Falernum
Shake with ice and strain into a cocktail coupe.

Andean Flamingo

The Hawthorne's Katie Emmerson riffed on of the El Presidente in 2013 to showcase the aromatics of Macchu Pisco's La Diablada.

1 1/2 oz Macchu Pisco La Diablada
3/4 oz Vya Dry Vermouth
1/2 oz Creole Shrubb Orange Liqueur
1 bsp Galliano l'Autentico
1 dash Peychaud's Bitters
Stir with ice and strain into a cocktail coupe.

AN

Andrea & the Governor

Local 149's tribute to The Walking Dead zombie apocalypse television series circa 2012.

1 oz Bastille French Whisky
1 oz Cocchi Americano
1 oz Dolin Blanc Vermouth
2 dash Mansinthe Absinthe
Stir with ice and strain into a rocks glass. In a pinch, substitute Irish whiskey for the Bastille.

Angel's Share

A seasonal drink made at The Gallows in 2010 that has also been made with Concord grapes.

6 Cranberries
1 Sugar Cube
2 oz Underwood Cellars Pinot Noir
3/4 oz Lemon Juice
3/4 oz Simple Syrup
1/4 oz Maraschino Liqueur
1/4 oz Campari
Muddle cranberries with sugar. Add the rest of the ingredients, shake with ice, strain into a cocktail glass, and garnish with 3 cranberries.

Angry Parrot

Eastern Standard's Hugh Fiore crafted this tropical libation for a Tiki night at the Citizen Public House that he guest bartended in 2013.

1 oz Lemon Hart 151 Rum
1 oz Old Monk Rum
1 oz Pineapple Juice
3/4 oz Lime Juice
1/2 oz Cinnamon Syrup
1/2 oz Curaçao
1/4 oz Grenadine
1 dash Angostura Bitters
Shake with ice, strain into a Collins glass, and fill with crushed ice. Garnish with a floated lime wheel and grated nutmeg; add a straw.

Antoine's Demise

At Woburn's Sichuan Garden II, Ran Duan paid homage in 2012 to Antoine Peychaud, the New Orleans pharmacist best known for his bitters.

1 1/2 oz Peychaud's Bitters
1 oz Passion Fruit Syrup
3/4 oz Lime Juice
Shake with ice, strain into a rocks glass with a large ice cube, and garnish with a few spritzes of St. Elizabeth Allspice Dram.

CRCRCRCRCRCRCRCRCRCRCRCRCRCR

Any Other Name

Dan Lynch and Augusto Lino riffed on the Attention Cocktail for the opening 2016 menu for Area 4's Ink Block location in Boston.

2 oz Brockman's Gin
1 oz Dolin Blanc Vermouth
1/4 oz Combier Liqueur de Rose
2 dash Absinthe
1 dash Orange Bitters
Stir with ice, strain into a cocktail coupe, float a rose petal, and garnish with lemon oil over the petal.

Apparition

A funky citrus and herbal beer cocktail created in 2014 by Jared Sadoian at Craigie on Main.

3/4 oz Cold River Gin
1/2 oz Amaro Nonino
1/2 oz Earl Grey Tea Syrup
1/4 oz Lemon Juice
Shake with ice and strain into a flute glass containing 3 oz Lambise Belgian Lambic.

Apricottage

Josh Cross created this "comfy cozy Summer sipper" for Backbar's menu's whiskey section in 2016.

1 oz Old Overholt Rye
3/4 oz Amaro Nonino
3/4 oz Amontillado Sherry
1/2 oz Giffard Apricot Liqueur
1 dash Orinoco (or other aromatic) Bitters
1 pinch Salt
Stir with ice and strain into a cocktail coupe.

April in Paris

Vannaluck Hongthong's herbal and spiced Collins at Sichuan Garden II's Baldwin Bar for the late Summer 2016 menu.

2 oz Salers Gentian Liqueur
1 oz Lemon Juice
3/4 oz Cardamom Syrup
1/2 oz Benedictine
Shake with ice and strain into a Collins glass containing 2 oz soda water. Fill with ice, garnish with a cherry and a (dehydrated) lemon wheel, and add a straw.

Archipelago

Bobby McCoy's 2014 Daiquiri Time Out tribute at Eastern Standard to Kevin "Kodiak" Martin who left the bar to work for the Privateer rum distillery; Bobby named this one after the islands where Kodiak bears live.

2 oz Privateer Silver Rum
1/2 oz Lime Juice
1/2 oz Cinnamon Syrup
1 dash Angostura Bitters
6 drop Pernod Pastis
Shake with ice and strain into a cocktail glass.

Ardent Spirit

Sean Maher's circa 2014 tribute at Barrel House in Beverly to the old alchemical sciences.

1 oz Old Ipswich Tavern Style Rum
1 oz Cynar
1 oz Cocchi Sweet Vermouth
Stir with ice, strain into a rocks glass, and garnish with an orange twist.

Arrack & A Hard Place

Crystal Kelley's Tiki creation and cocktail pun at Brick & Mortar for the Central Kitchen menu in 2013.

3/4 oz Batavia Arrack
3/4 oz Smith & Cross Rum
3/4 oz Combier Orange Liqueur
3/4 oz Amaretto
3/4 oz Lime Juice
Shake with ice, strain into a rocks glass, fill with crushed ice, garnish with 2 dashes Fee's Whiskey Barrel Bitters, and add straws.

Arthur Avenue

James Miranda crafted this tribute to the Bronx's Little Italy at Russell House Tavern in 2013.

1 1/4 oz Old Overholt Rye Whiskey
1 1/4 oz Aperol
3/4 oz Punt e Mes
3/4 oz Grapefruit Juice
1 dash Angostura Bitters
Shake with ice, strain into a cocktail glass, and garnish with grapefruit oil from a twist.

A Season of
Faith's Perfection,
Spoke Wine Bar

A Season of Faith's Perfection

Sam Karachi crafted this herbal malt bomb at Spoke Wine Bar circa 2013.

1 1/2 oz Bols Genever
1/2 oz Benedictine
1/2 oz Bonal Gentiane-Quina
1/2 oz La Grange Muscadet
(or other dry white wine)
2 dash Peychaud's Bitters
1 dash Jerry Thomas Decanter
Bitters
Stir with ice, strain into a cocktail coupe, and garnish with lemon oil from a twist.

Ask the Dust

Fred Yarm crafted this Scaffa for the Autumn 2014 Russell House Tavern menu.

2 oz Byrrh Quinquina
1 1/2 oz Mezcal
1/2 oz Tempus Fugit Crème de
Cacao
2 dash Angostura Bitters
1 scant bsp Butterfly Absinthe
Build in a snifter (or rocks) glass, and briefly stir to mix __without__ ice. Note: This is a room temperature cocktail.

Astra

Ryan Connelly created this as a low proof option for New Years Eve 2013 at Belly Wine Bar.

1 1/2 oz Dolin Blanc Vermouth
1/2 oz Laird's 7 1/2 Year Apple Brandy
1/2 oz CapRock Gin
1/2 oz Cardamaro
1 dash Regan's Orange Bitters
Stir with ice, strain into a rocks glass, and garnish with lemon oil from a twist.

Attitude Dancing

A spiced cocktail created at Brick and Mortar for a Spin the Bottle event in 2012 featuring Eastern Standard's Garrett Harker on the turntables.

1 1/2oz Pierre Ferrand 1840 Cognac
1 oz Fernet Branca
3/4 oz Combier Kümmel
1 oz Water
Build in a rocks glass, and briefly stir to mix __without__ ice. Note: This is a room temperature cocktail.

Auld Alliance

Kenny Belanger's creation at Brick & Mortar for a High & Mighty Brewery Spin the Bottle night in 2013 using another brewery's beer that High & Mighty had brought along.

1 1/2oz Grand MacNish Scotch
1/2 oz Crème de Cacao
1/4 oz Galliano Ristretto
1/2 oz Lemon Juice
Shake with ice, strain into rocks glass containing 2 oz of Page 24 Vieillie En Fût De Chêne (a barrel-aged brown ale), fill with ice, and add straws.

Autumn in Oahu

An adaptation of Ingrid Schneider's Fall Tiki drink at Little Donkey that utilized a housemade allspice syrup for their 2016 menu.

1 oz Foursquare Cask Rum
1 oz Old Monk Rum
1/2 oz Pineapple Syrup
1/2 oz Allspice Dram
1/2 oz Lime Juice
Shake with ice, strain into a rocks glass, fill with crushed ice, garnish with 4 dashes Peychaud's Bitters, and add straws.

Avalon

Carrie Cole's 2012 tribute at Eastern Standard to King Arthur's legendary island as well as Brian Ferry's hit song.

1/2 oz Old Port Rum
1/2 oz Yellow Chartreuse
1/2 oz Lime Juice
1/2 oz Grapefruit Juice
1/4 oz Cinnamon Syrup
1 dash Peychaud's Bitters
Shake with ice and strain into a flute glass containing 2 oz of dry sparkling wine.

Averna Cup

Sichuan Garden II's house riff on the Pimm's Cup that appeared on their menu in 2015.

1 oz Old Monk Rum
1 oz Averna
3/4 oz Lemon Juice
1/2 oz Giffard Crème de Fraise
Shake with ice and strain into a Collins glass containing 2 oz ginger ale. Fill with ice, garnish with mint sprigs and an orange twist, and add a straw.

Averna Diamond Fizz

Fred Yarm crafted this concept in 2016 for one of his regulars at Loyal Nine that drank either Averna or cava. That guest rejected the idea for he despised cocktails, but the combination turned out to be a winner with other patrons.

2 oz Averna
1/2 oz Demerara Syrup
1/2 oz Lemon Juice
1 dash Bittermens Mole Bitters
Shake with ice, strain into a white wine or flute glass containing 2 oz Bohigas Cava, and garnish with a lemon twist.

Backyard Bitter

A complex Cognac drink invented at the Cititzen Public House in 2013.

1 1/2 oz Pierre Ferrand 1840 Cognac
1/2 oz Aperol
1/2 oz Gran Classico
1/2 oz Lustau Oloroso Sherry
2 dash Jerry Thomas Decanter Bitters
Stir with ice, strain into a rocks glass, and garnish with grapefruit oil from a twist.

Bahia Sling,
Sichuan Garden II

Bahia Sling

Ran Duan's 2015 tropical Sling at the Baldwin Bar at Sichuan Garden II.

1 1/2 oz Avua Cachaça
3/4 oz Passion Fruit Syrup
1/2 oz Tempus Fugit Crème de Cacao
1 oz Lime Juice
Shake with ice and strain into a Collins glass. Fill with crushed ice, garnish with a mint sprig, edible orchid, and grated coffee bean, and add a straw.

Bairdley Legal

The inaugural 2015 menu at Yvonne's paid tribute to Scott Baird of San Francisco's Trick Dog with this tropical number.

1 oz Mezcal
1 oz Cynar
1 oz Passion Fruit Nectar
Shake with ice, strain into a tall glass containing 2 oz grapefruit soda, and fill with ice. Garnish with mint sprigs and add a straw.

Balboa

Sahil Mehta crafted this libation for his sherry-themed Christmas dinner at Estragon in 2012.

1 1/2 oz Ron Abuelo Rum
1/2 oz King's Ginger Liqueur
1/2 oz Lustau Pedro Ximenez Sherry
1/2 oz Lemon Juice
1 dash St. Elizabeth Allspice Dram
Shake with ice and strain into a cocktail glass.

Balmy Night

Fred Yarm merged two classics, the Balm and the Kingston Heights, for an allspice dram-themed online event in 2009.

1 oz Amontillado Sherry
1 oz Jamaican Rum
1/2 oz Orange Juice
1/4 oz Curaçao
1/4 oz Allspice Dram
1 dash Angostura Bitters
Shake with ice, strain into a cocktail glass, and garnish with an orange twist.

Bamboozled

Sam Treadway and Melinda Maddox at Backbar in 2013 riffed on the classic Bamboo Cocktail.

1 1/4 oz Amontillado Sherry
1 oz Cocchi Americano
1/2 oz Ford's Gin
1/8 oz Nux Alpina Walnut Liqueur
1/8 oz Simple Syrup
1 dash Angostura Bitters
Stir with ice and strain into a cocktail coupe.

Banana Cup No. 1

Sahil Mehta crafted this complex bitter and tropical Pimm's Cup for a drink of the day at Estragon in 2016.

1 1/2 oz Pimm's No. 1
1/2 oz Giffard Banane du Bresil
1/2 oz Cynar
1 oz Lemon Juice
Shake with ice and strain into a rocks glass containing 2 oz Barritts Ginger Beer. Fill with ice, garnish with a mint sprig, and add straws.

Bargellino

Josh Childs at Silvertone found this Brooklyn-esque recipe in his old notes, and he started serving this rediscovered tribute to a hotel in Italy circa 2013.

1 1/2 oz Old Overholt Rye
3/4 oz Dry Vermouth
1/2 oz Amaro Montenegro
1/4 oz Luxardo Maraschino
Stir with ice, strain into a rocks glass, and garnish with an orange twist.

Barnyard Punch

Shaher Misif created this as a large format punch before converting it to a single serving offering for the Highball Lounge menu circa 2015.

2 oz Woodford Reserve Bourbon
1/2 oz Suze Gentian Liqueur
1/2 oz Falernum
1/2 oz Lemon Juice
1/2 oz Simple Syrup
2 dash Celery Bitters
Shake with ice, strain into a rocks glass, fill with ice, garnish with a lemon slice and mint sprigs, and add straws.

Bartender's Bingo

In 2012, writer Luke O'Neil teamed up Temple Bar bartenders Evan Kenney and Sam Gabrielli to create a parody drink that was actually quite good; in fact, Trina's Starlite Lounge ended up putting it on their menu later that year.

1 1/2 oz Old Overholt Rye
1/2 oz Fernet Branca
1/2 oz Yellow Chartreuse
1/2 oz Maraschino Liqueur
1/2 oz Lemon Juice
1/2 oz Lime Juice
1 dash Angostura Bitters
1 dash Peychaud's Bitters
1 dash Orange Bitters
Shake with ice and strain into a rocks glass pre-rinsed with Del Maguel Mezcal Vida.

Basilica Cocktail

Evan Harrison's riff on the Old Hickory at Highland Kitchen that got published in a Boston.com Valentine's Day article in 2013.

1 oz Cocchi Americano
1 oz Sweet Vermouth
1/2 oz Suze Gentian Liqueur
1/2 oz Campari
1 dash Angostura Orange Bitters
Stir with ice, strain into an Old Fashioned glass with a large ice cube, and garnish with an orange twist.

CRUISE NORRECRUISE NORRECRUISE NORRECRUISE

Batavia Sazarrack

After my final shift at Russell House Tavern in 2013, the other bartenders took me to Park. There, I asked Nick Checchio for his take on a Batavia Arrack Sazerac. Bad decisions might have been made that night, but this was not one of them.

1 1/2 oz Batavia Arrack
1/2 oz El Dorado 3 Year Rum
1/2 oz Demerara Syrup
3 dash Peychaud's Bitters
2 dash Fee's Walnut Bitters
Stir with ice, strain into a rocks glass pre-rinsed with Velvet Falernum, and garnish with both lemon and orange twists.

Bath Salts

Trina's Starlite Lounge paid tribute in 2012 to the Zombie-inducing street drug with a Zombie-like Tiki treat.

3/4 oz Old Monk Rum
3/4 oz White Rum
1/2 oz Neisson Rhum Agricole Blanc
1 oz Apricot Liqueur
1/2 oz Simple Syrup
1/2 oz Lemon Juice
1/2 oz Lime Juice
1 dash Pernod
3 dash Bittermens Tiki Bitters
Shake with ice, strain into a pint glass containing 2 oz Barritts Ginger Beer, fill with ice, garnish with an orange slice and a brandied cherry, and add a straw.

Battle of Puebla

Lincoln Tavern in Southie's smoky, spicy, and herbal delight created circa 2015.

1 oz Del Maguey Crema de Mezcal
1 oz Ancho Reyes Chile Liqueur
1 oz Amaro Nonino
1/4 oz Crème de Cacao
1 dash Regan's Orange Bitters
Stir with ice, strain into a rocks glass, fill with ice, garnish with an orange twist, and add straws. Substitute a 9 part mezcal to 1 part agave nectar blend for the crema de mezcal.

BA-BE

Battle Over Dutch

One of the great sherry cocktails at Merrill & Co., and this one appeared on their menu in 2014.

1 oz Lustau East India Sherry
1 oz Kronan Swedish Punsch
1/2 oz Tempus Fugit Crème de Cacao
1/2 oz Lemon Juice
Shake with ice, strain into a cocktail coupe, and garnish with lemon oil from a twist.

Bayeux Cocktail

Craigie on Main's tribute in 2013 to where Lecompte Calvados is produced in Normandy.

1 1/2 oz Lecompte Calvados
1/2 oz Krogstad Aquavit
1/2 oz Benedictine
1/2 oz Earl Grey Tea Syrup
Stir with ice, strain into a cocktail glass, and garnish with orange oil from a twist.

Beacon Fix

An adaptation of Bergamot's vodka-based Beacon Fix circa 2011. Despite the name, it is not a classic Fix, but named by bartender Kai Gagnon after a methadone clinic he frequently passed by on the way to work.

1 1/2 oz Vodka (or Beefeater Gin)
1/2 oz Luxardo Triplum Orange Liqueur
1/2 oz Rooibos (or Earl Grey Tea) Syrup
1/2 oz Lemon Juice
Shake with ice and strain into a cocktail glass. Utilize MEM's rooibos-bergamot tea for the syrup if you can source it.

Becca's Blood & Sand

Silvertone's variation circa 2013 on the Scotch-based classic created for Rebecca of Girls Pint Out and later Puritan & Co.

3/4 oz Del Maguey Mezcal Vida
3/4 oz Carpano Sweet Vermouth
3/4 oz Maurin Quina
3/4 oz Orange Juice
Shake with ice and strain into a cocktail glass.

Before Night Falls

A rather savory herbal mezcal treat in 2016 from Sahil Mehta at Estragon.

1 oz Mezcal
1 oz Manzanilla Sherry
3/4 oz Green Chartreuse
1/4 oz Combier Kümmel
1/2 oz Lime Juice
Shake with ice and strain into a cocktail glass.

Bela Vista

No. 9 Park's rich and tropical Black Manhattan variation in 2015.

2 oz Old Overholt Rye
1 oz Amaro Ramazzotti
1/2 oz Giffard Banane du Bresil
Stir with ice, strain into a rocks glass with a large ice cube, and garnish with a cherry.

Belle Starr

For a Whiskey & Amari night at the Blue Room in 2013, Fred Yarm crafted this tribute to the Bandit Queen of the Wild West.

3/4 oz Bully Boy Aged Whiskey
3/4 oz Apple Brandy or Calvados
1 oz Bonal Gentiane-Quina
1/2 oz Strega
1 dash Orange Bitters
Stir with ice, strain into a cocktail coupe, and garnish with a lemon twist.

Bela Vista,
No. 9 Park

Benny & the Jets

One of Ryan Lotz's Tiki numbers at No. 9 Park resembling a Jet Pilot that he presented in 2015 at an event he did with Beachbum Berry here in Boston.

1 oz Pierre Ferrand 1840 Cognac
1 oz Smith & Cross Rum
1/2 oz Grapefruit Juice
1/2 oz Lime Juice
1/2 oz Benedictine
1/2 oz Demerara Syrup
3 dash Angostura Bitters
1 dash Kübler Absinthe
Shake with ice and strain into a Tiki mug. Fill with crushed ice, garnish with a spent lime shell, a cherry, and a mint sprig, and add a straw.

Betty Boop

An adaptation of Sam Spence's Tiki contribution to Audubon's cartoon-themed section of their 2015 menu.

3/4 oz Diplomatico Reserva Rum
3/4 oz Barbancourt 8 Year Rhum
1/2 oz Orgeat
1/2 oz Marie Brizard Crème de Cacao
1/2 oz Lemon Juice
2 dash Angostura Bitters
Shake with ice, strain into a tulip glass, fill with crushed ice, garnish with a paper parasol, and add straws.

Bezzera

Tyler Wang became intrigued by the pairing of Campari and coffee flavors at No. 9 Park, and he crafted this one in 2013 with a syrup made with Counter Culture's Rustico (now Hologram) coffee.

3/4 oz Campari
3/4 oz Cocchi Barolo Chinato
3/4 oz Wireworks Gin
1/2 oz Coffee Syrup
Stir with ice, strain into a cocktail glass, and garnish with an orange twist.

Bicycle Thief

California Gold helped to revamp the Blue Room's cocktail list in 2012 with this Little Italy riff.

1 1/2 oz Rittenhouse Rye
1/2 oz Bonal Gentiane-Quina
1/2 oz Cocchi Sweet Vermouth
1/2 oz Cynar
Stir with ice, strain into a rocks glass, and garnish with orange oil from a twist.

Bikini Bottom

A complex tropical libation with a cheeky name crafted at Brick & Mortar in 2016.

1 1/2 oz Plantation Pineapple Rum
3/4 oz Averna
3/4 oz Lime Juice
1/2 oz Simple Syrup
5 leaf Mint
Shake with ice, strain into a rocks glass, fill with crushed ice, garnish with a mint sprig and 3 spritzes Laphroaig Scotch, and add straws.

Bird Named Rufus

Chris Danforth created this at Spoke Wine Bar in 2015 in honor of the only birdcall his mom knew, that of a Rufous-crowned Tody Flycatcher.

1 oz Plantation 3 Star White Rum
1 oz Cynar
1/2 oz Yellow Chartreuse
1/2 oz Lemon Juice
4 leaf Mint
Shake with ice, strain into a rocks glass containing 1 oz soda water, fill with ice, garnish with a lemon twist, and add straws.

Bird's Eye View

Steve Shur's bitter, brown, and stirred offering at the Boston College Club circa 2012.

1 1/2 oz Eagle Rare Bourbon
3/4 oz Amaro Ramazzotti
1/2 oz Carpano Sweet Vermouth
1/4 oz Yellow Chartreuse
Stir with ice, strain into a cocktail glass, and garnish with lemon oil from a twist.

Birthday Suit

Joseph Cammarata created this drink in honor of Backbar's first anniversary in December 2012.

1 3/4 oz Four Roses Bourbon
1/2 oz Gran Classico
1/2 oz Lustau Pedro Ximenez Sherry
1/4 oz Cinnamon Syrup
1 dash Angostura Bitters
Stir with ice and strain into a cocktail coupe.

BI

Bitter Collins

Deep Ellum jazzed up the traditional Collins in 2013 with herbal citrus notes and distinctive coloration from Campari.

1 1/2 oz Damrak Gin
1/2 oz Campari
1 oz Lemon Juice
1 oz Simple Syrup
Shake with ice, strain into a Collins glass containing 3 oz soda water, and fill with ice. Garnish with a cherry-orange slice flag, and add a straw.

Bitter End

One part dessert and one part digestif at the Barrel House in Beverly circa 2014.

1 1/2 oz Fernet Branca
3/4 oz Coconut Cream
3/4 oz Pierre Ferrand 1840 Cognac
2 dash Bittermens Mole Bitters
1 Egg White
Shake once without ice and once with ice, and strain into a cocktail coupe.

Bitter Nail,
Ames Street Deli

Bitter Improv

Michael at Craigie on Main crafted this in 2008 in response to a request for a rye whiskey drink.

1 1/2 oz Rittenhouse Rye
1/2 oz Pimm's No. 1
1/2 oz Aperol
1/2 oz Cynar
1 dash Regan's Orange Bitters
Stir with ice, strain into a cocktail coupe, and garnish with an orange twist.

Bitter Monk

Tom Schlesinger-Guidelli crafted this libation at Island Creek Oyster Bar and it was later published in Esquire in 2012.

1 1/2 oz Old Monk Rum
3/4 oz Aperol
3/4 oz Lemon Juice
1 dash Bittermens Tiki Bitters
Shake with ice and strain into a cocktail coupe.

Bitter Nail

Iruma Shibuya's 2016 riff on the classic Rusty Nail at Ames Street Deli.

1 1/2 oz Great King Street Scotch
1/2 oz Drambuie
1/2 oz Cynar
1/2 oz Campari
Stir with ice, strain into a rocks glass, and add ice.

Bittersweet Aloha

Tracy Latimer's Negroni Week 2015 offering at J.M. Curley's.

1 oz Beefeater Gin
1/2 oz Campari
1/2 oz Cocchi Americano
1/2 oz Pineapple Syrup
1/2 oz Lime Juice
1 pinch Salt
Stir to dissolve the salt in the lime juice and pineapple syrup. Add the rest of the ingredients, shake with ice, and strain into a cocktail coupe.

Black Arrow

At Brick & Mortar, Matt Schrage paid tribute in 2014 to the first black player for the Scottish Celtics soccer team, and proceeds from the drink funded soccer teams in Jamaica.

1 1/2 oz Appleton Reserve Rum
3/4 oz Cinzano Sweet Vermouth
1/2 oz Pierre Ferrand Dry Curaçao
1/2 oz Lime Juice
1/2 oz Grenadine
Shake with ice and strain into a cocktail coupe.

BL

Black Douglas

Eastern Standard's 2013 tribute to James Douglas, a Scotsman who fought the Moors in Spain.

1 1/2 oz Johnnie Walker Red Scotch
3/4 oz Lustau East India Sherry
1/2 oz Licor 43
2 dash Angostura Bitters
Stir with ice and strain into a cocktail glass.

Black'd Out Shade

A 2012 beer riff on Eastern Standard's Prospect Park created by Jason Goodwin at Local 149 and named after a bartenders' tool use to catch up on sleep.

1/2 oz Campari
1/2 oz Maraschino Liqueur
1/2 oz Punt e Mes
Stir with ice and strain into a rocks glass containing 4 oz Sixpoint's Righteous Rye IPA beer.

Blackheart

A pirate-inspired beer cocktail crafted at Brick & Mortar in 2013.

1 1/2 oz Batavia Arrack
1/2 oz St. Elizabeth Allspice Dram
1/2 oz Molasses Syrup
1/2 oz Orange Juice
1/4 oz Lime Juice
1 dash Angostura Bitters
Shake with ice, strain into a rocks glass containing 2 oz of Notch Session Ale, fill with ice, and add straws.

Black Market

Deep Ellum's herbal Gin Sour crafted in 2011.

1 1/2 oz Death's Door Gin
3/4 oz Dolin Sweet Vermouth
1/2 oz Lemon Juice
1/2 oz Simple Syrup
2 dash Tea Bitters
Shake with ice, strain into a cocktail coupe, and garnish with a lemon twist.

Black Mercy

Tony Iamunno's 2014 tribute at Stoddard's to the Justice League Unlimited comic book.

2 oz Amaro Ramazzotti
3/4 oz Honey Syrup
1/2 oz Bols Orange Curaçao
3/4 oz Lemon Juice
Shake with ice and strain into a cocktail coupe.

Black Monk Julep

An adaptation of Bar Mezzana's dark herbal and fruity Julep for their opening Summer menu in 2016.

1 1/2 oz Evan Williams Bonded
  Bourbon
1 oz Averna
1/2 oz Blackberry Syrup
6-8 leaf Mint
Lightly muddle mint leaves in a double Old Fashioned glass, add the rest of the ingredients, and stir. Fill with crushed ice, garnish with mint sprigs, and add straws.

Black Sea Swizzle

For a Fernet Branca-themed week of drink of the day at Loyal Nine, Fred Yarm crafted this fruity-herbal number in 2017.

1 oz JM Rhum Agricole Blanc
1/2 oz Wray & Nephew White
  Overproof Rum
1/2 oz Benedictine
1/2 oz Passion Fruit Syrup
1/2 oz Lime Juice
Build in a Collins glass, fill with crushed ice, and swizzle to mix and chill. Add a straw, float 1/4 oz Fernet Branca, and garnish with a boat made out of citrus peels and toothpicks.

Black Snake

Myers and Chang honored 2013, the Year of the Black Snake in the Chinese Zodiac.

1 1/2 oz Cruzan Black Strap Rum
3/4 oz Cynar
1/2 oz Lime Juice
Shake with ice and strain into a Fizz glass containing 1 oz Coca Cola.

BL

Blackthorne (No. 9 Park's variation)

No. 9 Park riffed on the classic Blackthorn in 2012 by adding a Tipperary element of Green Chartreuse into the mix.

1 3/4 oz Jameson Black Barrel Irish Whiskey
1 oz Dolin Dry Vermouth
3/4 oz Green Chartreuse
1 bsp Kübler Absinthe
2 dash Angostura Bitters
Stir with ice and strain into a rocks glass.

Blade of Destiny

Tavern Road bartender Bruno Prado helped to create this complex digestif in 2014 for cocktailian Christopher "Blade" Kotelly.

1 oz Amontillado Sherry
1 oz Cynar
1 oz Nardini Amaro
Stir with ice, strain into a rocks glass with a large ice cube, and garnish with orange oil from a twist.

Bleeding Fog Swizzle

Ted Kilpatrick created this smokier riff on a Fog Cutter in 2013 at No. 9 Park with perhaps some elements lifted from his Burning Ice recipe.

1 1/2 oz Del Maguey Mezcal Vida
1/2 oz Swedish Punsch
3/4 oz El Maestro Sierra Pedro Ximenez Sherry
3/4 oz Lemon Juice
1 bsp Kübler Absinthe
Build in a goblet glass, fill with crushed ice, and swizzle to mix and chill. Garnish with 2 dashes Peychaud's Bitters and add a straw.

Blended Banana Ramos

For Mardi Gras 2017 at the Hawthorne, Jackson Cannon challenged Jared Sadioan to craft a blender-based Ramos, and it was subtitled on the menu "They said it couldn't be done."

1 1/2 oz Tanqueray 10 Gin
1 oz Coconut Cream
1/2 oz Heavy Cream
3/4 oz Simple Syrup
1/2 oz Lemon Juice
1/2 oz Lime Juice
3/4 oz Giffard Banane du Bresil
Blend with 6 oz ice, pour into a cup, and add a straw.

Blow-Up,
West Bridge

Blood Letter

An adaptation of Barrel House in Beverly's 2015 tribute to the badlands of Mexico originally made with a barspoon of hot pepper-infused vodka.

2 oz Peloton de la Muerte Mezcal
1/2 oz Carpano Bianco Vermouth
1/2 oz Salers Gentian Liqueur
2-3 drop Hot Sauce
2 dash Peychaud's Bitters
Stir with ice and strain into a rock glass.

Blood of My Enemies

A grassy and fruity number by Tony Iamunno at Stoddard's in 2012.

1 oz Clement Rhum Agricole
1 oz Aperol
3/4 oz Blood Orange Juice
1/2 oz Grenadine
2 dash Peychaud's Bitters
Shake with ice and strain into a cocktail coupe.

Blow–Up

Mike Fleming's movie tribute at West Bridge circa 2014.

3/4 oz Tanqueray Gin
3/4 oz Dimmi Liqueur
3/4 oz Amaro del Capo
3/4 oz Carpano Sweet Vermouth
Stir with ice, strain into a cocktail glass, and garnish with lemon oil from a twist.

Blue Hour

A complex fruit-driven creation by Stephen Shellenberger at Pomodoro in Brookline circa 2012.

3/4 oz Eau de Vie de Mirabelle
3/4 oz Pineau des Charentes
3/4 oz Aperol
3/4 oz Lime Juice
1 dash Peychaud's Bitters
Shake with ice, strain into a glass, and garnish with lime oil from a twist. Other fruit eaux de vie will work well here too.

Blue Point

Matthew Schrage at the Blue Room crafted this Green Point-like Manhattan in 2012.

1 1/2 oz Elijah Craig Bourbon
1/2 oz El Maestro Oloroso Sherry
1/2 oz Punt e Mes
1/2 oz Yellow Chartreuse
2 dash Jerry Thomas Decanter
Bitters
Stir with ice, strain into a rocks glass, and garnish with grapefruit oil from a twist.

Bokemon Daiquiri

Will Thomspon's Daiquiri at Brick & Mortar 2014 that appeared like a riff on Alex Day's Boukmon Daiquiri but named after the Japanese word meaning recklessly strong.

1 oz El Dorado 12 Year Rum
1 oz Pierre Ferrand 1840 Cognac
1/2 oz Cinnamon Syrup
1/2 oz Lemon Juice
1 dash Angostura Bitters
Shake with ice and strain into a cocktail coupe.

Bolsy Move

A gutsy cocktail crafted at J.M. Curley's in 2012.

1 1/2 oz Bols Genever
1/2 oz Yellow Chartreuse
1/2 oz Cherry Heering
3/4 oz Lemon Juice
1 dash Angostura Bitters
Shake with ice and strain into a cocktail coupe.

Bombos y Platillos

Sahil Mehta's 2015 take at Estragon on the 1930s Hoop La.

3/4 oz Batavia Arrack
3/4 oz Apricot Liqueur
3/4 oz Cocchi Americano
3/4 oz Lemon Juice
1 pinch Salt
Shake with ice and strain into a cocktail glass.

Bonatti & the Jets

Cory Buono named his Italian Alpine ingredient-laden drink at Brick & Mortar in 2013 after a famous Italian mountaineer who scaled K2.

1 1/2 oz Nardini Aquavite Bassano Riserva Aged Grappa
1/2 oz Benedictine
1/2 oz Cardamaro
1/2 oz Cocchi Sweet Vermouth
1 dash Angostura Bitters
Stir with ice, strain into a cocktail coupe, and garnish with grapefruit oil from a twist.

Bonnie & Clyde

Cory Buono's 2013 tribute at Brick & Mortar to the famed gunmen and perhaps the Serge Gainsbourg song as well.

1 1/2 oz Pierre Ferrand 1840 Cognac
1/2 oz Lustau Amontillado Sherry
1/2 oz Byrrh Quinquina
1/2 oz Benedictine
2 dash Angostura Bitters
Stir with ice and strain into a rocks glass.

Bonsoni
(Deep Ellum's variation)

Max Toste in 2010 at Deep Ellum riffed on Hugo Ensslin's 1916 classic digestif.

1 oz Dolin Sweet Vermouth
1 oz Punt e Mes
1 oz Fernet Branca
1/4 oz Cynar
Stir with ice, strain into a rocks glass, and garnish with lemon oil from a twist.

Bon-Vivant,
Eastern Standard

Bon–Vivant

Kit Paschal at Eastern Standard paid tribute to Jerry Thomas with this 2012 take on the classic Sherry Cobbler.

1 1/2 oz Lustau East India Sherry
1/2 oz Cruzan Black Strap Rum
3/4 oz Lemon Juice
1/2 oz Cinnamon Syrup
2 big Blackberries
Muddle blackberries in a rocks glass. Add rest of ingredients and fill with crushed ice. Stir, garnish with 2 sprigs of mint and a fresh blackberry, and add straws.

Bootlegger's Breakfast

Coffee and smoke notes are only the tip of the iceberg for this elegant split-spirit drink crafted in 2016 by Sahil Mehta at Estragon.

3/4 oz Appleton Signature Rum
1/2 oz Laphroaig Scotch
1/2 oz Old Granddad Bourbon
1/2 oz Cynar 70
1/2 oz Lustau Oloroso Sherry
1/4 oz Coffee Heering
Stir with ice and strain into a cocktail coupe.

Bourbon Milk Punch

Max Toste at Deep Ellum offered up his take on the New Orleans brunch drink in 2011.

1 1/2 oz Four Roses Bourbon
1/2 oz Diplomatico Reserva Rum
1 1/2 oz Milk
1/2 oz Cinnamon Syrup
2 dash Aromatic Bitters
Shake with ice, strain into a Highball glass, fill with ice, and garnish with freshly grated nutmeg.

Brautigan

Rendezvous' Scott Holliday tinkered with the Sloe Comfortable Screw Against the Wall-like drinks in 2011 and tried to give the fallen genre some dignity. His inspiration was a Richard Brautigan poem called "Fuck me like fried potatoes."

2 oz Rittenhouse Rye
1/2 oz Galliano l'Autentico
2 oz Orange Juice
Shake with ice, strain into a rocks glass, fill with ice, garnish with an orange twist, and add straws.

Braveheart

An adaptation of a blender drink that the Hawthorne's Scott Marshall crafted for a Drambuie-sponsored Tales of the Cocktail 2012 send-off party at the Franklin Southie.

1 1/2 oz Bacardi 8 Year Rum
1/2 oz Drambuie
1/2 oz Orgeat
3/4 oz Lime Juice
2 dash Angostura Bitters
Shake with ice, strain into a rocks glass, and fill with crushed ice. Garnish with freshly grated nutmeg and add straws.

Brazilian Million

Todd Maul's circa 2012 cachaça variation at Clio of the classic Millionaire; his original formulation utilized sloe gin before switching over to damson.

2 oz Germana Cachaça
1/2 oz Averell Damson Gin (or Plymouth Sloe Gin)
1/2 oz Bitter Truth Apricot Liqueur
1 oz Lime Juice
1 dash Grenadine
Shake with ice, strain into a rocks glass, and fill with ice. Garnish with a lime wheel and add straws.

BR

Breakfast

A drink crafted in 2013 by John Henderson of Scholars for one of the Blue Room's Whiskey & Amari nights.

2 oz John L. Sullivan Irish Whiskey
1 oz Galliano Ristretto
1 dash Chocolate Bitters
Stir with ice and strain into a rocks glass pre-rinsed with Laphroaig Scotch.

Breakfast of Champions

Matt Baber's rich dessert Flip circa 2016 at Craigie on Main; other styles of rich dark beer have been utilized in this recipe.

2 oz Cruzan Black Strap Rum
2 oz Breckenridge Vanilla Porter
1/2 oz Demerara Syrup
2 dash Mole Bitters
1 Whole Egg
Stir the beer to de-gas it and add the rest of the ingredients. Shake once without ice and once with ice, strain into a tulip beer glass, and garnish with freshly grated nutmeg.

Br'er Rabbit

Scott Holliday at Rendezvous created this for a customer's request in 2012 for something blackberry-esque and bitter.

2 oz Old Overholt Rye
1/2 oz Crème de Cassis
1/2 oz Salers Gentian Liqueur
Stir with ice, strain into a rocks glass, and fill with ice. Float a barspoon of absinthe, garnish with a lemon twist, and add straws.

Broadside

Sean Frederick at the Citizen Public House competed in the 2012 Angostura competition with this cocktail.

2 oz Hayman's Royal Dock Navy Strength Gin
3/4 oz Lime Juice
3/4 oz Rooibos Tea Syrup
5 dash Angostura Bitters
Shake with ice and strain into a rocks glass (optional: smoke the glass by lighting a cinnamon stick, covering it with a glass, and let it smolder before use).

Broken Crown

Tyler Wang crafted this tequila Twentieth Century (a/k/a P.D.T.'s 21st Century) crossed with a Jack Rose at Kirkland Tap and Trotter in 2013.

1 1/2 oz El Tesoro Tequila
1/2 oz Laird's Bonded Apple Brandy
1/2 oz Tempus Fugit Crème de Cacao
1/2 oz Lime Juice
1 bsp Grenadine
1 dash Celery Bitters
Shake with ice and strain into a cocktail coupe.

Brooklyn Roasting Company

At Deep Ellum, Max Toste crafted this amaro-forward cocktail in 2012 around the coffee liqueur component.

1 1/2 oz Bacardi 8 Year Rum
1/2 oz Galliano Ristretto
1/2 oz Meletti Amaro
1/2 oz Fernet Branca
2 dash Orange Bitters
Stir with ice, strain into a rocks glass, and garnish with orange oil from a twist.

Bruce's Heart

Sahil Mehta crafted this nutty, smoky, and spiced number at Estragon in 2016.

2 oz Lustau Amontillado Sherry
1/2 oz Laphroaig Scotch
1/2 oz King's Ginger Liqueur
1/2 oz Orgeat
1/2 oz Lemon Juice
1 dash Angostura Bitters
Shake with ice and strain into a cocktail glass.

Budokan

An adaptation of Hojoko's 2015 rum Sazerac riff.

1 oz Hamilton's 151 Proof Demerara Rum
1 oz Sandeman Rainwater Madeira
1/4 oz Demarara Syrup
2 dash Angostura Bitters
Stir with ice and strain into a rocks glass pre-rinsed with absinthe.

BU

Bull Fight

*Sinclair's refreshingly spicy
Tequila Buck on their 2013 menu.*

1 1/2 oz El Jimador Reposado
  Tequila
3/4 oz Drambuie
3/4 oz Falernum
1/2 oz Lime Juice
*Shake with ice and strain into a
Highball glass containing 2 oz
ginger beer. Fill with ice, garnish
with a lime wedge, and add a straw.*

Burning Ice

*No. 9 Park's Ted Kilpatrick
designed this riff on the Modern
Cocktail in 2012 for a Whisky Live
event in Boston.*

1 1/2 oz Laphroaig Scotch
3/4 oz Pedro Ximenez Sherry
3/4 oz Lemon Juice
1/2 oz Swedish Punsch
1 bsp Kübler Absinthe
2 dash Peychaud's Bitters
*Shake with ice and strain into a
rocks glass.*

Busy Bee

*Stephen Shellenberger's 2012
Norwegian Bee's Knees variation
at Pomodoro.*

1 1/2 oz Linie Aquavit
3/4 oz Cristinalda Brandymel
  Honey Liqueur
3/4 oz Lemon Juice
*Shake with ice and strain into a
cocktail glass. Honey syrup will
work here in place of the
brandymel.*

Butchertown

*For a 2013 Bärenjäger competi-
tion, Sahil Mehta at Estragon
created this tribute to the part
of Louisville where German
immigrants settled.*

2 oz Manzanilla Sherry
1/2 oz Bärenjäger Bourbon &
  Honey
1/2 oz Combier Kümmel
*Stir with ice, strain into a cocktail
coupe, and garnish with lemon oil
from a twist. Substitute 1/2 oz
Bourbon and a barspoon of honey
syrup for the Bourbon & Honey.*

Butterfly Skeletons

Sahil Mehta in 2015 created a four equal parter at Estragon that he prefers over the Last Word.

3/4 oz Berkshire Greylock Gin
3/4 oz Cynar
3/4 oz Avèze Gentian Liqueur
3/4 oz Lime Juice
Shake with ice and strain into a cocktail coupe.

Butterfly Sting

A slight adaptation of Tony Iamunno's tribute to Muhammad Ali at Stoddard's circa 2017.

1 1/2 oz Four Roses Bourbon
1/2 oz Punt e Mes
1/2 oz Kronan Swedish Punsch
1/2 oz Demerara Syrup
2 dash Regan's Orange Bitters
Stir with ice, strain into a cocktail coupe, and garnish with an orange twist.

Butterfly Sting,
Stoddard's

CA

Cadet

Aaron Feder showcased his first cocktail creation, a cross between a Toronto and a Junior, at Backbar as a drink of the day in 2012.

1 1/2 oz Old Overholt Rye
1/2 oz Benedictine
1/2 oz Fernet Branca
1/2 oz Lime Juice
Shake with ice and strain into a cocktail glass.

Calamity Jane

A tribute by Katie Emmerson of the Hawthorne to a brave whiskey-drinking sharpshooter at the Women of the Wild West night at the Blue Room in 2013.

1 1/2 oz Beefeater Gin
3/4 oz Luxardo Amaro Abano
1/2 oz Lemon Juice
1/2 oz Ginger Syrup
2 slice Orange
Shake with ice and strain into a cocktail glass.

Calico Jack

An adaptation of a rum Manhattan of sorts at The Independent circa 2014; it was named for John "Jack" Rackham who terrorized the Caribbean in the early 18th with his pirating.

1 oz Old Monk Rum
1 oz Becherovka
1/2 oz Cherry Heering
1/2 oz Punt e Mes
Stir with ice and strain into a rocks glass. Fill with ice, garnish with an orange twist, and add straws.

Cambridge Tea

Paul Manzelli as a child used to be served English Breakfast Tea as Cambridge Tea, and here is his adult variation at Bergamot circa 2012.

1 1/2 oz Benedictine
3 oz English Breakfast Tea (Hot)
4 1/2 oz Steamed Milk
Build in a pre-warmed heat resistant Highball, rocks glass, or mug.

Camellia

Sahil Mehta at Estragon made a sherry and citrus riff on the classic Chrysanthemum aperitif in 2014.

2 oz Amontillado Sherry
3/4 oz Benedictine
1/2 oz Lemon Juice
1/4 oz Absinthe
Shake with ice, strain into a cocktail coupe, and garnish with a lemon twist.

Campbell Town Rock

Vannaluck Hongthong paid tribute to Privateer Rum distiller Maggie Campbell with this bitter-tropical Hurricane-esque libation at the Baldwin Bar at Sichuan Garden II in 2016.

2 oz Privateer Silver Rum
1 oz Passion Fruit Syrup
1/2 oz Gran Classico
1 oz Lemon Juice
2 dash Bittermens Tiki Bitters
Shake with ice, strain into a Collins glass, and fill with crushed ice. Garnish with mint sprigs and a lemon-cherry flag, and add a straw.

Campeche

Fred Yarm was influenced by Derek Brown's Bitter Peach and created this aperitif-style drink in 2012 originally with peach syrup.

1 1/2 oz Dry Vermouth
1/2 oz Gin
1/2 oz Campari
1/2 oz Crème de Peche
1 dash Peychaud's Bitters
Stir with ice and strain into a cocktail glass.

Capovolto

John Nugent of the Citizen Public House created this capsized Red Hook recipe for the Piccola Italia "educational soirée" at the Villa Victoria Center hosted by the Fratelli Branca company in 2012.

1 3/4 oz Punt e Mes
1 1/4 oz Jim Beam Rye
1/4 oz Maraschino Liqueur
1 dash Angostura Bitters
Stir with ice and strain into a cocktail coupe.

Cappelletti Smash

Straight Law's 2014 Smash inspired by Dominic Venegas' Aperol one.

2 oz Cappelletti Aperitivo
1/2 Lemon (cut into 6 pieces)
2 heaping tsp Sugar
Muddle the lemon pieces, shake with ice, strain into a rocks glass, and fill with ice. Garnish with a mint sprig and add straws.

Captain Sheehan Sour

Fred Yarm paid tribute to his chef at Loyal Nine in 2016 with this egg white Sour; the drink is normally garnished at the bar with Angostura Bitters spritzed through a stencil of chef's face.

1 1/2 oz Privateer Silver Rum
1/2 oz Rothman & Winter Apricot Liqueur
1/2 oz Kronan Swedish Punsch
1/2 oz Lime Juice
1 Egg White
Shake once without ice and once with ice, strain into a large cocktail coupe, and garnish with a few drops of Angostura Bitters swirled with a toothpick.

Cara_Me_Away

The Regal Beagle's Andy Holub competed in the Bombay Sapphire East competition with this recipe in 2012, but he later found that the drink really shined with Ransom's Old Tom.

1 1/2 oz Ransom Old Tom Gin
1/2 oz Combier Kümmel
1/2 oz Carpano Sweet Vermouth
1/2 oz Leopold Maraschino
2 dash Fee's Rhubarb Bitters
Stir with ice, strain into a cocktail glass, and garnish with a flamed lemon twist.

Carlsbad Flip, Bergamot

Cardinal O'Malley

Saloon's 2012 tribute to the Archbishop of Boston.

1 1/2 Irish Whiskey
3/4 oz Cardamaro
3/4 oz House Red Wine
1/2 oz Lemon Juice
1/2 oz Simple Syrup
Shake with ice, strain into a cocktail coupe, and garnish with a cherry.

Cardo Bendito

Katie Emmerson at the Hawthorne created this for a 2014 Wall Street Journal article about port cocktails.

1 oz Siete Leguas Reposado Tequila
1 oz Taylor Fladgate Tawny Port
1/2 oz Cardamaro
1/2 oz Dolin Dry Vermouth
Stir with ice, strain into a rocks glass, and garnish with a cherry.

Caribbean Collins

Fred Yarm concocted this drink of the day in the midst of Loyal Nine's 2016 patio season.

2 oz Barbancourt 8 Year Rhum
1/2 oz Hibiscus Tea Syrup
1/2 oz Lime Juice
1 bsp St. Elizabeth Allspice Dram
Shake with ice, strain into a Collins glass containing 2 oz soda water, fill with ice, garnish with a lime wheel, and add a straw.

Carlsbad Flip

Paul Manzelli crafted this at Bergamot in 2013 for a guest who wanted Egg Nog, and he named after the town where Becherovka is made.

1 1/2 oz Becherovka
3/4 oz Pierre Ferrand Pineau
   des Charentes
1/2 oz Heavy Cream
1/2 oz Honey Syrup
1 bsp Simple Syrup
1 Whole Egg
Shake once without ice and once with ice, strain into a rocks glass, and garnish with freshly grated nutmeg.

Category 1

For Tales of the Cocktail's Hurricane competition in 2014, Estragon's Sahil Mehta crafted this complex beer cocktail utilizing a malty English-style IPA.

1 1/2 oz Batavia Arrack
1 oz Passion Fruit Syrup
1 oz Lime Juice
1/2 oz Campari
1 pinch Salt
Shake with ice and strain into a Highball glass containing 3 oz of Left Hand 400 Pound Monkey IPA. Fill with ice, garnish with a lime wheel and a dash of Angostura Bitters, and add a straw.

Celery Stalker

Sahil Mehta created this vegetal wonder in 2013 at Estragon.

1 1/2 oz Del Maguey Mezcal Vida
3/4 oz Manzanilla Sherry
1/2 oz Falernum
1/4 oz Lime Juice
1 inch piece Celery
Muddle the celery. Add the rest of the ingredients, stir with ice, and strain into a rocks glass rimmed with celery salt and containing 1 oz soda water. Fill with ice, garnish with a celery stalk's leafy end, and add straws.

Césaire Daiquiri

Ashish Mitra at Russell House Tavern in 2017 paid tribute to Aimé Césaire, a French poet from Martinique, with this Daiquiri Time Out.

2 oz Clement Premiere Canne
  Rhum Agricole
1/2 oz Bacardi 8 Year Rum
3/4 oz Honey Syrup
3/4 oz Lime Juice
2 dash Regan's Orange Bitters
Shake with ice, strain into a single Old Fashioned glass, and garnish with a lime twist.

Cesare

At Estragon in 2013, Sahil Mehta captured his interest in the Vatican with this tribute to Pope Alexander VI's son, Cesare Borgia.

1 1/2 oz Del Maguey Mezcal Vida
1 oz Lustau Palo Cortado Sherry
1/2 oz Yellow Chartreuse
1/4 oz Avèze Gentian Liqueur
1 dash Angostura Bitters
Stir with ice and strain into a cocktail coupe.

Chachalaca

Sahil Mehta at Estragon circa 2016 took a tropical direction with this cachaça-herbal number.

1 1/2 oz Leblon Cachaça
1/2 oz Green Chartreuse
1/2 oz Passion Fruit Syrup
1/2 oz Coconut Cream
1 oz Lime Juice
Shake with ice and strain into a rocks glass. Fill with ice, garnish with a mint sprig, and add straws.

Chappe Telegraph

At Estragon, Sahil Mehta paid tribute in 2015 to other wireless forms of communicaction with this abstraction of the Marconi Wireless.

1 oz Laird's Applejack
1 oz Bonal Gentiane-Quina
1/2 oz Amontillado Sherry
1/2 oz Amaro Ramazzotti
1 dash Regan's Orange Bitters
Stir with ice, strain into a cocktail coupe, and garnish with an orange twist.

Charles in Charge

Ran Duan's Manhattan variation created in 2015 at the Baldwin Room at Sichuan Garden II either named after the television show or as an inside joke about bartender Charles Coykendall.

1 1/2 oz Four Roses Bourbon
1 oz Carpano Dry Vermouth
1/4 oz Benedictine
1/4 oz Gran Classico
1/2 oz Water
Stir with ice, strain into a cocktail glass, and garnish with a lemon twist.

Charles Roy

Sam Cronin had a request for a smoky Manhattan at Ames Street Deli in 2016, and he merged a Rob Roy with both a Red Hook and a Green Point.

1 1/2 oz Great King Street Scotch
1/2 oz Laphroaig Scotch
1/2 oz Punt e Mes
1/4 oz Maraschino Liqueur
1/4 oz Yellow Chartreuse
Stir with ice, strain into a rocks glass, and garnish with a spritz of Laphroaig Scotch.

CH

Charterhouse

A sherry-driven libation at Viale created circa 2014.

1 1/4 oz Cesar Florido Oloroso Sherry
3/4 oz Green Chartreuse
1/2 oz Lime Juice
1/2 oz Simple Syrup
Shake with ice and strain into a cocktail glass.

Chasing Fireflies

Stoddard's Tony Iamunno created this for Trina's Starlite Lounge's "Tasty Drinks From Good People" section of their 2013 menu.

1 1/2 oz El Jimador Blanco Tequila
1/2 oz Green Chartreuse
1/2 oz Orgeat
1/2 oz Orange Juice
1/2 oz Lime Juice
Shake with ice and strain into a rocks glass. Fill with ice, garnish with a lime wedge, and add straws.

Chipileño

Sahil Mehta at Estragon mixed these Mexican and Italian ingredients into a flavorful Daisy circa 2016.

1 oz Milagro Tequila
1 oz Punt e Mes
1/2 oz Passion Fruit Syrup
1/2 oz Cinnamon Syrup
1/2 oz Lime Juice
Shake with ice and strain into a cocktail coupe.

Chipilo

Sahil Mehta created this Mexican-Italian cocktail at Estragon in 2015, and he dubbed it after a city in Puebla with a large Italian population.

1 oz Mezcal
1 oz Lustau Oloroso Sherry
1/2 oz Campari
1/2 oz Cynar
1 dash Orange Bitters
1 pinch Salt
Stir with ice, strain into a cocktail coupe, and garnish with an orange twist.

Choke Up

Backbar's baseball-themed Whiskey Sour riff on the Tradesman section of their 2014 menu.

1 oz Old Overholt Rye
1 oz Cynar
1/2 oz Lemon Juice
1/2 oz Simple Syrup
Shake with ice, strain into a cocktail glass, and garnish with a dash of Angostura Bitters.

Chasing Fireflies,
Trina's Starlite
Lounge

Chutes & Ladders

At Russell House Tavern, Fred Yarm riffed on the Metexa from 1937's Café Royal Cocktail Book and took it in a Margarita direction in 2013.

1 1/2 oz Zapopan Blanco Tequila
1 oz Kronan Swedish Punsch
1 oz Cocchi Americano
1/2 oz Lime Juice
Shake with ice, strain into a single Old Fashioned glass, and garnish with orange oil from a twist.

Cisco Bay

A refreshing herbal libation crafted by Ran Duan in 2013 at Sichuan Garden II.

1 1/2 oz St. George Botanivore Gin
3/4 oz Passion Fruit Syrup
1/2 oz Campari
3/4 oz Lemon Juice
3/4 oz Grapefruit Juice
Shake with ice, strain into a Collins glass, fill with ice, garnish with a grapefruit twist, and add a straw.

CI-CO

Citizen's Arrest

A lighter libation created by Danielle Berman at Fairsted Kitchen as an attempt to slow down one's pace.

1 1/4 oz El Maestro Oloroso Sherry
1 oz Dolin Sweet Vermouth
3/4 oz Punt e Mes
1 pinch Salt
Stir with ice and strain into a rocks glass. Fill with ice, garnish with orange oil from a twist, and add straws.

Cleansing Tonic

Franklin Café's cure-all circa 2013.

1 1/2 oz Olmeca Altos Plata Tequila
1/2 oz Cocchi Americano
1/2 oz Simple Syrup
1/2 oz Lemon Juice
4 dash Celery Bitters
Shake with ice and strain into a cocktail glass.

Cobbler Noir

Sahil Mehta's complex take on the 19th century Cobbler at Estragon in 2014.

1 1/4 oz Zucca Rabarbaro Amaro
1 1/4 oz Cocchi Americano
1/4 oz Maraschino Liqueur
1/4 oz Lemon Juice
Shake with ice and strain into a wine glass. Fill with crushed ice, garnish with lemon and orange slices, and add straws.

Cocktail à La Salle

A variation on the Cocktail à la Louisiane that Fred Yarm crafted for a Mixology Monday event in 2013.

1 oz Reposado Tequila
1 oz Oloroso Sherry
1 oz Benedictine
3 dash Peychaud's Bitters
3 dash Absinthe
Stir with ice and strain into a cocktail glass.

Cocoa Puff Smash

Sam Gabrielli developed this popular brunch libation at Russell House Tavern in 2014; the original utilized a cereal-infused Chartreuse but this was the way the drink was made when that ran out.

2 oz Green Chartreuse
1/2 oz Tempus Fugit Crème de Cacao
3 wedge Lemon
6-8 leaf Mint
24 piece Cocoa Puff Cereal
Muddle lemon wedges, mint leaves, and Cocoa Puffs. Add rest of ingredients, shake with ice, and strain into a rocks glass. Fill with crushed ice, garnish with mint sprigs and a few Cocoa Puffs, and add straws.

Columbus Exchange

Chris Danforth at the Blue Room circa 2013 captured the history of New World-Old World sharing.

1 1/2 oz Ron Pampero Rum
1/2 oz Amaro S. Maria al Monte
1/2 oz Cocchi Sweet Vermouth
1/4 oz Grand Marnier
1/4 oz Velvet Falernum
Stir with ice, strain into a rocks glass, and garnish with orange oil from a twist.

Come Dancing!

Matt Schrage from Brick & Mortar crafted this Swizzle in 2014 for Central Kitchen downstairs.

3/4 oz St. George Terroir Gin
3/4 oz Amontillado Sherry
3/4 oz Dolin Blanc Vermouth
3/4 oz Grapefruit Juice
Build in a Collins glass, add crushed ice, and swizzle to mix and chill. Garnish with 3 dashes of Fee's Whiskey Barrel Bitters and add a straw.

Commercial Free

An intriguing and dark equal parts cocktail by Tony Iamunno circa 2015 at Trina's Starlite Lounge.

3/4 oz Old Monk Rum
3/4 oz Cynar
3/4 oz Velvet Falernum
3/4 oz Grapefruit Juice
Shake with ice and strain into a single Old Fashioned glass.

CO

Company Swizzle,
The Hawthorne

Company Swizzle

Katie Emmerson's spiced mezcal Swizzle at the Hawthorne in 2013 paid tribute to the house Swizzle formula at her previous bar, Death & Co.

1 oz Del Maguey Espadin Especial Mezcal
1 oz Lustau Amontillado Sherry
3/4 oz Lime Juice
1/2 oz Velvet Falernum
1/2 oz Ginger Syrup
Build in a Collins glass, add crushed ice, and swizzle to mix and chill. Garnish with a mint sprig, 2 dashes Fee's Whiskey Barrel Bitters, and 2 dashes Bittermens Mole Bitters, and add a straw.

Confederation Bridge

The staff at Backbar riffed on the classic Prince Edward cocktail in 2012 and named it after the bridge that connects Nova Scotia and Prince Edward Island.

1 1/2 oz Bulleit Rye
1/2 oz Cynar
1/2 oz Drambuie
1/2 oz Dolin Blanc Vermouth
1 dash Angostura Bitters
Stir with ice, strain into a cocktail glass, and garnish with orange oil from a twist.

Consigliere

Ashish Mitra's 2014 tribute at Russell House Tavern to independent Italian businessmen everywhere.

1 1/4 oz Branca Menta
1 1/4 oz Cocchi Americano
3/4 oz Meletti Anisette
1/2 oz Lime Juice
2 dash Angostura Bitters
Shake with ice, strain into a single Old Fashioned glass, and garnish with grapefruit oil from a twist.

Conspiracy Theory

Created by Mike Fleming at West Bridge in 2014.

1 1/2 oz Dewar's Scotch
3/4 oz Meletti Amaro
1/2 oz Apricot Liqueur
1/2 oz Lemon Juice
Shake with ice and strain into a rocks glass.

Contrarian Collins

A light offering at the Baldwin & Sons Trading Co. at Sichuan Garden II in 2016.

3/4 oz Privateer Gin
3/4 oz Cynar
3/4 oz Simple Syrup
3/4 oz Lemon Juice
1 bsp Apricot Liqueur
Shake with ice, strain into a Collins glass containing 2 oz soda water, fill with ice, garnish with a cherry-lemon peel flag, and add a straw.

Cooper

An elegant Manhattan variation at the Barrel House in Beverly, MA, created circa 2013.

1 1/2 oz Riverboat Rye
3/4 oz Pineau des Charentes
3/4 oz Averna
Stir with ice and strain into a rocks glass.

CO

Copper Canyon

Adapted from a Twentieth Century riff created by Drink's Will Thompson in 2012 and named after another famous train line.

1 1/2 oz El Tesoro Reposado Tequila
1/2 oz M. Brizard Crème de Cacao
1/2 oz Salers Gentian Liqueur
1/2 oz Lemon Juice
1 dash Fee's Whiskey Barrel Bitters
1 dash Hot Sauce

Shake with ice, strain into a rocks glass containing a large ice cube, and garnish the ice cube with a pinch of salt. The original recipe called for a barspoon of long pepper tincture instead of hot sauce.

Copper Swizzle

A citrusy, tropical Swizzle at the Highball Lounge circa 2015.

1 1/2 oz Peloton de la Muerte Mezcal
3/4 oz Manzanilla Sherry
1/2 oz Honey Syrup
1/2 oz Falernum
1/2 oz Lemon Juice
2 oz San Pellegrino Grapefruit Soda

Build in a Collins glass, fill with crushed ice, and swizzle to mix and chill. Add 3-4 dashes Angostura Bitters and swizzle to mix the bitters into the top layer. Garnish with a cucumber slice and add a straw.

Copp's Hill

Mike Wyatt of Ward Eight competed in the Libations for Preservations competition hosted at the GrandTen Distillery in 2014 with this tribute to a historic cemetery located near his bar.

1 1/2 oz GrandTen Wire Works Gin
3/4 oz St. Germain
3/4 oz Lemon Juice
1/4 oz Campari

Shake with ice, strain into a cocktail glass, and garnish with an orange twist.

Cormac McCarthy

At Local 149, John Mayer crafted this tribute to the Western and Southern Gothic author in 2012 after being moved by Blood Meridean.

1 oz High West Silver Whiskey
1/2 oz Punt e Mes
1/2 oz Cynar
1 dash Bitter Truth Mole Bitters
Stir in a mixing glass, add 5 oz Pretty Things Saint Botolph's Town brown ale, and pour into a snifter glass.

Corpse Reviver #6

The Citizen Public House riffed on the Savoy Cocktail Book classic to create this Winter-spiced variation in 2012.

3/4 oz Beefeater Gin
3/4 oz Becherovka
3/4 oz Cocchi Americano
3/4 oz Lemon Juice
1/4 oz Honey Liqueur or Syrup
Shake with ice, strain into a rocks glass, fill with ice, garnish with a lemon twist, and add straws.

Corpse Reviver #33

Beau Sturm's Wednesday drink of the day at Trina's Starlight Lounge in 2012 was an elegant summery Corpse Reviver #2 riff.

3/4 oz Gin
3/4 oz Cocchi Americano
3/4 oz Triple Sec
3/4 oz Lemon Juice
3 dash Absinthe
2 chunk Watermelon (~1 1/2 oz)
Muddle the watermelon chunks. Add the rest of the ingredients, shake with ice, and strain into a cocktail coupe. Garnish with a small wedge of watermelon.

Corpse Reviver Fizz

Fred Yarm's Easter Brunch 2016 offering at Loyal Nine.

1 oz Berkshire Greylock Gin
1 oz Lillet Blanc
1/2 oz Creole Shrubb Orange Liqueur
1/2 oz Lemon Juice
2 dash St. George Absinthe
1 1/2 oz Heavy Cream
1 Egg White
Shake once without ice and once with ice, strain into a Collins glass containing 2 oz soda water, garnish with an orange twist, and add a straw.

Cosmopari (or Camparipolitan)

Fred Yarm made this riff on the classic Cosmo when he received a drink request for a Campari-based cocktail at Russell House Tavern one night in 2014.

1 1/2 oz Campari
3/4 oz Creole Shrubb Orange Liqueur
3/4 oz Lime Juice
1/2 oz Cranberry Juice
1 pinch Salt
Shake with ice, strain into a cocktail glass, and garnish with an orange twist.

Count Camillo's Derby

Fred Yarm's Julep variation for Negroni Week 2014.

1 oz Beefeater Gin
1 oz Dolin Sweet Vermouth
1 oz Campari
8 leaf Mint
In a Julep cup, muddle the mint in Campari. Add the rest of the ingredients, fill with crushed ice, stir to mix and chill, garnish with mint, and add a straw.

Cover Letter

Tyler Wang's motley collection of ingredients at Kirkland Tap and Trotter in 2014 reminded him of the interview process of tying together disparate aspects.

1 1/4 oz Tuthilltown Half Moon Gin
1/2 oz Sotol
3/4 oz Lustau Amontillado Sherry
1/4 oz Maraschino Liqueur
1/4 oz Honey Syrup
1 dash Fee's Whiskey Barrel Bitters
Stir with ice, strain into a cocktail coupe, and garnish with orange oil from a twist.

Cravan Cocktail

Inspired by Matt Schrage's Hugo Ball, Fred Yarm named his drink in 2009 after a Dada poet and man of mystery, Arthur Cravan.

1 1/2 Bourbon
3/4 oz Grapefruit Juice
1/2 oz Maraschino Liqueur
1/4 oz Campari
1 dash Angostura Bitters
Shake with ice, strain into a cocktail glass, and garnish with either an orange twist or a short mint sprig.

Crimson Crow #1

Russell House Tavern's Daisy tribute to neighboring Harvard University that they first put on the menu in 2010; although two later variations were created, this one still gets requested.

1 1/4 oz Sobieski Vodka
1 1/4 oz Aperol
3/4 oz Lemon Juice
3/4 oz Raspberry Syrup
Shake with ice and strain into a cocktail glass.

Crimson Daiquiri

Sinclair's Daiquiri Time Out in 2013 as a tribute to their Harvard neighborhood.

1 1/2 oz Santa Teresa Claro Rum
3/4 oz Crème Yvette
3/4 oz Cocchi Americano
1/2 oz Lime Juice
Shake with ice and strain into a cocktail coupe.

Cover Letter,
Kirkland Tap &
Trotter

ꝏꝏꝏꝏꝏꝏꝏꝏꝏꝏꝏꝏ

(The) Cross & the Switchblade

Fred Yarm's 2012 tribute to the Mau Maus, a Puerto Rican street gang in New York during the 1950s.

1 oz Puerto Rican White Rum
1 oz Dry Vermouth
1/2 oz Crème de Cacao
1/2 oz Lime Juice
2 dash Bittermens Burlesque
  Bitters
Shake with ice and strain into a cocktail coupe.

Crossroads Highball

One of Backbar's drinks of the day in 2016 created by Carlo Caroscio that began as a riff on a Champs-Élysées.

1 1/2 oz Pierre Ferrand 1840
  Cognac
1/4 oz Smith & Cross Rum
1/2 oz Yellow Chartreuse
1/4 oz Honey Syrup
1/2 oz Lemon Juice
Shake with ice and strain into a Highball glass containing 2 oz sparkling wine. Fill with ice, garnish with a lemon twist and 2 dashes Angostura Bitters, and add a straw.

Cruella

Crafted at Tavern Road by Will Tomlinson in 2013 as perhaps a 101 Dalmations tribute.

1 1/2 oz Leblon Cachaça
1/2 oz Galliano l'Autentico
1/2 oz Crème de Cacao
1/4 oz Lemon Juice
1 bsp Maraschino Liqueur
2 dash Peychaud's Bitters
1 Lemon Peel (twist and include)
Stir with ice, strain into a cocktail coupe, and garnish with lemon oil from another twist.

Curandero

John Gertsen and Misty Kalkofen at Drink crafted this originally with a Barolo Chinato before switching to another quinquina in 2010.

2 oz Del Maguey Mezcal Vida
3/4 oz Bonal Gentiane-Quina
1/4 oz Crème de Cacao
Stir with ice, strain into a cocktail glass, and garnish with orange oil from a twist.

Cynar Buck

Patrick Andrew's spicy digestif Highball in 2016 at the Baldwin Bar at Sichuan Garden II.

1 1/2 oz Cynar
1/2 oz Velvet Falernum
1/2 oz Lime Juice
Shake with ice, strain into a Collins glass containing 3 oz ginger beer, fill with crushed ice, garnish with mint sprigs and freshly grated nutmeg, and add a straw.

Cynar Fizz

Scott Holliday was inspired by the simplicity of the Cynar Flip and crafted this Silver Fizz at Rendezvous in 2011.

2 oz Cynar
1 oz Lemon Juice
1 Egg White
Shake once without ice and once with ice, and strain into a Fizz glass or Champagne flute containing 1 1/2 oz soda water.

Cypress

Bobby McCoy's "view from the concourse" at Eastern Standard in 2014.

1 1/2 oz Bacardi 8 Year Rum
3/4 oz Lime Juice
1/2 oz Grapefruit Juice
3/4 oz Maple Syrup
1/4 oz Honey Syrup
Shake with ice, strain into a Collins glass, fill with crushed ice, and add a straw.

Czech Matador

Backbar's flavorful take on a Blood & Sand on the Tradesman section of their 2013 menu.

1 oz Old Overholt Rye
1 oz Jelinek Fernet
1/2 oz Orange Juice
1/2 oz Cherry Heering
Shake with ice, strain into a cocktail coupe, and garnish with a cherry.

Czech Remedy

A 2012 smoke and spice Daisy created as a group effort by the bartenders at Backbar.

1 oz Dewar's Scotch
1 oz Becherovka
1/2 oz Lemon Juice
1/2 oz Honey Syrup
Shake with ice, strain into a cocktail glass, and garnish with a spritz of Laphroaig Scotch.

Dakkar Grotto

Fred Yarm paid tribute in 2016 to Jules Verne and Captain Nemo with this grassy number at Loyal Nine.

1 1/2 oz JM Rhum Agricole Blanc
1/2 oz Punt e Mes
1/2 oz Green Tea Syrup
1/2 oz Lime Juice
Shake with ice, strain into a cocktail coupe, and garnish with a grapefruit twist.

Daley Fix

Belly Wine Bar's 2013 tribute to Central Bottle's chef Stacey Daley.

1 1/2 oz Amontillado Sherry
1/2 oz Rothman & Winter Apricot
   Liqueur
3/4 oz oz Pineapple Syrup
1/2 oz Lemon Juice
Shake with ice, strain into a rocks glass, and fill with crushed ice. Garnish with a mint sprig and 1-2 dash Angostura Bitters, and add a straw.

Da Nang,
Tiger Mama

Dame En Rouge

At the Sichuan Garden II's Baldwin Bar in 2016, Ran Duan crafted this refreshing vermouth Collins as a tribute to an old Barbara Stanwyck movie.

2 oz Maurin Sweet Vermouth
3/4 oz Lime Juice
3/4 oz Simple Syrup
Shake with ice and strain into a Collins glass containing 2 oz soda water. Fill with crushed ice, garnish with a mint sprig and a lime wedge-cherry flag, and add a straw.

Damp Hands of Melancholy

Daren Swisher discussed with reporter Luke O'Neil the trials and tribulations of being a writer, and this 2012 drink at Park Restaurant was named after a James Thurber quote.

1 1/2 oz Carpano Sweet Vermouth
1 oz Amaro Montenegro
3/4 oz Shooting Star Syrah
2 dash Jerry Thomas Decanter Bitters
Stir with ice, strain into a rocks glass containing a large ice cube, and garnish with a flamed orange twist.

Da Nang

Tiger Mama's circa 2015 fruity, floral, and complex crowd pleaser that is rather good with rum or gin in place of the vodka.

3/4 oz Tito's Vodka
3/4 oz St. Germain
3/4 oz Aperol
1/2 oz Passion Fruit Syrup
3/4 oz Lime Juice
Shake with ice, strain into a cocktail coupe, and garnish with a lime wheel-cherry flag.

Danger Zone

Fred Yarm based this Swizzle on both Matt Schrage's Soekarno and a rum-based Junior for Loyal Nine's Yacht Rock Sundays in 2015.

1 1/2 oz Old Monk Rum
1/2 oz Batavia Arrack
1/2 oz Benedictine
1/2 oz Lime Juice
1 dash Angostura Bitters
Build in a Collins glass, fill with crushed ice, and swizzle to mix and chill. Garnish with 3 lime wheels submerged along the side of the glass, a mint sprig, and freshly grated nutmeg, and add a straw.

DA

Daq in Black

Luc Thiers' drink of the day at Backbar in 2016 showcases his love of amaro-laden Daiquiri variations as well as the band AC/DC.

1 oz Blackwell Jamaican Rum
1/2 oz Cognac
1/2 oz Meletti Amaro
1/2 oz Demerara Syrup
1/2 oz Lime Juice
1 dash Fee's Walnut Bitters
Shake with ice, strain into a cocktail coupe, and garnish with a lemon peel lightning bolt.

Darkness 'til Dawn

Misty Kalkofen named her drink after a Carly Simon song for the 2012 Spin the Bottle event featuring Eastern Standard's Garrett Harker on the turntables.

1 oz Laird's Bonded Apple Brandy
3/4 oz Cherry Heering
3/4 oz Fernet Branca
1/2 oz Lemon Juice
Shake with ice and strain into a rocks glass.

Darkwing Duck

Tyler Wang's autumnal delight on Audubon's cartoon-themed section of their 2015 menu.

1 oz Royal Thistle Scotch
1/2 oz Laird's Bonded Apple Brandy
1 oz Carpano Sweet Vermouth
1/2 oz Russo Nocino Walnut Liqueur
1 dash Angostura Bitters
Stir with ice, strain into a rocks glass, and garnish with a cherry.

(A) Dash and Three Dots

Fred Yarm riffed on the Three Dots and a Dash in 2016 and turned it into a gin drink. A dash and three dots is Morse code for B (is for Bee's Knees).

2 oz Berkshire Greylock Gin
1 oz Lemon Juice
1/2 oz Honey Syrup
1/4 oz Creole Shrubb Orange Liqueur
1/4 oz Velvet Falernum
1 bsp St. Elizabeth Allspice Dram
1 dash Angostura Bitters
Shake with ice, strain into a Collins glass, and fill with crushed ice. Garnish with either a dash and three dots imagery (such as a rectangular lemon wedge and three cherries) or a citrus peel honey bee. A lemon twist would work in a pinch.

ↁↂ੭ↂ੭ↂↄↂↄↂↄↂↄↂↄↂↄↂↄↂↄↂↄↂↄↂↄↂↄↂↄ

Dashboard Hula Girl

Tainah Soares at Trina's Starlite Lounge in 2016 paid tribute to the name of a bartender at Parlor Sports' old band. The drink was originally on the menu with Amaro Montenegro before switching to Averna.

1 1/2 oz Plantation Pineapple Rum
3/4 oz Lustau Amontillado Sherry
3/4 oz Averna
Stir with ice, strain into a cocktail coupe, and garnish with flamed orange oil from a twist.

Day 3ish

In the midst of a 14 day rally during restaurant week at Rialto, Todd Maul when asked how he was doing replied "Day 3ish"; Todd later brought the drink with him to Clio.

2 oz Frapin VS Cognac
1/2 oz Gran Classico
1/2 oz Dolin Dry Vermouth
1/2 oz Lemon Juice
Shake with ice and strain into a cocktail glass.

D.C. Flip

West Bridge's egg-laden 2014 abstraction of the El Presidente.

3/4 oz Plantation 3 Star Silver Rum
3/4 oz Old Monk Rum
1/2 oz Velvet Falernum
3/4 oz Cocchi Americano Rosa
1/2 oz Grenadine
1 Whole Egg
Shake once without ice and once with ice, strain into a cocktail glass, and garnish with orange oil from a twist and with freshly grated cinnamon.

Deadline

One of the last drinks created by Ryan Lotz at Lineage in Brookline in 2011 before he departed for the Hawthorne.

1 1/2 oz Bully Boy White Whiskey
1/2 oz St. Germain
1/2 oz Benedictine
3/4 oz Lime Juice
Shake with ice, strain in a cocktail glass, and garnish with a lemon twist.

DE

Death or Glory

Beau Sturm crafted this libation at Trina's Starlite Lounge in 2013, and I was drawn to it for The Clash reference and because Angostura Bitters was listed third in the description.

3/4 oz Smith & Cross Rum
3/4 oz Old Monk Rum
1/2 oz Angostura Bitters
1 oz Cherry Heering
1/2 oz Lemon Juice
Shake with ice, strain into a rocks glass, and garnish with a lemon twist.

Declaration

Sam Olivari crafted this elegant libation at No. 9 Park in 2015 after having tried the Two Caravels at Brick & Mortar.

2 oz Plymouth Gin
1/2 oz Rare Wine Co. Bual Madeira
1/2 oz Lemon Juice
1/2 oz Demerara Syrup
2 dash Angostura Bitters
Shake with ice and strain into a cocktail coupe.

Deep Six

At Drink, Palmer Matthews was inspired in 2012 by reading in the Flavor Bible about how artichoke and mint work well together.

2 oz Cynar
1/2 oz Lemon Juice
1/2 oz Simple Syrup
Leaves of 2 Mint Sprigs
1 pinch Salt
Shake with ice and strain into a cocktail coupe.

De La Vega

Bruno Prado crafted this straight spirits rum drink at Tavern Road circa 2013.

1 1/2 oz Bacardi 8 Year Rum
1/2 oz Amaro Nardini
1/2 oz Amontillado Sherry
1/4 oz Maraschino Liqueur
2 dash Fee's Old Fashioned Bitters
Stir with ice, strain into a cocktail coupe, and garnish with a cherry.

Delores Haze

An adaptation of a drink Patrick Andrew served at the Barrel House in Beverly in 2015; Patrick was then at New Hampshire's Bar Tek-Nique before switching over to Sichaun Garden II a few months later.

1 1/2 oz Reposado Tequila
3/4 oz Dolin Sweet Vermouth
3/4 oz Aperol
2 dash Chocolate Bitters
Stir with ice, strain into a cocktail glass pre-rinsed with Laphroaig Scotch, and garnish with a lemon twist.

De La Vega,
Tavern Road

Demerara Smash

Nicole Lebedevitch's 2009 rum riff on Eastern Standard's Whiskey Smash.

2 oz Renegade Guyana Rum
1 oz Yellow Chartreuse
2 wedge Lemon
3 wedge Lime
6-8 leaf Mint
Muddle lemon wedges, lime wedges, and mint. Add rum and Yellow Chartreuse, shake with ice, and strain into a rocks glass. Fill with crushed ice, garnish with a mint sprig, and add straws.

De Moda

Daren Swisher of Hojoko offered this funky rum drink in 2017 at The Automatic's first industry night.

1 1/4 oz Plantation O.F.T.D.
   Overproof Dark Rum
1 1/4 oz Lustau East India Sherry
1/2 oz Demerara Syrup
1 dash Angostura Bitters
6 drop Scrappy's Cardamom
   Bitters
Stir with ice, strain into a rocks glass, and garnish with orange oil from a twist.

123

DE

Dengue Fever

Tony Iamunno at Trina's Starlite Lounge utilized a house pineapple-infused rum (here, substituted with a commercial equivalent) to make this Tiki libation in 2016.

2 oz Plantation Pineapple Rum
3/4 oz Velvet Falernum
1/2 oz Benedictine
3/4 oz Lime Juice
1/2 oz Orange Juice
2 dash Angostura Bitters
Shake with ice, strain into a Collins glass, and fill with ice. Float 1/2 oz DonQ 151 Proof Rum, garnish with an orange-cherry flag, and add a straw.

Derby Scaffa

Backbar veers away from pure Scaffa structure in 2015 with this delightfully floral room temperature number.

1 1/2 oz Four Roses Bourbon
1/2 oz Amaro Montenegro
1/2 oz Punt e Mes
1/2 oz St. Germain
1/2 oz Water
2 drop Lavender Bitters
Build in a rocks glass, briefly stir to mix <u>without</u> ice, and garnish with orange oil from a twist. Note: This is a room temperature cocktail.

Dessert L'Italienne

At Belly Wine Bar, Ryan Connelly's 2013 post-meal answer to the classic Appetizer L'Italienne.

1 oz Amaro S. Maria al Monte
1 oz Amaro Braulio
1/2 oz Carpano Sweet Vermouth
1/2 oz Galliano l'Autentico
1/4 oz Espresso Liqueur
Stir with ice and strain into a rocks glass.

Destreza

Fred Yarm crafted this as a mezcal "White Lucien Gaudin" at Loyal Nine in 2016 to mirror the White Negroni. The recipe worked as a gin variation as well.

1 oz Mezcal Amaras
1 oz Lillet Blanc
1/2 oz Creole Shrubb Orange Liqueur
1/2 oz Baska Snaps Malört
Stir with ice, strain into a cocktail coupe, and garnish with an orange twist.

Devil's Curve

Tyler Wang crafted this libation at No. 9 Park in 2013 riffing on the Supreme, and it got named after its similarity to the bar's Figure Eight recipe.

1 1/2 oz Beefeater Gin
1 oz Dolin Dry Vermouth
1/2 oz Velvet Falernum
1/2 oz Lemon Juice
1 dash Peychaud's Bitters
Shake with ice and strain into a cocktail glass.

Devil's Left Hand

A Tiki libation on the opening 2016 menu of The Automatic.

1 oz Plantation 3 Star White Rum
1 oz Old Monk Rum
1/2 oz Campari
1/2 oz Orgeat
1/2 oz Cinnamon Syrup
1/2 oz Lime Juice
Shake with ice, strain into a tall glass, fill with crushed ice, float 1/2 oz Plantation O.F.T.D. Overproof Dark Rum, garnish with an orange twist, and add a straw.

Devil Walking Next to Me

In tinkering for Loyal Nine's Yacht Rock Sundays in 2015, Fred Yarm merged a Floridita with a Sinnerman Swizzle.

1 1/4 oz Batavia Arrack
1/2 oz Sweet Vermouth
1/2 oz Lime Juice
1/2 oz Salers Gentian Liqueur
1/4 oz St. Elizabeth Allspice Dram
Shake with ice, strain into a cocktail coupe, and garnish with a lime wheel.

Diaspora

An adaptation of Sahil Mehta's spice-driven rum drink at Estragon that originally included muddled curry leaves.

2 oz Ron Abuelo Rum
1/2 oz St. Germain
1/4 oz King's Ginger Liqueur
1/4 oz Combier Kümmel
1/2 oz Lime Juice
Shake with ice and strain into a cocktail glass.

Dissenter,
Puritan & Co.

Diddlin' Dora

Fred Yarm created this tribute to one of Dora DuFran's brothels in the Wild West for a 2013 Whiskey and Amari night at the Blue Room.

1 oz Lustau Amontillado Sherry
1 oz Cocchi Sweet Vermouth
1 oz Pimm's No. 1
3/4 oz Fernet Branca
1/4 oz Maraschino Liqueur
Build in a Highball glass, fill with crushed ice, garnish with an orange twist and freshly grated nutmeg, and add a straw.

Diener

Fanny Katz created this sherry and vermouth wonder circa 2013 for one of Belly Wine Bar's regulars.

1 1/2 oz Lustau Amontillado
  Sherry
3/4 oz Cocchi Sweet Vermouth
3/4 oz Punt e Mes
1/4 oz Lustau Pedro Ximenez
  Sherry
2 dash Bittermens Mole Bitters
2 dash Orange Bitters
Stir with ice, strain into a cocktail glass, and garnish with an orange twist.

Dissenter

One of the lighter drinks on the Puritan & Co.'s 2014 cocktail menu.

1 1/2 oz Zucca Rabarbaro Amaro
1 1/2 oz Carpano Sweet Vermouth
1 bsp Crème de Cassis
Stir with ice and strain into a rocks glass.

Diversionary Dam

During Restaurant Week 2013 at No. 9 Park, two regulars at the bar served as a hiding place for Ted Kilpatrick and he created this libation for their service.

1 1/2 oz Green Chartreuse
1 oz Angostura Bitters
1 oz Lime Juice
1 bsp Kübler Absinthe
Shake with ice and strain into a cocktail glass.

Dogger Bank

Sean Maher crafted this light summery number at the Barrel House in Beverly in 2014 and named it after the bit of ocean between England and Sweden.

1 1/2 oz Pimm's No. 1
3/4 oz Lemon Juice
3/4 oz Simple Syrup
1/2 oz Kronan Swedish Punsch
Shake with ice and strain into a cocktail glass.

Domo Arigato

Ran Duan noticed how well mezcal paired with a sesame dish, and he concocted this drink at Sichuan Garden II in 2012 as a result.

2 oz Del Maguey Mezcal Vida
3/4 oz Lime Juice
1/2 oz Simple Syrup
1 bsp Sesame Oil
Shake with ice, strain into a Collins glass containing 3 oz ginger beer, fill with ice, garnish with a lime wheel, and add a straw.

Don't Fight It

Fred Yarm created this Swizzle for Loyal Nine's Yacht Rock Sundays in 2015 to satisfy the chef's request for a tribute to the Loggins-Perry duet.

1 oz Berkshire Greylock Gin
1 oz Lillet Blanc
1/2 oz Green Chartreuse
1/2 oz Lime Juice
Build in a Collins glass, fill with crushed ice, and swizzle to mix and chill. Garnish with 2-3 dashes Angostura Bitters and a mint sprig, and add a straw.

DO

Don't Flip Out

Russell House Tavern's Sam Gabrielli crafted this rich wonder for a 2012 Branca Fratelli event called Piccola Italia.

1 oz Fernet Branca
1 oz Hennessy VS Cognac
1/2 oz Punt e Mes
1/2 oz Caffè Borghetti Espresso
   Liqueur
1 Whole Egg
Shake once without ice and once with ice, strain into a cocktail coupe containing 1 oz soda water, and garnish with freshly grated dark roast coffee.

Dose

Dan Myers created this Corpse Reviver #2 riff at Spoke, and it later appeared on the Loyal Nine cocktail menu.

3/4 oz Mezcal Amaras
3/4 oz Creole Shrubb Orange
   Liqueur
3/4 oz Lillet Blanc
3/4 oz Lime Juice
1 dash St. George Absinthe
Shake with ice and strain into a cocktail glass.

Double Entendre

Green Street's complex sipper from their Summer 2016 menu.

1 1/2 oz Gordon's Gin
1/2 oz Lustau Oloroso Sherry
1/2 oz Cynar
1/2 oz Luxardo Maraschino
2 dash Regan's Orange Bitters
Stir with ice, strain into a rock glass, and garnish with a cherry.

Dove & Daisy

Tyler Wang in 2013 crossed a Margarita with a Paloma at No. 9 Park.

1 1/2 oz Milagro Blanco Tequila
1 oz Combier Orange Liqueur
1/2 oz Aperol
3/4 oz Lime Juice
3 inch swath Grapefruit Peel
Shake with ice and strain into a salt-rimmed Collins glass containing 2 oz soda water. Fill with ice and garnish with an additional grapefruit twist.

Down & Brown

Ryan McGrale crafted this stirred rye whiskey drink for the inaugural Tavern Road menu in 2013.

2 oz Riverboat Rye
3/4 oz Fernet Branca
1/2 oz Benedictine
1/4 oz Maraschino Liqueur
Stir with ice, strain into a rocks glass, and garnish with a flamed orange twist.

Down for the Count

Fred Yarm merged the Negroni with the Remember the Maine for a Cherry Heering-themed week of drinks of the day at Loyal Nine. The name pays tribute to both Count Camillo Negroni and sinking ships.

1 oz Berkshire Greylock Gin
1 oz Punt e Mes
1/2 oz Cherry Heering
1/2 oz Campari
10 drop St. George Absinthe
1 dash Angostura Bitters
Stir with ice, strain into a rocks glass, fill with ice, garnish with an orange twist, and add straws.

Downtown at Dawn

To replace the Laguna Sunrise at Russell House Tavern, Fred Yarm in 2013 opted for the all-nighter angle of early morning via a Richard Hell song title.

1 oz Del Maguey Mezcal Vida
1 oz Laird's Bonded Apple Brandy
3/4 oz Benedictine
3/4 oz Cocchi Sweet Vermouth
1/2 oz Lime Juice
Shake with ice and strain into a single Old Fashioned glass.

Dragon's Bane

Scott Holliday riffed on the Martinez in 2014 at Rendezvous.

1 1/2 oz St. George Terroir Gin
1 1/2 oz Punt e Mes
1/4 oz Dolin Genepy des Alpes
Stir with ice, strain into a rocks glass, and garnish with lemon oil from a twist.

Dreadlock Holiday

Green Street's Caribbean number for Summer 2016.

1 1/2 oz Jamaican Rum
1/2 oz Creole Shrubb Orange Liqueur
1/2 oz Cinnamon Syrup
1/2 oz Lemon Juice
1 dash Angostura Bitters
Shake with ice, strain into a rocks glass, fill with ice, garnish with an orange slice, and add straws.

Drink Has No Name

Benjamin Kweskin dubbed his 1794 riff in 2016 after a Games of Thrones reference at Craigie on Main.

1 oz Rittenhouse Rye
1 oz Cardamaro
1 oz Lustau East India Sherry
2 dash Orange Bitters
Stir with ice, strain into a rocks glass, and garnish with orange oil from a twist.

Drink One Up

Dave Werthman at the Sinclair created this drink using a few of his favorite ingredients for the DrinkOne charity in 2013 that helped the Boston Marathon victims.

1 1/2 oz Reposado Tequila
1 oz Drambuie
3/4 oz Punt e Mes
1/2 oz Grapefruit Juice
1/4 oz Lime Juice
Shake with ice and strain into a cocktail glass.

Dusty Trail

Craigie on Main's 2013 hybrid of a Rum Old Fashioned and a Pirate's Cocktail.

2 oz Privateer Silver Rum
1/4 oz Cocchi Sweet Vermouth
1/4 oz Vanilla Syrup
2 dash Bittermens Mole Bitters
1 dash Peychaud's Bitters
Stir with ice and strain into a rocks glass.

ෙ෨ඣෙ෨ඣ෨ඣ෨ඣ෨ඣ෨ඣ෨ඣ෨ඣ෨ඣ෨

Dutch Courage

From Eastern Standard's Old Fashioned section on their 2009 menu, this tribute to pre-battle medication utilized Anchor's Dutch-style gin.

2 oz Anchor Genevieve
1/2 oz Bauchaunt Orange Liqueur
1 heaping bsp Sugar
1 dash Angostura Bitters
1 dash Angostura Orange Bitters
Dissolve sugar in a splash of water. Add rest of the ingredients, stir with ice, and strain into a rocks glass. Fill with ice, garnish with an orange twist, and add straws.

Dutch Revival

Sahil Mehta elegantly paired Genever with kümmel at Estragon circa 2013.

1 1/2 oz Bols Genever
1/2 oz Combier Kümmel
1/2 oz Velvet Falernum
3/4 oz Lime Juice
Shake with ice and strain into a cocktail glass.

Dusty Trail,
Craigie on Main

DU-EA

Dutch Totem

Bar Mezzana offered this complex amaro-forward Tiki drink in 2016.

2 oz Bols Genever
1 oz Amaro Ramazzotti
1/2 oz Honey Syrup
3/4 oz Pineapple Juice
3/4 oz Lime Juice
2 dash Angostura Bitters
1 dash Absinthe
Shake with ice, strain into a Tiki mug, fill with crushed ice, garnish with a pineapple slice and freshly grated nutmeg, and add a straw.

Dwarf Leopard

Sahil Mehta at Estragon's 2013 Tiki tribute to the Panamanian ocelot.

2 oz Ron Abuela Rum
1 oz Lime Juice
1/2 oz Velvet Falernum
1/2 oz Green Chartreuse
1 dash Allspice Dram
1 Egg White
Shake once without ice and once with ice, and strain into a rocks glass.

Early Fog

An adaptation of a hot dessert drink crafted by Jordan Marshall on Art Bar's autumnal 2012 menu.

1 1/2 oz Lepanto Spanish Brandy
1/2 oz Snap Ginger Liqueur
1/2 oz Cointreau
1/2 oz Earl Grey Syrup
1 dash Angostura Bitters
Heat a cocktail glass with boiling water. Stir ingredients without ice. Dump hot water out of cocktail glass, pour in stirred ingredients, and top with 2 oz steamed (or hot) milk. Spoon froth on top (if steamed) and garnish with freshly grated nutmeg.

Earthbound

An excellent Tequila Daisy at The Independent circa 2014.

1 1/2 oz Chinaco Blanco Tequila
1 oz Aperol
3/4 oz Honey Syrup
3/4 oz Lime Juice
Shake with ice, strain into a cocktail coupe, and garnish with a grapefruit twist.

CRBDBOCRBDBOCRBDBOCRBDBOCRBDBOCRBDBOCRB

Eastern Promise

Ted Gallagher named this 2012 Craigie on Main creation after his friend's word that he would bring him back a bottle of Jeppsen's Malört from Chicago.

1 1/2 oz Pierre Ferrand Ambre Cognac
1 oz Cocchi Barolo Chinato
1/2 oz Zucca Rabarbaro Amaro
1 bsp Jeppsen's Malört
Stir with ice and strain into a cocktail coupe pre-rinsed with Caol Ila Scotch.

Eastern Slopes

Seth Freidus' dual spirits drink at Alden & Harlow circa 2014.

1 oz Old Overholt Rye
1 oz Macchu Pisco La Diablada
3/4 oz Amaro S. Maria al Monte
1/4 oz Orgeat
1 dash Reagan's Orange Bitters
Stir with ice, strain into a rocks glass, and fill with ice. Garnish with an orange twist and add straws.

Easy E

At Backbar, Luc Thiers took a New Orleans-inspired direction on the Improved Japanese Cocktail for a drink of the week in 2015.

1 1/2 oz Four Roses Bourbon
1/2 oz Pimm's No. 1
1/2 oz Orgeat
1/2 oz Lemon Juice
2 dash Peychaud's Bitters
Shake with ice, strain into a cocktail coupe, and garnish with an 'E' shaped lemon twist.

Echo Lake

No. 9 Park's herbal egg white Sour circa 2014.

1 oz Del Maguey Chichicapa Mezcal
1 oz Green Chartreuse
1 oz Lime Juice
1/2 oz Simple Syrup
2 dash Orange Bitters
1 Egg White
Shake once without ice and once with ice, and strain into a cocktail coupe.

ED

Eddie Lynch

At Steel & Rye, Ted Gallagher paid tribute in 2013 to his grandfather, a Canadian Club salesman, who as a youth successfully protested the order of the stoplight to better mimic the Irish flag.

2 oz Canadian Club Whisky
1/2 oz Lemon Juice
1/4 oz Orange Juice
1/4 oz Cocchi Sweet Vermouth
2 dash Green Chartreuse
Shake with ice and strain into a Highball glass containing 2 oz soda water. Fill with ice, garnish with an "upside-down traffic light" (from top to bottom: cherry, lemon twist, and lime twist on a pick), and add a straw. See photo below.

Edgar Allen Poe

Sahil Mehta crafted this literary tribute for Estragon's Dead Poet Halloween dinner party in 2013.

1 1/2 oz Laird's Applejack
1/2 oz Alvear Amontillado Sherry
1/2 oz Frangelico
1/4 oz Luxardo Maraschino
3/4 oz Lemon Juice
Shake with ice, strain into a cocktail glass, and float a dash of allspice dram. Garnish with a fennel frond if available.

Eddie Lynch,
Steel & Rye

Eldridge

The "house Negroni" at Viale created by Patrick Gaggiano in 2014.

1 oz Edinburgh Gin
1/2 oz Dolin Dry Vermouth
1/2 oz Cinzano Sweet Vermouth
1 oz Amaro Montenegro
Stir with ice, strain into a rocks glass with a large ice cube, and garnish with an orange twist.

Electrical Storm Julep

One of Ted Kilpatrick's curious Julep creations at No. 9 Park circa 2013.

2 oz Bols Genever
3/4 oz Wray & Nephew White
   Overproof Rum
1/2 oz Cocchi Americano
1/2 oz Crème de Cacao
Leaves of 1 Mint Sprig
Muddle the leaves from a mint sprig at the bottom of a Julep cup, add the rest of the ingredients, fill with crushed ice, and stir to mix and chill. Garnish with mint sprigs, float 1/4 oz Gantous & Abou Raad Arak (sub absinthe or pastis), and add a straw.

Elegy

Sahil Mehta of Estragon crafted this recipe for an Angostura Bitters competition in 2012.

1 1/2 oz Daron Calvados
3/4 oz Lillet Blanc
1/2 oz Averna
1/2 oz Lemon Juice
2 dash Angostura Bitters
Shake with ice, strain into a rocks glass, fill with ice, garnish with a lemon twist, and add a straw.

Elementary My Dear

An adaptation of Ben Kweskin's basic sparkling wine cocktail at Craigie on Main in 2017 that was originally made with lemon cordial syrup and lemon juice.

3/4 oz Beefeater Gin
3/4 oz Aperol
1/2 oz Lime Cordial Syrup
1/2 oz Lime Juice
Shake with ice, strain into a flute glass with 2 oz Cristalino sparkling wine, and garnish with a grapefruit twist.

EL-EM

Elena

An aperitif created by Nick Korn at the Citizen Public House in 2012.

1 oz Carpano Sweet Vermouth
1 oz Amaro Montenegro
1 oz Lustau Amontillado Sherry
Stir with ice and strain into a rocks glass.

El Morro

At Russell House Tavern in 2014, Ashish Mitra captured memories of tropical nights in Puerto Rico.

1 1/4 oz Lustau Amontillado Sherry
3/4 oz Tres Agaves Blanco Tequila
1/2 oz Byrrh Quinquina
1/2 oz Grenadine
8 drop Hibiscus (or other flower) Water
1 dash Peychaud's Bitters
Stir with ice and strain in to a cocktail coupe. If substituting another flower water, a lighter touch might be needed.

Elvis & the Mexican Ghost

Sahil Mehta crafted this South of the Border-inspired number in 2016 for Estragon's Bar Go-Go nights on Sundays.

1 oz Milagro Blanco Tequila
3/4 oz Giffard Banane du Bresil
1/2 oz Ancho Reyes Chile Liqueur
3/4 oz Lime Juice
Shake with ice and strain into a cocktail coupe.

Emperor's New Clothes

Sahil Mehta's herbal number at Estragon circa 2013.

1 oz Bourbon
3/4 oz Cynar
3/4 oz Bittermens Citron Sauvage
1/2 oz Green Chartreuse
Stir with ice and strain into a cocktail coupe.

Endicott Cobbler

Fred Yarm paid tribute to the oldest living cultivated fruit tree in North America, the Endicott Pear Tree in Danvers, MA, for the Russell House Tavern 2014 menu.

1 1/2 oz Lustau Amontillado Sherry
1 1/2 oz St. George Spiced Pear Liqueur
1 oz Averna
2 dash Peychaud's Bitters
Build in a Collins glass, fill with crushed ice, garnish with an orange twist, and add a straw.

(An) End to Feral Days

Chris Danforth's funky bitter, brown, and stirred tribute at West Bridge circa 2014.

1 1/2 oz Avuá Aged Cachaça
1/2 oz Lustau East India Sherry
1/2 oz Amaro del Capo
1/2 oz Averna
2 dash Mole Bitters
1 dash Reagan's Orange Bitters
Stir with ice and strain into a cocktail coupe.

Esperanto

Jackson Cannon of the Hawthorne and Eastern Standard was a finalist in the 2012 Vinos de Jerez Cocktail Competition with this smoky drink.

2 oz Del Maguey Crema de Mezcal
3/4 oz La Cigarrera Manzanilla Sherry
1/2 oz Carpano Sweet Vermouth
1 dash Regan's Orange Bitters
Stir with ice, strain into a rocks glass, and garnish with lemon oil from a twist. Substitute a 9 part mezcal to 1 part agave nectar blend for the crema de mezcal.

Espionage

Kevin Martin balanced a trio of herbal liqueurs on a premise of earthy vodka at Eastern Standard in 2012.

1 1/2 oz Fair Trade Quinoa Vodka
3/4 oz Yellow Chartreuse
1/2 oz Amaro Montenegro
1/2 oz Cynar
Stir with ice, strain into a rocks glass, and garnish with lemon and orange oil from twists.

Essex

Saloon paid tribute in 2012 to rum finally being made again in Essex County, Massachusetts.

1 1/2 oz Privateer Amber Rum
1/2 oz Dry Vermouth
1/2 oz Creole Shrubb Orange
  Liqueur
1/2 oz Cynar
2 dash Angostura Bitters
Stir with ice, strain into a rocks glass, and garnish with a lemon twist.

Etched in Time

Sahil Mehta's amber-colored creation at Estragon for the Angostura 2013 competition.

1 1/2 oz Angostura 7 Year Rum
1/2 oz Luxardo Maraschino
1/2 oz Luxardo Amaretto
1/4 oz Luxardo Amaro Abano
1/4 oz Angostura Bitters
1/2 oz Lemon Juice
Stir with ice, strain into a cocktail coupe, and garnish with a small dried rosebud.

Everell's Nightwatch

An autumnal creation by Stephen Shellenberger of Pomodoro in Brookline in 2013.

3/4 oz Old Overholt Rye
3/4 oz Hispaniola Mamajuana
  Spiced Rum
3/4 oz Nocino Walnut Liqueur
3/4 oz Pineau des Charentes
Stir with ice and strain into a rocks glass.

Everybody Wants to Rule the World

An autumnal Swizzle crafted by Fred Yarm for the tail end of Loyal Nine's Yacht Rock Sundays in 2015.

3/4 oz Chinaco Blanco Tequila
3/4 oz Morin Selection Calvados
1/2 oz Kronan Swedish Punsch
1/2 oz Cinnamon Syrup
1/2 oz Lime Juice
Build in a Collins glass, fill with crushed ice, and swizzle to mix and chill. Garnish with an orange twist and freshly grated nutmeg, and add a straw.

Etched in Time, Estragon

Everything Nice

Brick & Mortar in 2016 offered sugar and spice in this nursery rhyme of a Cognac libation.

1 1/2 oz Pierre Ferrand 1840 Cognac
3/4 oz St. George Spiced Pear Liqueur
3/4 oz Pineau des Charentes
1/2 oz St. Elizabeth Allspice Dram
Stir with ice, strain into a rocks glass, and garnish with an orange twist.

Exchange Place Fizz

Dave Delaney at the Citizen in Worcester crafted this Fizz in 2011 as a spin-off of his Imbibe Magazine cover drink since he had to keep the winning recipe under wraps until Tales of the Cocktail that July.

2 oz Redemption Bourbon
1 oz Pineapple Shrub
1/2 oz Lemon Juice
1/2 oz Simple Syrup
1/4 oz Allspice Dram
Shake with ice, strain into a High-ball glass containing 2 oz soda water, fill with ice, garnish with a mint sprig, and add a straw.

Expatriot

Trina's Starlite Lounge rich, nutty Rob Roy variation in 2012.

1 1/2 oz Cutty Sark Scotch
3/4 oz Carpano Sweet Vermouth
3/4 oz Nocino Walnut Liqueur
1 dash Fee's Walnut Bitters
Stir with ice and strain into a cocktail glass.

Exporter

Alex Howell and Josh Taylor crafted this recipe to appear on a Drambuie event menu at West Bridge but it ended up on the regular cocktail menu in 2013 instead.

1 oz Bols Genever
3/4 oz Drambuie
1/2 oz Becherovka
1/4 oz Falernum
1/2 oz Lemon Juice
1 dash Fee's Whiskey Barrel Bitters
Shake with ice, strain into a rocks glass, and garnish with lemon oil from a twist.

Eye of the Storm

Ashish Mitra's 2015 Tiki drink riff on a Dark & Stormy at Russell House Tavern.

1 oz Smith & Cross Rum
1 oz Clement Premiere Canne
   Rhum Agricole
3/4 oz Lime Juice
1/2 oz Caffè Borghetti
1/2 oz Vanilla Syrup
1 dash Angostura Bitters
Shake with ice, strain into a Collins glass containing 2 oz ginger ale, fill with ice cubes alternating with lime wheels (3 lime wheels total), and add a straw.

Face for Radio

An adaptation of a recipe John Mayer created at Local 149 for a Bacardi competition circa 2013. The drink was named as such to make light of the drink's murky appearance.

1 1/2 oz Bacardi 8 Year Rum
3/4 oz Becherovka
1/2 oz Orgeat
1/2 oz Lime Juice
1/4 oz Cinnamon Syrup
Shake with ice and strain into a cocktail glass.

Fairwell & Adieu

John McElroy's nightcap tribute to Quint's song in Jaws that he created at Russell House Tavern in 2012. At 4 ounces of 80 proof spirit, the name is quite apt.

1 1/2 oz Del Maguey San Luis
  Del Rio Mezcal
1 1/2 oz Privateer Amber Rum
1/2 oz Benedictine
1/2 oz Drambuie
2 dash Angostura Bitters
Stir with ice and strain into a cocktail coupe.

Fangataufa

Sahil Mehta at Estragon added to sherry Tiki gestalt in 2014.

2 oz Manzanilla Sherry
1/2 oz Green Chartreuse
1/2 oz Cynar
1/2 oz Passion Fruit Syrup
1/2 oz Lime Juice
Shake with ice, strain into a cocktail coupe, and garnish with a lime wheel.

Fannie Porter

A tribute to a brothel owner who sheltered outlaws in the Wild West; crafted by the Hawthorne's Katie Emmerson for a 2013 Women of the Wild West night at the Blue Room.

1 1/2 oz Rittenhouse Rye
3/4 oz Pierre Ferrand Dry Curaçao
3/4 oz Nardini Amaro
1 dash Bittermens Mole Bitters
Stir with ice and strain into a cocktail coupe.

Father's Advice

Ran Duan won the Bacardi Legacy Competition 2015 with this cocktail created at the Baldwin Bar at Sichuan Garden II.

1 1/2 oz Bacardi Gold Rum
1/2 oz Cardamaro
1/2 oz Punt e Mes
1/2 oz Amontillado Sherry
1/4 oz Giffard Banane du Bresil
Stir with ice, strain into a cocktail glass, and garnish with an orange twist-cherry flag.

Ferrari Colada,
Backbar

Feliz Flip

Kobie Ali crafted this Flip in 2015 at Backbar to make people happy!

1 1/2 oz El Buho Mezcal
1/2 oz Lemon Juice
1/2 oz Honey Syrup
1/4 oz Cinnamon Syrup
1/4 oz Angostura Bitters
1 bsp Allspice Dram
1 Whole Egg
Shake once without ice and once with ice, strain into a rocks glass, and garnish with 3 drops of Jerry Thomas Decanter Bitters.

Fenway Flip

A Flip Ryan Lotz created in 2011 while doing a guest shift at Lineage, and he served it shortly thereafter at the Hawthorne.

1 oz Bulleit Rye
1 oz Pimm's No. 1
3/4 oz Cinnamon Syrup
1 Whole Egg
Shake once without ice and once with ice, strain into a single Old Fashioned glass, and garnish with a few drops of Fee's Whiskey Barrel Bitters.

Fernet Alexander

Fred Yarm created this dessert nightcap in 2009 while working through the 100 Drink List by Houston's Anvil that left the spirit part for the Alexander open.

1 oz Fernet Branca
1 oz Crème de Cacao
1 oz Heavy Cream
Shake with ice, strain into a cocktail glass, and garnish with freshly grated nutmeg.

Fernet Fix

Fred Yarm updated the 19th century drink style in 2011 with a more modern bartender flavor profile. It later spawned the Kitty Leroy (page 189) in 2013.

2 oz Fernet Branca
3/4 oz Pineapple Syrup
1/2 oz Lime Juice
Shake with ice, strain into a rocks glass, fill with crushed ice, dress the top with berries in season, and add straws.

Fernet Flip

A robust Flip served at Eastern Standard in 2008 with perhaps some input from Ben Sandrof then of No. 9 Park. I have had good luck with using brown sugar syrup here in place of the simple.

2 oz Fernet Branca
1 oz Simple Syrup
1 Whole Egg
Shake once without ice and once with ice, strain into cocktail glass, and garnish with a few drops of Fee's Whiskey Barrel Bitters.

Ferrari Colada

Luc Thiers at Backbar combined the Fernet-Campari shoot with the classic Piña Colada in 2015.

1/2 oz Plantation Trinidad Rum
1/2 oz Rhum Clement Select Rhum Agricole
1/2 oz Campari
1/2 oz Fernet Vallet
1 1/2 oz Pineapple Juice
1/2 oz Coconut Cream
1/4 oz Demerara Syrup
Shake with ice, strain into a Tiki mug, fill with crushed ice, garnish with a lime wheel coated with a dash of Angostura Bitters, and add a straw.

FI

Fight in Silence

A bitter dark orange number created by Tony Iamunno at Stoddard's in 2013.

1 1/2 oz Clement VSOP Rhum Agricole
1 oz Amaro Ramazzotti
1 oz Orange Juice
1/2 oz Brown Sugar Syrup
2 dash Angostura Bitters
Shake with ice, strain into a cocktail coupe, and garnish with an orange twist.

Figure Eight

An adaptation of a curious drink created by Ted Kilpatrick at No. 9 Park circa 2012; it was named after how the drink alternated between a rhum-tropical and a gin-vermouth focus, and this flip-flopping reminded Ted of the infinity symbol.

1 3/4 oz Anchor Junipero Gin
3/4 oz Velvet Falernum
3/4 oz Dolin Blanc Vermouth
3/4 oz Lemon Juice
Shake with ice and strain into a rocks glass pre-rinsed Neisson Rhum Agricole.

Fishnets & Fangs

Ryan McGrale's vampy homage for Tavern Road's inaugural 2013 menu.

3/4 oz Peychaud's Bitters
3/4 oz Lime Juice
1/2 oz Drambuie
1/2 oz Raspberry Syrup
1/2 oz El Buho Mezcal
Shake with ice, strain into a cocktail coupe, and garnish with a lemon twist.

Five Points Pop-in

At Drink in 2013, Will Thompson paid tribute to an old style of drink brought back at Dead Rabbits in the Five Points neighborhood in Manhattan.

1 oz Pierre Ferrand 1840 Cognac
1 oz St. Teresa 1796 Rum
3/4 oz Demerara Syrup
1 Whole Egg
Shake once without ice and once with ice, strain into a Highball glass containing 2 oz Barney Flats Oatmeal Stout, and garnish with freshly grated nutmeg.

CRBCRCBCRCBCRCBCRCBCRCBCRCBCRCB

Fleming Fizz

Fred Yarm's 2015 cross of a Penicillin and a French 75 at Russell House Tavern that was named after Alexander Fleming who discovered the drug Penicillin.

1 1/2 oz Great King Street Scotch
3/4 oz Lemon Juice
1/2 oz Honey Syrup
1/4 oz Ginger Syrup
Shake with ice, strain into a flute glass containing 2 oz of sparkling wine, float a barspoon Laphroaig Scotch, and garnish with a lemon twist.

Flintlock

A smoky aperitif served at Thirst Boston 2013 that was created by Sean Frederick at the Citizen Public House.

2 oz Lillet Blanc
1 oz Savory & James Amontillado Sherry
3/4 oz Montelobos Mezcal
1 dash Angostura Orange Bitters
1 pinch Salt
Stir to dissolve salt, add ice and stir again, strain into a cocktail glass, and garnish with an orange twist.

Flip Cup

Eastern Standard's Pimm's Cup variation for Summer 2015 named after the infamous beer drinking game.

1 1/2 oz Pimm's No. 1
3/4 oz Lemon Juice
3/4 oz Simple Syrup
Shake with ice, strain into a Highball glass containing 3 oz Newburyport Belgian-style Wit Beer, fill with ice, garnish with a cucumber slice, and add a straw.

Flowers of Romance

Sahil Mehta's 2014 Public Image Ltd. tribute Sidecar riff at Estragon.

1 1/2 oz Pierre Ferrand Ambre Cognac
3/4 oz Breckenridge Bitters
1/4 oz Chamomile Tea Syrup
1/2 oz Lemon Juice
1 dash Angostura Bitters
Shake with ice, strain into a cocktail coupe, and garnish with a few dried chamomile flowers.

FL-FO

Flower Sour

Ted Gallagher's floral Bourbon drink at Craigie on Main to greet the blooms in 2012.

1 oz W.L. Weller Bourbon
1 oz Cardamaro
3/4 oz Lemon Juice
1/2 oz Honey Syrup
1 Egg White
Shake once without ice and once with ice, strain into a rocks glass, fill with ice, garnish with a lemon slice and either a pinch of dried lavender flowers or a spritz of lavender tincture, and add straws.

Flushing – Main Street

Tiger Mama's Manhattan variation on their opening 2015 menu.

2 oz Akashi White Oak Japanese Whisky
1/2 oz Dolin Blanc Vermouth
1/4 oz Green Chartreuse
1/4 oz Tempus Fugit Crème de Cacao
2 dash Angostura Bitters
Stir with ice, strain into a cocktail coupe, and garnish with a flamed lemon twist.

Forbidden Fruit

Ran Duan created this egg white Sour at the Baldwin Room at Sichuan Garden II and served it at the Hawthorne for the Bombay Sapphire and GQ's "Most Imaginative Bartender" event in 2014 held in his honor.

1 1/2 oz Bombay Sapphire Gin
3/4 oz Passion Fruit Syrup
1/2 oz Campari
1/2 oz Lemon Juice
1/4 oz Yuzu Juice
1 Egg White
Shake once without ice and once with ice, strain into a cocktail coupe, and garnish with a spritz (or a few drops) of St. Elizabeth Allspice Dram.

Forte Four

Drink outdid their Four Rum Old Fashioned with a 4 rum-4 bitters Old Fashioned in 2009.

1 oz Plantation Jamaican Rum
1 oz Lemon Hart 151 Rum
1/2 oz La Favorite Rhum Agricole
1/2 oz Old Monk Rum
2 dash Angostura Bitters
2 dash Regan's Orange Bitters
2 dash Fee's Whiskey Barrel Bitters
2 dash Bittermens Mole Bitters
1 Demerara Sugar Cube
Muddle sugar cube with a 1/4 oz of water until dissolved. Add rest of ingredients, stir with ice, strain into a rocks glass with a large ice cube, and garnish with an orange twist.

Fort Français

Ryan Sullivan's 2015 French ingredient riff on the Vieux Carré at La Brasa.

1 oz Pierre Ferrand 1840 Cognac
1 oz La Favorite Rhum Agricole Ambre
1 oz Pierre Ferrand Dry Curaçao
1 bsp Benedictine
1 dash Peychaud's Bitters
1 dash Angostura Bitters
Stir with ice, strain into a rocks glass with a large ice cube, and garnish with a lemon twist.

Flower Sour,
Craigie on Main

❧❧❧❧❧❧❧❧❧❧❧❧❧❧❧❧❧❧❧❧❧❧❧

Four Rum Manhattan

Max Toste crafted this spirited mix resembling a Pirate's Cocktail in 2009 at Deep Ellum.

1/2 oz Berkshire Rum
1/2 oz Ron Matusalem 10 Yr Rum
1/2 oz La Favorite Rhum Agricole Vieux
1/2 oz Diplomático Añejo Rum
1/2 oz Dolin Dry Vermouth
1/2 oz Dolin Blanc Vermouth
1 cube Demerara Sugar
2 dash Aromatic Bitters
Muddle the sugar cube with the bitters, add the rest of the ingredients, stir with ice, and strain into a rocks glass. Fill with ice, garnish with a lemon twist, and add straws.

Four Rum Old Fashioned

Drink gathered four rums from four parts of the world in 2009 to one up Don the Beachcomber's quote of "What one rum can't do, three rums can."

1/2 oz Batavia Arrack
1/2 oz Ron Pampero Anniversario
1/2 oz JM Rhum Agricole Blanc
1/2 oz Barbancourt 8 Year Rhum
1/2 oz Cinnamon Syrup
2 dashes Fee's Whiskey Barrel Bitters
2 dashes Angostura Orange Bitters
Stir with ice, strain into a rocks glass with a large ice cube, and garnish with lime and orange oil from twists.

Four Vices

Ryan Connelly created this equal-parts recipe at Belly Wine Bar in 2013 that was named by the restaurant's owner, Nick Zappia.

3/4 oz Pierre Ferrand Cognac
3/4 oz Dry Amontillado Sherry
3/4 oz Amaro Montenegro
3/4 oz Cocchi Sweet Vermouth
1 dash Angostura Bitters
1 dash Orange Bitters
Stir with ice, strain into a cocktail glass, and garnish with orange oil from a twist.

Franklin Bearse

Misty Kalkofen's shotgun blast of a cocktail at Brick and Mortar in homage to a Cape Cod rum runner; the drink was created in August 2012 as a way of teaching returning students how to drink.

2 oz Smith & Cross Rum
1/2 oz Yellow Chartreuse
1/2 oz Combier Orange Liqueur
1 dash Angostura Bitters
Stir with ice and strain into a rocks glass.

Fratelli Sling

Adam Hockman crafted this Fernet Sling at Russell House Tavern in 2012.

2 oz Rittenhouse Rye
3/4 oz Fernet Branca
1/2 oz Honey Syrup
1/2 oz Lemon Juice
Shake with ice, strain into a Collins glass glass containing 2 oz soda water, and fill with ice cubes. Float a 1/4 oz of Fernet Branca, garnish with an orange twist, and add a straw.

French Derby

At Rendezvous, Scott Holliday riffed on the gin-based Derby and took it in a pear direction in 2011.

2 1/2 oz Citadelle Gin
1/2 oz Matilde Pear Liqueur
2 dash Fee's Whiskey Barrel Bitters
2 sprig Mint
Muddle mint with other ingredients, remove mint, stir with ice, and strain into a rocks glass.

French Film

Fred Yarm riffed on Sable's Board of Directors to create this clean, crisp number for Loyal Nine's low proof section of the menu in 2016.

1 1/2 oz Dolin Dry Vermouth
1/2 oz Benedictine
1/2 oz Honey Syrup
1/2 oz Lemon Juice
Shake with ice, strain into a rocks glass, fill with ice, garnish with a lemon twist, and add straws.

French Laundry

The Franklin Café's circa 2013 tribute to one of the best restaurants in the world.

1 1/2 oz Citadelle Gin
3/4 oz St. Germain
1/2 oz Lime Juice
1/4 oz Luxardo Maraschino
3 dash Bitter Truth Grapefruit Bitters
Shake with ice and strain into a cocktail glass.

Frequent Flier

Phil MacLeod's 2013 funky Rum Buck at Brick & Mortar.

1 1/2 oz St. Teresa Rum
1/2 oz Cynar
1/2 oz St. Elizabeth Allspice Dram
1/2 oz Lime Juice
1 dash Angostura Orange Bitters
Shake with ice and strain into a Collins glass containing 2 oz ginger beer. Fill with ice, garnish with an orange twist, and add a straw.

Friar Tuck

Tyler Knight's contribution to Audubon's 2015 cartoon-themed menu section.

1 oz Perry's Tot Gin
1 oz Cocchi Americano
1/2 oz Combier Peche
1/2 oz Amargo Vallet
Stir with ice, strain into a cocktail coupe, and garnish with a grapefruit twist.

Frosty the Julep, Backbar

Frisco Rose

For a Loyal Nine drink of the day in 2016, Fred Yarm merged the Frisco Sour with the Jack Rose to create a fruity, herbal, and spiced libation.

3/4 oz Rittenhouse Rye
3/4 oz Morin Selection Calvados
1/2 oz Benedictine
1/2 oz Grenadine
1/2 oz Lemon Juice
1 dash Peychaud's Bitters
Shake with ice, strain into a cocktail coupe, and garnish with a lemon twist.

From the Hip

A complex Swizzle Matthew Schrage created for Ribelle's opening 2013 menu that he later put on the list at the Highball Lounge.

1 oz Del Maguey Mezcal Vida
3/4 oz Velvet Falernum
1/2 oz Lime Juice
2 sprig Mint
Muddle mint sprigs at the bottom of a Collins glass. Add the rest of the ingredients, fill with crushed ice, swizzle to mix and chill but leaving the mint at the bottom, and layer 1/2 oz Campari over the top. Garnish with fresh mint sprigs and a dash of Angostura Bitters, and add a straw.

Front Street

Sam Olivari at No. 9 Park named his Toronto variation in 2012 after a neighborhood in that city.

2 oz Sazerac 6 Year Rye
3/4 oz Amaro S. Maria al Monte
1/2 oz Cinnamon Syrup
2 dash Mole Bitters
Stir with ice, strain into a rocks glass, and garnish with flamed orange oil from a twist.

Frosty the Julep

Josh Cross at Backbar in 2017 was inspired to make a Winter Julep "because Frosty melted."

2 oz Old Granddad Bonded Bourbon
1/2 oz Peppermint Tea Syrup
1/2 oz St. George Geijer Glögg
Build in a Julep cup, fill with crushed ice, and stir. Garnish with "all manner of festive accoutrements" (a cinnamon stick, sage leaf, mint sprig, and rosemary sprig, and dust leaves with powdered sugar), and add a straw.

FU-GA

Full Sail Swizzle

Stephen Bookman's spiced Swizzle off of the secret 2015 Tiki menu at Highball Lounge.

1 1/2 oz Appleton Rum
1/2 oz Becherovka
1/2 oz Ginger Syrup
1/2 oz Grenadine
1/2 oz Lime Juice
Build in a Pilsner glass, fill with crushed ice, and swizzle to mix and chill. Garnish with 3 dashes Angostura Bitters and add a straw.

Funky Kingston

James Miranda at Russell House Tavern in 2017 paid tribute to the Sons of Liberty distillery's location in Kingston, RI, by naming this tropical number after a reggae song.

1 1/2 oz Sons of Liberty True Born Genever-style Gin
3/4 oz Pierre Ferrand Dry Curaçao
3/4 oz Velvet Falernum
1/2 oz Lime Juice
3 dash Angostura Bitters
2 slice Ginger Root
Muddle the ginger slices, add the rest of the ingredients, shake with ice, and strain into a double Old Fashioned glass. Fill with crushed ice, garnish with freshly grated nutmeg, and add straws.

Further Moore

At Viale in 2014, Patrick Gaggiano paid tribute with this beer cocktail to the person who turned him on to Cardamaro.

1 1/2 oz El Buho Mezcal
3/4 oz Cardamaro
1/2 oz Yellow Chartreuse
1/2 oz Honey Syrup
1/2 oz Lemon Juice
1 dash Angostura Bitters
Shake with ice, strain into a Collins glass containing 2 oz Jack's Abby Jabby Brau Lager, fill with ice, and add a straw.

Galleon

One of Sahil Mehta's recipe ideas at Estragon for the 2016 Vino de Jerez competition.

1 oz Dos Maderas 5+3 Rum
1 oz Lustau Palo Cortado Sherry
1/2 oz Bonal Gentiane-Quina
1/2 oz Benedictine
1 dash Angostura Bitters
1 dash Peychaud's Bitters
Stir with ice, strain into a rocks glass, and garnish with a lemon twist.

Gambit

Lena Webb at Spoke crafted this Scaffa in 2013 based off of her love of the pisco-Oloroso sherry pairing.

3/4 oz Bols Genever
3/4 oz Pisco
3/4 oz El Maestro Sierra Oloroso Sherry
3/4 oz Kina L'Avion d'Or
1 pinch Salt
Build in a rocks glass, briefly stir to mix __without__ ice, and garnish with orange oil from a twist. Note: This is a room temperature cocktail.

Garden of Good and Evil

Sahil Mehta at Estragon crafted this spicy vegetal mezcal drink for the Angostura Bitters competition in 2013.

1 1/2 oz Del Maguey Mezcal Vida
1 oz Velvet Falernum
1/2 oz Lime Juice
1/4 oz Angostura Bitters
2 slice Cucumber
Muddle 2 slices of cucumber, add the rest of the ingredients, and shake with ice. Strain into a rocks glass half-rimmed with celery salt, fill with ice, garnish with a cucumber slice, and add straws.

Genie in a Bottle

At Backbar in 2015, Luc Thiers was inspired by the classic Blue Hawaiian.

1 oz El Buho Mezcal
1 oz El Dorado 3 Year Rum
2 oz Pineapple Juice
1/2 oz Drambuie
1/2 oz Blue Curaçao
1/2 oz Lemon Juice
1/2 oz Simple Syrup
Shake with ice, strain into a flower vase (or Collins glass), fill with crushed ice, and add a straw.

Gens du Monde

An adaptation of a 2013-vintage drink created by John Mayer of Local 149.

1 oz Bookers Bourbon
1 oz Maurin Quina
1 oz Amaro Nonino
2 dash Angostura Bitters
2 dash Angostura Orange Bitters
2 dash Bittermens Mole Bitters
Stir with ice and strain into a snifter glass.

Get the Wolfe

Rob Ficks' Bobby Burns-like creation at Craigie on Main circa 2016.

1 1/2 oz Grant's Scotch
3/4 oz Punt e Mes
1/4 oz Lustau East India Sherry
1/4 oz Lustau Amontillado Sherry
1/4 oz Cynar
1 dash Angostura Orange Bitters
Stir with ice, strain into a cocktail coupe, and garnish with a flamed orange twist.

Ghost of Castle Island

John Mayer created this recipe for a Bacardi contest circa 2013, and it got dubbed after the 19th century lore of a military base a short distance away from Local 149. Edgar Allen Poe was stationed at that base nearly two centuries ago, and the legend of the walled up officer inspired his short story, "The Cask of Amontillado."

1 1/2 oz Bacardi Select Rum
3/4 oz Green Chartreuse
3/4 oz Pedro Romero Oloroso Sherry
1/2 oz La Favorite Blanc Rhum Agricole
Stir with ice, strain into a rocks glass, and garnish with orange oil from a twist.

Gianopulos

At Sichuan Garden II in Woburn, Ran Duan made this tribute in 2012 to his friend who loves Amaro Nardini.

1 1/2 oz El Dorado 12 Year Rum
1/2 oz Campari
1/2 oz Amaro Nardini
1/2 oz Punt e Mes
3 dash Angostura Bitters
Stir with ice, strain into a cocktail glass, and garnish with a cherry.

Gin Cobbler (Ames Street Deli's variation)

An adaptation of Ames Street Deli's Gin Cobbler created in 2014.

1 1/2 oz Ford's Gin
1 oz Lustau Amontillado Sherry
1/4 oz Maple Syrup
1/4 oz Allspice Dram
1/4 oz Giffard Apricot Liqueur
Build in a Highball glass or Julep cup, fill with crushed ice, and add straws. Garnish with a dried apricot if available.

Gin Cobbler,
Ames Street Deli

Girlfriend's Dilemma

At Brick and Mortar in 2012, Evan Harrison was faced with the girlfriend of one of the investors wanting something lighter in alcohol.

1 oz Pierre Ferrand 1840 Cognac
1 oz Cocchi Americano
1/2 oz Cynar
1/2 oz Lemon Juice
3/4 oz Pineau des Charentes
1/2 oz St. Elizabeth Allspice Dram
Shake with ice and strain into a rocks glass.

Girl from Ipanema

A refreshing and tropical egg white Sour created in 2016 at the Baldwin & Sons Trading Co. upstairs at Sichuan Garden II.

1 oz Avua Cachaça
1 oz Tempus Fugit Crème de Menthe
3/4 oz Passion Fruit Syrup
3/4 oz Lemon Juice
1 Egg White
Shake once without ice and once with ice, strain into a cocktail coupe, and garnish with lemon oil from a twist and three drops of Angostura Bitters.

GI-GO

Giuseppe's Lady

Will Isaza's 2014 cross at Fairsted Kitchen between a Little Giuseppe and a Pink Lady.

1 1/4 oz St. George Terroir Gin
1/2 oz Cynar
3/4 oz Grenadine
1/2 oz Lime Juice
1 dash Angostura Bitters
Shake with ice, strain into a cocktail coupe, and garnish with lemon oil from a twist.

Gloamin Dwines

Scott Holliday crafted this tribute to the fading dusk at Rendezvous in 2012.

2 oz White Horse Scotch
1 oz Cynar
1/2 oz Cocchi Americano
1 dash Scrappy's Celery Bitters
Stir with ice, strain into a rocks glass pre-rinsed with Caol Ila Scotch, and garnish with lemon oil from a twist.

Golden-Eyed Treefrog

After the El Dorado Rum distiller Shaun Caleb spoke at Felipe's in Harvard Square in 2015, the bartenders served up this Tiki libation named after one of the common sounds heard in Guyana's forest.

1 1/2 oz El Dorado 12 Year Rum
1 1/2 oz Grapefruit Juice
3/4 oz Falernum
3/4 oz Simple Syrup
1/2 oz Lime Juice
1 dash Angostura Bitters
Shake with ice, strain into a Tiki mug, fill with crushed ice, garnish with a spent lime shell "hat" filled with 1/4 oz El Dorado 151 Rum, and ignite the overproof rum.

Golden Fiddle

For Appleton's 2012 Remixology contest, No. 9 Park's Tyler Wang was inspired by Charlie Daniels' The Devil Went Down to Georgia to riff on Trader Vic's El Diablo.

2 oz Appleton Estate Reserve Rum
3/4 oz Lime Juice
1/2 oz Crème de Cassis
1/2 oz Willet Rye
1 bsp Kübler Absinthe
2 dash Angostura Bitters
Build in a Collins glass, fill with crushed ice, swizzle to mix and chill, garnish with a flamed spritz of Angostura Bitters, and add a straw.

CRBEDBOCRBEDBOCRBEDBOCRBEDBOCRBEDBOCRBEDBOCRB

Golden Temple Fizz

A complex bitter-citrus Golden Fizz crafted by Ran Duan in 2013 at Sichaun Garden II.

1 oz Campari
1 oz Peychaud's Bitters
1 oz Combier Pamplemousse
  Liqueur
1 oz Lime Juice
1/4 oz Yuzu Juice
1/2 oz Simple Syrup
1 Egg Yolk
Shake once without ice and once with ice, strain into a Highball glass containing 2 oz soda water, garnish with a grapefruit twist-cherry flag, and add a straw.

Good Buddy

Scott Shoer's variation on the Old Pal at Sycamore circa 2013.

1 1/2 oz Four Roses Bourbon
3/4 oz Dolin Blanc Vermouth
3/4 oz Campari
2 dash Orange Bitters
Stir with ice, strain into a cocktail coupe, and garnish with an orange twist.

Good Cuban

Steel & Rye's take on the neo-classic, the Old Cuban, in 2013.

1 oz Plantation 3 Star White Rum
1/2 oz Lime Juice
1/2 oz Mint Syrup
1/2 oz Kina L'Avion d'Or
1 dash Bittermens Mole Bitters
Shake with ice and strain into a cocktail glass containing 2 oz dry sparkling wine.

Gorillas on Deck

Highball Lounge's riff on the classic Piña Colada in 2016 that was served with a warning about how much the mix hides the boozy potency.

1 oz Clement Premiere Canne
  Rhum Agricole
1 oz Plantation Overproof Dark
  Rum
1 oz Pineapple Juice
1 oz Coconut Cream
1/2 oz Ginger Syrup
1/2 oz Lime Juice
Shake with ice, strain into a Collins glass, fill with crushed ice, garnish with mint sprigs and 5 dashes Angostura Bitters, and add a straw.

Green Harbor,
Island Creek
Oyster Bar

Graduate

*Upstairs on the Square's
sparkling 2013 abstraction of the
Teresa from Gary Regan's The Joy
of Mixology.*

3/4 oz Campari
3/4 oz Crème de Cassis
3/4 oz Lemon Juice
*Shake with ice, strain into a flute
glass containing 2 oz dry sparkling
wine, and garnish with an orange
twist.*

Grandpa's Drunk

*An adaptation of a Trina's Starlite
Lounge nightcap circa 2017.*

2 oz Pierre Ferrand Cognac
1/2 oz Crème de Cacao
1/2 oz Benedictine
1 dash Molé Bitters
*Stir with ice and strain into a rocks
glass.*

Grand Tour

*This tour started circa 2013 at
Craigie on Main and offers
complex sherry and agave notes
in a Fix-like format.*

1 oz Lustau Amontillado Sherry
1/2 oz Herradura Reposado
    Tequila
3/4 oz Pineapple Syrup
3/4 oz Lime Juice
1 dash Regan's Orange Bitters
*Shake with ice, strain into a rocks
glass, fill with ice, garnish with a
lime wedge, and add straws.*

Grease Lightning

Sahil Mehta crafted this aperitif reminiscent of a Chrysanthemum in 2016 at Estragon.

1 1/2 oz Dolin Dry Vermouth
1 oz Bonal Gentiane-Quina
1/2 oz Benedictine
1 dash Peychaud's Bitters
Stir with ice, strain into a double Old Fashioned glass, fill with ice, and garnish with a lemon twist.

Green Harbor

Vikram Hedge named this refreshing tall drink at Island Creek Oyster Bar in 2012 after a beach at his wife's hometown of Marshfield.

1 oz Green Chartreuse
1 oz Cocchi Americano
4 wedge Lime
2 sprig Mint
2 dash Bittermens Grapefruit Bitters
Muddle the lime wedges and mint sprigs. Add the rest of the ingredients, shake with ice, and strain into a Collins glass containing 3 oz soda water. Fill with ice, garnish with mint sprigs, and add a straw.

Green Hornet

A great nightcap from John Wierszchalek circa 2015 at Barrel House in Beverly.

2 oz Old Overholt Rye
1/2 oz Cognac
1/2 oz Amaro Nardini
1 bsp Green Chartreuse
2 dash Orange Bitters
Stir with ice and strain into a cocktail glass.

Guadalajara

Ashish Mitra crafted this Old Cuban-style drink at Russell House Tavern in 2015 using the Southside as inspiration.

2 oz Olmeca Altos Plata Tequila
1/2 oz Lemon Juice
1/2 oz Simple Syrup
2 dash Regan's Orange Bitters
6-8 leaf Mint
Shake with ice, strain into a cocktail glass containing 1 oz sparkling wine, and garnish with a lemon twist.

GU-HA

Guiding Light

At Russell House Tavern in 2015, Joe Slavinski paid tribute in his first cocktail to everyone who taught him the trade.

2 oz Xicaru Mezcal
3/4 oz Gran Classico
1/2 oz Creole Shrubb Orange Liqueur
1/4 oz St. Elizabeth Allspice Dram
1 dash Peychaud's Bitters
Stir with ice, strain into a rocks glass, and garnish with an orange twist.

Gullistan

Sahil Mehta at Estragon was inspired in 2011 by the Dutch's fascination with tulips to name this Genever drink after a 13th century Persian poet whose name translates to "flower garden."

1 oz Bols Genever
3/4 oz Amaro Montenegro
1/2 oz Aperol
1/2 oz Massenez Crème a la Fraise
1/2 oz Lemon Juice
Shake with ice, strain into a cocktail coupe, and garnish with a lemon twist.

Haitian Monk

Ryan Lotz crafted this Daiquiri variation at Lineage in 2010, and luckily he chose this name over my more irreverent suggestion of the Popa Docquiri.

2 oz Barbancourt 8 Year Rhum
1/2 oz Lime Juice
1/2 oz Simple Syrup
1/4 oz Green Chartreuse
2 dash Fee's Peach Bitters
1 dash Angostura Bitters
Shake with ice and strain into a cocktail glass.

Halfway to Havana

Dan Braganca's 2016 drink of the day at Backbar that riffed on the Floradita and Hemingway Daiquiris by adding Don's Mix #2 flavors.

1 1/4 oz Plantation Barbados Rum
1/2 oz Carpano Sweet Vermouth
1/2 oz Lime Juice
1/2 oz Grapefruit Juice
1/4 oz Cinnamon Syrup
Shake with ice, strain into a cocktail coupe, and garnish with lime oil from a twist.

Hampshire

One of Fanny Katz's recipes from the sherry section of the Belly Wine Bar's 2013 cocktail menu.

1/2 oz Lustau Pedro Ximenez Sherry
3/4 oz Pierre Ferrand Dry Curaçao
1/2 oz Aperol
1/2 oz Lemon Juice
Shake with ice, strain into a Highball glass with 3 oz soda water, fill with crushed ice, garnish with an orange twist, and add a straw.

Harrison Bergeron

Patrick Andrew's 2016 Boulevardier riff tribute to Kurt Vonnegut at Sichuan Garden II.

1 oz Four Roses Bourbon
1 oz Carpano Sweet Vermouth
1 oz Amaro Montengro
Stir with ice, strain into a double Old Fashioned glass, fill with ice, and garnish with an orange twist.

Harris Shrub

A whiskey refresher by Charles Coykendall on Tiger Mama's inaugural drink menu in 2015.

3/4 oz Four Roses Bourbon
3/4 oz Cardamaro
3/4 oz Aperol
3/4 oz Lemon Juice
1 oz Pineapple Shrub
Shake with ice and strain into a Collins glass. Fill with ice, garnish with a pineapple fruit leaf, and add a straw.

Harvard Yard #1

Russell House Tavern's original tribute in 2010 to the nearby campus.

2 1/2 oz Pikesville Rye
1 oz Dubonnet Rouge
1/2 oz Benedictine
Stir with ice and strain into a cocktail glass pre-rinsed with St. Elizabeth Allspice Dram.

Harvard Yard #2

After a few years, the staff at Russell House Tavern reformulated their neighborhood-focused whiskey drink circa 2012.

2 oz Buffalo Trace Bourbon
1 oz Cocchi Sweet Vermouth
1/2 oz Becherovka
1 dash Angostura Bitters
Stir with ice and strain into a rocks glass pre-rinsed with St. Elizabeth Allspice Dram.

HA-HE

Haumea

A sparkling tribute to the Hawaiian goddess of fertility and childbirth crafted at Blue Dragon circa 2013.

1/2 oz Lemon Hart 151 Rum
1/2 oz Yellow Chartreuse
1/4 oz Cinnamon Syrup
1/2 oz Grapefruit Juice
1/2 oz Lime Juice
1 dash Peychaud's Bitters
Shake with ice, strain into a Champagne flute containing 2 oz cava, and garnish with an orange twist.

Heads or Tails

Ran Duan created this beer cocktail for the local St. George's sales rep in 2013, and the name reflects the odds that the bar had Heady Topper on hand.

1 1/2 oz St. George Terroir Gin
3/4 oz Honey Syrup
1/2 oz Lime Juice
1 dash Scrappy's Celery Bitters
Shake with ice and strain into a cocktail glass containing 1 1/2 oz Heady Topper (or Green Flash) IPA.

Heat of the Moment

A Julep created by Fred Yarm for Loyal Nine's Yacht Rock Sundays in 2015.

1 1/2 oz Rittenhouse Rye
1/2 oz Zucca Rabarbaro Amaro
1/2 oz Amaro Montenegro
1/2 oz Demerara Syrup
4 leaf Mint
Muddle mint in syrup and liqueurs in a double Old Fashioned glass. Remove mint, add rye, fill with crushed ice, garnish with mint sprigs, and add straws.

Hedy Lamarr

West Bridge's Mike Fleming crafted this complex mixture of strong and light ingredients in 2013 and named it after an actress who played the heroine in Samson and Delilah.

1 1/2 oz Laird's Bonded Apple Brandy
3/4 oz Meletti Amaro
1/2 oz Punt e Mes
1/4 oz Honey Syrup
1 dash Angostura Bitters
Stir with ice and strain into a rocks glass.

Helen of Troy Does Countertop Dancing

One of the curious drinks on The Independent's 2014 menu reminiscent of the Trinidad Sour and named after a Margaret Atwood poem.

1 1/2 oz Laird's Applejack
1 oz Orgeat
1/2 oz Angostura Bitters
1/2 oz Lemon Juice
Shake with ice and strain into a cocktail coupe.

Hernando's Hideaway

Danielle Berman at Deep Ellum named her 2012 agave drink after a song about a speakeasy from The Pajama Game musical.

1 oz Reposado Tequila
1 oz Mezcal
1/2 oz Dolin Dry Vermouth
1/2 oz Fair Trade Coffee Liqueur
1 bsp Cinnamon Syrup
3 dash Mole Bitters
Stir with ice, strain into a rocks glass, and garnish with orange oil from a twist.

Heat of the Moment,
Loyal Nine

HE-HI

Herr Professor

A rum Manhattan of sorts created by Sahil Mehta in 2016 for his Sunday night Bar GoGo events at Estragon.

1 1/2 oz Lustau Oloroso Sherry
1 oz Dos Maderas 5+5 PX Rum
1/4 oz Avèze Gentian Liqueur
1/4 oz Luxardo Maraschino
1 dash Regan's Orange Bitters
Stir with ice, strain into a rocks glass, and garnish with orange oil from a twist.

Hey Heywood!

Fred Yarm was inspired by the Hoop La and members of the Algonquin Round Table for this popular drink of the day at Loyal Nine that made it to the regular menu in 2016.

3/4 oz Berkshire Greylock Gin
3/4 oz St. George Spiced Pear Liqueur
3/4 oz Yellow Chartreuse
3/4 oz Lemon Juice
Shake with ice and strain into a cocktail coupe.

Hiding Nemo

The bartenders at Backbar created a tribute to Blizzard Nemo for the drink of the day before the storm hit in 2013.

1 oz Plantation Barbados Rum
1 oz Aperol
1/4 oz Maraschino Liqueur
1/4 oz Grenadine
1/2 oz Orange Juice
1 dash Angostura Bitters
1 Egg White
Shake once without ice and once with ice, strain into a cocktail coupe, and garnish with a submerged Swedish Fish (or perhaps a fish carved from a citrus peel).

High Five, So Am I

Laura Ganci's complex herbal Sour at J.M. Curley's circa 2015.

1 1/2 oz Milagro Reposado Tequila
1/2 oz Rothman & Winter Apricot Liqueur
1/2 oz Cynar
1/2 oz Honey Syrup
1/2 oz Lemon Juice
Shake with ice and strain into a cocktail coupe.

Hires Fizz

Joel Atlas at Sichuan Garden II crafted this earthy and desserty New Orleans Fizz in 2013.

1 1/2 oz Cynar
3/4 oz Cherry Heering
3/4 oz Lemon Juice
1 oz Heavy Cream
1 Egg White
3 dash Angostura Bitters
Shake once without ice and once with ice, strain into a Collins glass containing 2 oz root beer, garnish with cherries, and add a straw.

Hit & Run

Josh Childs at Silvertone created this charity cocktail in 2013 to benefit bartender Alex Homans who was injured in a bicycling accident.

2 oz Four Roses Bourbon
3/4 oz Maple Syrup
3/4 oz Lemon Juice
3 dash Regan's Orange Bitters
Shake with ice, strain into a rocks glass, and garnish with an orange twist.

Holy Diver

An adaptation of Palmer Matthews' 2014 riff on the classic Pearl Diver and Skin Diver for Drink's Tiki Sunday where the spice rum is complemented by the hops. Instead of the beer and demerara syrup, there was originally 3/4 oz beer syrup.

2 oz Sailor Jerry Spiced Rum
3/4 oz Orange Juice
1/2 oz Lemon Juice
1/2 oz IPA Beer
1/2 oz Coconut Cream
1/2 oz Demerara Syrup
2 dash Angostura Bitters
Shake with ice, strain into a Tiki mug, fill with crushed ice, and add a straw.

Holy Molé!

The Hawthorne's creation for the William & Grant party to wrap up Boston Thirst 2016.

1 1/2 oz Glenfiddich Scotch
3/4 oz Giffard Banane du Bresil
1/2 oz Ginger Syrup
1/2 oz Lemon Juice
1 dash Bittermens Mole Bitters
Shake with ice and strain into a cocktail coupe.

HO

Homère Punch

Fred Yarm's drink was a finalist for the Rhum Clement 'Ti Punch Cup in 2015, and he later put his creation on the Loyal Nine menu as listed. Named after Homère Clement who decided on Martinique to distill sugarcane like an eau de vie and create rhum agricole.

2 oz JM Rhum Agricole Blanc
1/2 oz Benedictine
1/4 oz Creole Shrubb Orange
   Liqueur
1/4 oz Lime Juice
Stir with ice, strain into a rocks glass, fill with ice, garnish with a lime wheel floated on the ice, and add straws.

Home Wrecker

A drink John Nugent created for the soirée with Count Branca at Silvertone in 2013; John's influence here was Misty Kalkofen's Maximilian Affair.

1 1/2 oz Old Overholt Rye
1/2 oz Punt e Mes
1/2 oz St. Germain
1/2 oz Lemon Juice
Shake with ice and strain into a cocktail glass.

Honey Bee, Yvonne's

Honey & Thistle

Matthew Schrage at the Blue Room in 2013 paid tribute to the honey in the Sibilla and the blessed thistle in the Cardamaro in this refreshing tall drink.

1 1/2 oz Cardamaro
3/4 oz Cocchi Americano
1/4 oz Amaro Sibilla
Stir with ice, strain into a Highball glass with 2 oz tonic water, fill with ice, garnish with an orange twist, and add a straw.

Honey Bee (Yvonne's variation)

Yvonne's updated the Honey Bee in 2016 by changing the rum origin and adding pear brandy, egg white, and a bitters garnish.

2 oz Plantation Barbados Rum
1/4 oz St. George Pear Eau de Vie
3/4 oz Honey Syrup
3/4 oz Lemon Juice
1 Egg White
Shake once without ice and once with ice, strain into a cocktail coupe, and garnish with 10 drops of Angostura Bitters.

Hopping Through The Frothy Waves

Fred Yarm created this Hurricane riff for Loyal Nine's The Walrus & The Carpenter event in 2015 and it made it on to the regular menu shortly after.

1 1/2 oz Chinaco Blanco Tequila
1/2 oz Dolin Blanc Vermouth
1/2 oz Passion Fruit Syrup
1/2 oz Lemon Juice
Shake with ice, strain into a tall glass, fill with crushed ice, garnish with 2-3 dashes Peychaud's Bitters and a mint sprig, and add a straw.

Hoptimum Pine

Ashley Ruest's Transformer tribute beer cocktail on the Firebrand Saints 2016 menu.

1 oz Denizen White Rum
3/4 oz Pineapple Shrub
1/2 oz Orgeat
3/4 oz Lemon Juice
Shake with ice, strain into a Collins glass containing 2 oz Dogfish Head 60 Minute IPA, fill with crushed ice, garnish with a pineapple fruit leaf, and add a straw.

HO-HU

Hotel Homans

Backbar's Seelbach riff to raise money for bartender Alex Homans' recovery after Alex was hit by a car while biking to work in 2013.

1 oz Partida Tequila
1/2 oz Pierre Ferrand Dry Curacao
7 dash Angostura Bitters
7 dash Peychaud's Bitters
Shake with ice, strain into a flute glass containing 2 1/2 oz sparkling wine, and garnish with an orange twist.

Hoti Hoti

Robert Sanford's Tiki number on the Summer 2016 Russell House Tavern cocktail menu.

1 1/2 oz Pyrat Rum
1 oz Lime Juice
1 oz Grapefruit Juice
1 oz Velvet Falernum
3/4 oz Cocchi Sweet Vermouth
2 dash Absinthe
Build in a Collins glass, fill with crushed ice, swizzle to mix and chill, garnish with 4-5 dashes Angostura Bitters and a grapefruit twist, and add a straw.

Howling Winds

Adam Hockman's variation on the Champs Élysées for the Autumn 2013 menu at Russell House Tavern.

1 3/4 oz Ansac VS Cognac
3/4 oz Yellow Chartreuse
3/4 oz Lemon Juice
1/2 oz Cinnamon Syrup
1 bsp St. George Absinthe
2 dash Angostura Bitters
Shake with ice, strain into a rocks glass, and garnish with a lemon twist.

Hullabaloo

Sahil Mehta named this complex tropical number at Estragon in 2015 after a popular Indian children's book Hullabaloo in the Guava Orchard.

1 1/2 oz Beefeater Gin
1/2 oz Avèze Gentian Liqueur
1/2 oz Guava Syrup
1/2 oz Lemon Juice
1 dash Angostura Bitters
Shake with ice and strain into a cocktail coupe.

Human Rocket

Misty Kalkofen crafted this recipe for a 2013 Spin the Bottle event at Brick and Mortar featuring Hollis Bulleit as the evening's DJ.

1 1/2 oz Bulleit Bourbon
1/2 oz Rothman & Winter Apricot Liqueur
1/2 oz Nux Alpina Walnut Liqueur
1/2 oz Suze Gentian Liqueur
Stir with ice and strain into a rocks glass.

Hungry Eyes

Fred Yarm crafted this Daisy with a curious garnish for Loyal Nine's Yacht Rock Sundays in 2015. Citrus peel eyes (perhaps punched out with a plastic straw) would work in a pinch as the garnish.

1 1/2 oz Berkshire Greylock Gin
1/2 oz Yellow Chartreuse
1/2 oz Green Tea Syrup
1/2 oz Lemon Juice
1 dash Angostura Bitters
Shake with ice, strain into a cocktail coupe containing 1 oz soda water, and garnish with 6-8 pre-swelled Thai basil seeds (also known as tukmaria and falooda).

Hungry Like The Wolf

Fred Yarm created this Pimm's Cup crossed with a Bourbon Buck for Loyal Nine's Yacht Rock Sundays in 2015 before it made it to the main menu and became the restaurant's top seller.

1 oz Four Roses Bourbon
1 oz Pimm's No. 1
1/2 oz St. Elder Elderflower Liqueur
1/2 oz Lemon Juice
Shake with ice, strain into a rocks glass containing containing 2 oz ginger beer, fill with crushed ice, garnish with a lemon twist, and add straws.

Hurly-Burly

An adaptation of Paul Manzelli's 2013 riff of the Hoop La at Bergamot.

3/4 oz Pierre Ferrand Amber Cognac
3/4 oz Amaro Montenegro
3/4 oz Lillet Blanc
3/4 oz Lemon Juice
Shake with ice and strain into a cocktail glass.

HU-ID

Hurricane Caesar

Backbar's Joe Cammarata won the Tales of the Cocktail 2014 cocktail competition with this Hurricane variation.

1 1/2 oz Bacardi 8 Year Rum
1 oz Clement VSOP Rhum Agricole
3/4 oz Passion Fruit Syrup
3/4 oz Lime Juice
1/2 oz Orgeat
1/4 oz Honey Syrup
Shake with ice, strain into a Hurricane glass, fill with crushed ice, float 1/2 oz Campari, garnish with freshly grated nutmeg and a cherry-lime wheel flag, and add a straw.

Ibsen's Door

Hannah Moore's 20th Century tribute to theatrical moments created at Russell House Tavern in 2014.

1 1/2 oz Spring 44 Old Tom Gin
3/4 oz Amaro Braulio
1/2 oz Tempus Fugit Crème de Cacao
1/2 oz Lemon Juice
Shake with ice and strain into a cocktail glass.

I Can't Dance

Fred Yarm sought the 19th century style of refreshment for Loyal Nine's Yacht Rock Sundays cocktail menu in 2015.

2 1/4 oz Blandy's Sercial Madeira
3/4 oz Averna
2 dash Bittermens Mole Bitters
3 slice Orange
Muddle orange slices, add the rest of the ingredients, shake with ice, and strain into a Collins glass. Fill with crushed ice, garnish with a fresh orange slice, and add a straw.

Ideal Manhattan

Joy Richard crafted this fruit and floral-tinged Manhattan at the Citizen Public House in Boston circa 2011.

1 1/2 oz Maker's Mark Bourbon
3/4 oz St. Germain
1/2 oz Cinzano Sweet Vermouth
2 dash Angostura Bitters
1 dash Bitter Truth Grapefruit Bitters
Stir with ice, strain into a cocktail glass, and garnish with a grapefruit twist.

170

Hurricane Caesar,
Backbar

Idle Class

At Loyal Nine, Fred Yarm riffed on the Chaplin from ZigZag in Seattle and named the new recipe after one of Charlie Chaplin's films in 2015.

1 oz Amber Rum
1 oz Verdelho or Sercial Madeira
1 oz Amaro Ramazzotti
1 bsp Orange Liqueur
2 dash Orange Bitters
Stir with ice, strain into a cocktail glass, and garnish with a lemon twist.

Iguaçu

Andrew Ianazzi at State Park loves Cardamaro and Blood & Sands, and he put them together in this 2015 creation.

3/4 oz Novo Fogo Cachaça
1 1/2 oz Cardamaro
1/2 oz Demerara Syrup
1/2 oz Orange Juice
1 dash Angostura Bitters
Shake with ice, strain into a rocks glass with a large ice cube, and garnish with an orange twist.

'I'iwi Bird

At No. 9 Park, Jenna Rycroft paid tribute to Hawaii's honeycreeper in 2015, and she brought the recipe with her to Bar Mezzana in 2016.

2 oz Privateer Tiki Gin
1/2 oz Passion Fruit Syrup
1/2 oz Aperol
1/2 oz Lime Juice
Shake with ice and strain into a cocktail coupe.

I Know You Know

Matt Schrage of Brick & Mortar won the Lustau Brandy competition in 2014 with this tribute to jazz musician Esperanza Spalding.

1 oz Lustau Brandy
3/4 oz Lustau Amontillado Sherry
3/4 oz St. George Spiced Pear Liqueur
1/2 oz Averna
1 dash Fee's Whiskey Barrel Bitters
Stir with ice, strain into a cocktail coupe, and garnish with grapefruit oil from a twist.

I'll Have Another

Bergamot's Paul Manzelli paid tribute to the biggest upset in the history of the Kentucky Derby (which he also bet money on in 2012 and won).

1 1/2 oz Eagle Rare Bourbon
1/2 oz Lemon Juice
1/2 oz Simple Syrup
1 dash Angostura Bitters
6-8 leaf Mint
Shake with ice, strain into a rocks glass containing a large ice cube and 1 oz ginger beer, and garnish with a mint leaf.

Illusion Travels by Street Car

Sahil Mehta discovered at Estragon that his drink tasted better as it warmed up to room temperature, so he eschewed ice completely in the next iteration. He dubbed this 2016 creation after a quirky 1954 Buñuel movie.

1 1/2 oz Lustau Oloroso Sherry
1 oz Cimarron Blanco Tequila
1/2 oz Cynar
1/4 oz Maraschino Liqueur
1 dash Angostura Bitters
1 dash Regan's Orange Bitters
3/4 oz Water
Build in a cocktail coupe, and briefly stir to mix __without__ ice. Note: This is a room temperature cocktail.

I'm on a Boat

A 2013 split spirits and split citrus Mai Tai-Jet Pilot riff crafted at Stoddard's.

1 oz Cognac
1 oz Sailor Jerry's Spiced Rum
1/2 oz Marie Brizard Curaçao
1/2 oz Orgeat
1/2 oz Grapefruit Juice
1/2 oz Lime Juice
2 dash Angostura Bitters
Shake with ice, strain into a rocks glass, fill with crushed ice, garnish with a pineapple fruit leaf, an orange twist, and a cherry, and add a straw.

Improper Scaffa

Sam Treadway and the other bartenders at Backbar in 2014 created something that is not quite a Scaffa just how Scaffas are not quite cocktails.

1 1/2 oz Pierre Ferrand Ambre Cognac
1/2 oz Cardamaro
1/2 oz St. George Spiced Pear Liqueur
1/2 oz Maraschino Liqueur
1/2 oz Water
1 dash Angostura Bitters
Build in a rocks glass, and briefly stir to mix <u>without</u> ice. Note: This is a room temperature cocktail.

Improved Ping Pong

The early 20th century classic was augmented at a Plymouth industry night at the Franklin Southie in 2010.

1 oz Plymouth Gin
1 oz Plymouth Sloe Gin
1/2 oz Crème Yvette
1/2 oz Lemon Juice
Shake with ice, strain into a cocktail glass, and garnish with a lemon twist.

Independent

A smoke and citrus Manhattan (or Hoots Mon) of sorts at the Citizen Public House circa 2012.

1 1/2 oz Miltonduff Scotch
1/2 oz Punt e Mes
1/2 oz Cocchi Americano
1/2 oz Pierre Ferrand Dry Curaçao
2 dash Angostura Orange Bitters
Stir with ice and strain into a cocktail coupe.

IN

Inman Swizzle,
East Coast Grill

Industry Fav

Tenzin Samdo's great stomach settler at Trade circa 2013.

1 3/4 oz Nolet's Gin
3/4 oz Fernet Branca
1 oz Ginger Syrup
1 oz Lemon Juice
Shake with ice, strain into a rocks glass, fill with ice, garnish with a lemon wedge, and add straws.

Infanta

Ryan Connolly's creation for Belly Wine Bar's vermouth cocktail section of their 2013 menu.

1 1/2 oz La Cigarrera Amontillado
  Sherry
3/4 oz Amaro Braulio
1/2 oz Carpano Sweet Vermouth
1/4 oz Punt e Mes
Stir with ice, strain into a cocktail glass, and garnish with grapefruit oil from a twist.

In Fashion

Kevin Mabry's 2012 abstraction of a new-fashioned Old Fashioned at J.M. Curley's.

2 oz Four Roses Bourbon
3/4 oz Kasteel Rouge Cherry
  Lambic Beer
3/4 oz Averna
1 Orange Slice
1 Sugar Cube
Muddle the sugar cube with the orange slice, add the rest of the ingredients, stir with ice, and strain into a rocks glass.

174

Inman Swizzle

An adaptation of a Swizzle that Joe McGuirk created for the relaunch of the East Coast Grill in 2017; it was named after the restaurant's Cambridge location.

2 oz Barbancourt 8 Year Rhum
3/4 oz Velvet Falernum
1/2 oz Lime Juice
Build in a double Old Fashioned glass, fill with crushed ice, and swizzle to mix and chill. Garnish with 2 dashes of Angostura Bitters, a lime wedge, and a cinnamon stick, and add straws.

Intercept

For one of Loyal Nine's drinks of the day in 2016, Fred Yarm crossed the Boulevardier with the Slope to create the Intercept.

1 oz Four Roses Bourbon
1 oz Punt e Mes
1/2 oz Rothman & Winter Apricot Liqueur
1/2 oz Campari
1 dash Angostura Bitters
Stir with ice, strain into a rocks glass, fill with ice, garnish with an orange twist, and add straws.

In The Bond

J.M. Curley's spiced apple cocktail created 2012.

2 oz Laird's Bonded Apple Brandy
1/2 oz King's Ginger Liqueur
1/2 oz Cinnamon Syrup
4 dash Angostura Bitters
Stir with ice, strain into a rocks glass, fill with ice, garnish with a lemon twist, and add straws.

Inventor

Tyler Wang created this Sazerac-inspired Flip in 2013 at No. 9 Park.

2 oz Pierre Ferrand 1840 Cognac
1/4 oz Peychaud's Bitters
1/4 oz Kübler Absinthe
1 oz Simple Syrup
1 Whole Egg
Shake once without ice and once with ice, strain into a rocks glass, and garnish with lemon oil from a twist.

IN-IT

In Vida Veritas

Mezcal is the truth serum at Brick & Mortar in Cambridge circa 2012.

1 1/2 oz Del Maguey Mezcal Vida
3/4 oz Nux Alpina Walnut Liqueur
3/4 oz Zirbenz Stone Pine Liqueur
1/2 oz Benedictine
1 dash Fee's Whiskey Barrel Bitters
Stir with ice, strain into a rocks glass, and garnish with orange oil from a twist.

Irish Rover

Trina's Starlite Lounge paid tribute to the Irish folk song with this beer cocktail in 2013.

1 1/2 oz Jameson Irish Whiskey
5 drop Liquid Smoke
2 dash Fee's Walnut Bitters
10 oz Berkshire Brewing Company Coffee Porter
Build in a Highball glass and top with the beer.

Island of Misfit Toys

A drink created at Brick & Mortar for a Christmas time "Drinkle Bells" Spin the Bottle event in 2012 featuring DJ Brother Cleve.

2 oz Del Maguey Mezcal Vida
1/2 oz Meletti Amaro
1/2 oz Combier Kümmel
1 dash Angostura Bitters
Stir with ice, strain into a rocks glass, and garnish with orange oil from a twist.

Italian Greyhound

John Gertsen in 2006 riffed on the vodka-based Greyhound at No. 9 Park.

2 oz Punt e Mes
2 oz Grapefruit Juice
Shake with ice, strain into a double Old Fashioned glass half-rimmed with salt, and fill with ice.

Italian Stallion

Fred Yarm's 2016 riff on Michael McIlroy's Rome with a View for Loyal Nine's low proof section of the menu.

1 oz Aperol
3/4 oz Avèze Gentian Liqueur
3/4 oz Lime Juice
1/2 oz Passion Fruit Syrup
Shake with ice, strain into a Collins glass containing 2 oz soda water, fill with ice cubes, garnish with an orange twist, and add a straw.

It's Arrack!

For Backbar's 2013 Star Wars week, Sam Treadway challenged Kyle Powell with the drink name as a pun on Admiral Ackbar's "It's a trap" and let Kyle do the rest.

1 oz Batavia Arrack
1 oz Amontillado Sherry
1/2 oz Yellow Chartreuse
1/2 oz Lemon Juice
Shake with ice, strain into a Collins glass containing 2 oz ginger beer, fill with ice, garnish with a dash of Angostura Bitters, and add a straw.

It Was Ritten

Vannaluck Hongthong's 2016 nod to both a Nas song and the bonded rye whiskey with this nightcap at the Baldwin Bar at Sichuan Garden II.

1 1/2 oz Rittenhouse Rye
3/4 oz Punt e Mes
1/2 oz Fernet Branca
1/4 oz Bigallet China China
2 dash Aromatic Bitters
1 dash Angostura Bitters
Stir with ice, strain into a cocktail glass, and garnish with a cherry.

Jab Molassie

Sean Frederick crafted this libation at the Citizen in 2013 to recreate his Trinidad Carnivale experience and capture it in a glass.

2 oz Scarlet Ibis Rum
1/2 oz Lime Juice
1/2 oz Simple Syrup
1/4 oz Coconut Cream
1/4 oz Angostura Bitters
1 pinch Salt
Shake with ice and strain into a cocktail coupe.

Jackalope

Carlo Caroscio's drink of the day at Backbar in 2016 was his riff on the Applejack Rabbit that utilized his favored pairing of orgeat and maple syrups.

2 oz Laird's Bonded Apple Brandy
1/2 oz Lemon Juice
1/4 oz Orgeat
1/4 oz Maple Syrup
2 dash Peychaud's Bitters
Shake with ice, strain into a cocktail coupe, and garnish with lemon oil from a twist.

Jack Frost

Eric Cross paid tribute in 2013 to the long Winter season with this number at Stoddard's.

1 1/2 oz Laird's Applejack
1/2 oz Sheep Dip Scotch
1/2 oz Lemon Juice
1/2 oz Cinnamon Syrup
2 dash Absinthe
Shake with ice, strain into a rocks glass containing a large ice cube, and garnish with a lemon twist.

Jack Ward

Steve Schnelwar at GrandTen Distillery's bar merged the Jack Rose with the Ward Eight in 2016 to craft something more enjoyable than the Boston original.

1 1/2 oz GrandTen's North County
  Apple Brandy
1/2 oz Orange Juice
1/2 oz Lemon Juice
1/2 oz Grenadine
Shake with ice and strain into a cocktail coupe.

Jade Mountain

An adaptation of Myers and Chang's 2013 riff on the classic Bijou.

1 1/2 oz Bols Genever
1 oz Sweet Vermouth
1/2 oz Green Chartreuse
1 dash Angostura Bitters
Stir with ice and strain into a cocktail glass.

Jamaican Bobsled

Mick Kellogg's Olympics 2016-themed Tiki drink on the Baldwin Bar's menu at Sichuan Garden II.

1 1/2 oz Smith & Cross Rum
3/4 oz Lime Juice
3/4 oz Pineapple Juice
3/4 oz Cinnamon Syrup
1/4 oz Allspice Dram
Shake with ice, strain into a rocks glass, fill with crushed ice, garnish with an edible orchid (or perhaps a lime wheel instead), and add straws.

Jarabe Tapatío

Ran Duan's 2013 tribute to the Mexican Hat Dance at Sichuan Garden II in Woburn.

1 1/2 oz Del Maguey Chichicapa
  Mezcal
3/4 oz Grenadine
1/2 oz Campari
1 oz Lime Juice
3 dash Bittermens Boston Bittahs
Shake with ice, strain into a cocktail glass, and garnish with a dash of freshly ground black pepper.

Javanese Crusta

An exotic islander take on the Crusta by Fred Yarm in 2009.

1 1/2 oz Batavia Arrack
1/4 oz Orgeat
1/4 oz Cinnamon Syrup
1/4 oz Lime Juice
1 dash Angostura
Shake with ice, strain into a small wineglass rimmed with sugar, and garnish with a wide lime peel looped around the inside of the glass' opening.

Javari Mai Tai

For the Mai Tai Challenge on Instagram in 2015, Fred Yarm paid tribute to the border of Peru and Brazil with this grassy and funky tropical number.

1 oz Cachaça
1 oz Pisco
3/4 oz Lime Juice
1/2 oz Orange Liqueur
1/2 oz Orgeat
Shake with ice, strain into a rocks glass, fill with crushed ice, garnish with a spent half lime shell and mint sprigs, and add straws.

Jack Frost, Stoddard's

Jenna Haze

Kevin Mabry's 2012 companion piece at J.M. Curley's to Sam Gabrielli's Taylor Rain with his own tribute to an American film starlet.

1 1/4 oz Drambuie
3/4 oz Fighting Cock Bourbon
1 oz Lemon Juice
1/4 oz Amaretto
1 Egg White
Shake once without ice and once with ice, strain into a rocks glass, fill with ice, garnish with an orange twist-cherry flag, and add straws.

(The) Jerk

Melinda Johnson-Maddox paid tribute to the old time soda jerks with this 2015 libation at Backbar.

1 oz Old Monk Rum
1/2 oz Coconut Milk
1/2 oz Orgeat
1/2 oz Root Liqueur
1/2 oz Pernod Pastis
Shake with ice, strain into a Highball glass containing 2 oz soda water, garnish with an orange twist, and add a straw.

Jersey Isle Julep

Barrel House in Beverly gave the Rum Julep a light summery Tiki feel in 2015.

1 oz Privateer Amber Rum
1 oz Amaro Montenegro
1 oz Grapefruit Juice
1/2 oz Simple Syrup
4-6 leaf Mint
Muddle mint in simple syrup in a Julep cup or tulip glass. Add the rest of the ingredients, fill with crushed ice, stir, garnish with a mint sprig and freshly grated nutmeg, and add straws.

Jets to Brazil

Will Thompson and Matt Schrage crafted this "Jungle Bird sans pineapple juice" for a 2015 emo-themed night at Brick & Mortar.

1 1/2 oz Plantation Pineapple Rum
1/2 oz Lime Juice
1/2 oz Demerara Syrup
1/4 oz Campari
1/4 oz Aperol
Shake with ice and strain into a cocktail coupe.

Jim Rose

A whiskey-laden Jack Rose tribute at Merrill & Co. in 2014 to a circus sideshow ringleader.

2 oz Bourbon
1/2 oz Grenadine
1/2 oz Lime Juice
1 bsp Fernet Branca
Shake with ice, strain into a rocks glass, and garnish with a cherry.

Joan Miró

Sahil Mehta's unusual herbal drink at Estragon in 2014 named for an unusual Spanish artist.

1 1/2 oz Cynar
1 1/2 oz Dry Vermouth
1/2 oz St. Germain
1/2 oz Lime Juice
1 inch piece Celery
Muddle celery, add the rest of the ingredients, and shake with ice. Strain into a rocks glass rimmed with a celery salt-sugar mix, fill with ice, and garnish with a celery leaf.

Joie de Julep

Corey Bunnewith at Drink placed second in the Tales of the Cocktail 2009 Mint Julep competition with this recipe.

1 1/2 oz Rye Whiskey
1/2 oz Simple Syrup
1/4 oz Green Chartreuse
1/4 oz Lemon Juice
1 dash Peychaud's Bitters
4-6 leaf Mint
Muddle mint in the simple syrup in a Julep cup. Add the rest of the ingredients, fill with crushed ice, stir to mix and chill, garnish with mint sprigs, and add a straw.

Jook Sing

An adaptation of Markus Yao's 2014 Manhattan variation at Shojo.

1 1/2 oz Rittenhouse Rye
1/2 oz Cynar
1/2 oz Punt e Mes
1/2 oz Amaro Montenegro
2 dash Angostura Bitters
Stir with ice and strain into a rocks glass with a large ice cube.

Josephine's Bath

At Steel & Rye in 2013, Ted Gallagher named this rhum agricole Negroni variation after a Martician pool where Napoleon's empress used to bathe.

1 1/4 oz JM Rhum Agricole Blanc
1 oz Dolin Dry Vermouth
3/4 oz Gran Classico
Stir with ice, strain into a rocks glass containing a large ice cube, and garnish with grapefruit oil from a twist.

Juan's Flying Burrito

A complex sparkler from Tyler Wang at No. 9 Park in 2012 named after a Mexican restaurant in New Orleans.

1 1/4 oz La Puritita Verda Mezcal Joven
1/2 oz Lime Juice
1/2 oz Combier Triple Sec
Shake with ice, strain into a flute glass containing 2 1/2 oz Crémant de Bourgogne Brut sparkling wine, and float 3 dashes Peychaud's Bitters.

Julep En Fuego, No. 9 Park

Juglans Regia

Sahil Mehta at Estragon named this nutty Bobby Burns riff in 2015 on the Linnaean name for walnuts.

1 1/2 oz Pig's Nose Scotch
1 oz Lustau Oloroso Sherry
1/2 oz Nocino Walnut Liqueur
2 dash Fee's Walnut Bitters
1 dash Orange Bitters
Stir with ice, strain into a cocktail coupe, and garnish with an orange twist.

Jukebox Opera

Christa Manalo's complex gin tipple at Gloucester's Short & Main in 2016.

1 oz St. George Terroir Gin
1 oz Sweet Vermouth
1/2 oz Fernet Branca
1/2 oz Campari
1/2 oz Luxardo Maraschino
Stir with ice, strain into a rocks glass with a large ice cube, and garnish with an orange twist.

Julep En Fuego

Ted Kilpatrick's crafted this spicy Julep for one of his No. 9 Park regulars in 2011 and considered calling it the Julep Peligroso.

2 oz Booker's Bourbon
3/4 oz Smith & Cross Rum
1/2 oz Simple Syrup
1/4 oz Angostura Bitters
1 dash Cholula Hot Sauce
10-12 leaf Mint
Muddle mint leaves with the simple syrup in a Julep cup. Add rest of ingredients and crushed ice, stir until the cup is frosted over, and then top with crushed ice. Garnish with mint sprigs and freshly cut hot pepper rings if available, and add straws.

Jungle Madness

Jason Cool's Mr. Bali Hai-Pago Pago fusion for one of Citizen Public House's Tiki Tuesdays in 2014.

1 1/2 oz Sailor Jerry Spiced Rum
3 oz Pineapple Juice
1/2 oz Coffee Liqueur
1/4 oz Crème de Cacao
1/4 oz Green Chartreuse
2 dash Angostura Bitters
Shake with ice, strain into a Tiki mug, fill with crushed ice, garnish with mint sprigs and freshly grated nutmeg, and add a straw.

JU-KA

Jungle Stirred

Matty Durgin crafted this straight-spirits riff on the Jungle Bird in 2016 at Brick & Mortar.

1 oz Plantation Jamaica Rum
1 oz Plantation Pineapple Rum
3/4 oz Campari
1/4 oz Velvet Falernum
1 dash Angostura Bitters
Stir with ice, strain into a cocktail coupe, and garnish with lime oil from a twist.

Jupiter's Dilemma

A food-friendly aperitif created by Ryan Lotz in 2011 at Lineage.

1 1/2 oz Dolin Blanc Vermouth
3/4 oz Beefeater Gin
1/2 oz Combier Orange Liqueur
1/4 oz Cynar
Stir with ice, strain into a rocks glass, and garnish with an orange twist.

Kafka Does Jalisco

No. 9 Park's 2015 agave take on Eastern Standard's Metamorphosis.

1 oz Pueblo Viejo Blanco Tequila
1 oz Becherovka
3/4 oz Lime Juice
3/4 oz Honey Syrup
Shake with ice and strain into a cocktail coupe.

Kamayurá

A complex tropical number from Sahil Mehta at Estragon in 2016.

2 oz Leblon Cachaça
1/2 oz Campari
1/2 oz Orgeat
3/4 oz Lime Juice
2 dash Angostura Bitters
4-6 leaf Mint
Muddle the mint in a shaker tin with the orgeat, add the rest of the ingredients, shake with ice, and strain into a Collins glass. Fill with crushed ice, garnish with a mint sprig, and add a straw.

CЯ৪Ɔ৪ƆCЯCЯ৪Ɔ৪ƆCЯCЯ৪Ɔ৪ƆCЯCЯ৪Ɔ৪ƆCЯCЯ৪Ɔ৪ƆCЯCЯ৪Ɔ৪ƆCЯ

Kanaloa

Fred Yarm developed this bright libation as a brunch Tiki drink for Loyal Nine's Sunday morning menu in 2015.

2 oz Privateer Silver Rum
1/2 oz Lime Juice
1/2 oz Grapefruit Juice
1/2 oz Kronan Swedish Punsch
1/2 oz Chamomile Tea Syrup
1 dash Angostura Bitters
10 drop St. George Absinthe
Shake with ice, strain into a rocks glass, fill with crushed ice, garnish with a lime wheel, and add straws.

Kan Shibuya

A herbal Japanese Manhattan of sorts crafted in 2016 by Schuyler Hunton and Charles Coykendall at Tiger Mama.

2 oz Suntory Toki Whisky
1/2 oz Lustau East India Sherry
1/4 oz Yellow Chartreuse
1/4 oz Amaro Montenegro
1 dash Mole Bitters
Stir with ice, strain into a cocktail coupe, and garnish with a lemon twist.

Kapuna Kane

The Independent's 2015 Tiki tribute to the Hawaiian author.

1 1/2 oz Salers Gentian Liqueur
1 oz Macchu Pisco
3/4 oz Pineapple Juice
1/2 oz Lime Juice
1/4 oz Cinnamon Syrup
1/4 oz Honey Syrup
6 dash Angostura Bitters
Shake with ice, strain into a rocks glass, and garnish with a spritz of mezcal.

Kartini

At the Citizen Public House in 2013, Sean Frederick crafted this upon a request for a drink with Batavia Arrack and sherry, and it got dubbed after an Indonesian heroine.

2 oz Batavia Arrack
3/4 oz Lime Juice
1/2 oz Orgeat
1/2 oz Lustau Pedro Ximenez
   Sherry
1/4 oz Angostura Bitters
Shake with ice, strain into a cocktail coupe, and garnish with freshly grated nutmeg.

Kekua

Joe Cammarata in 2014 crossed Ben Sandrof's Esmeralda and Josie Packard's Prosecutor at Backbar.

1 1/2 oz Avuá Cachaça
1/2 oz St. Germain
1/2 oz Green Chartreuse
1/2 oz Lime Juice
Shake with ice, strain into a rocks glass, and garnish with a spritz of Del Maguey Chichicapa Mezcal.

Kentucky Proper

Bergamot's whiskey variation on the Old Cuban circa 2012.

1 1/2 oz Old Weller Antique
   Bourbon
3/4 oz Lemon Juice
1/2 oz Simple Syrup
1 dash Fee's Whiskey Barrel
   Bitters
Shake with ice, strain into a cocktail glass containing 1 oz dry sparkling wine, and garnish with a mint leaf.

Kentucky Shuffle

An adaptation of Spoke Wine Bar's Kentucky Buck variation in 2015.

1/2 oz Rittenhouse Rye
1/2 oz White Horse Scotch
1 oz Meletti Amaro
1/2 oz Lemon Juice
1/2 oz Ginger Syrup
2 dash Jerry Thomas Decanter
   Bitters
Shake with ice, strain into a Collins glass containing 2 oz soda water, fill with ice, garnish with a lemon twist, and add a straw.

Key Largo

Fred Yarm riffed on the Jet Pilot for Loyal Nine's Yacht Rock Sundays menu in 2015.

1 oz Turkey Shore Tavern Style
   Rum
1 oz Lustau Brandy
1/2 oz Grapefruit Juice
1/2 oz Lemon Juice
1/2 oz Passion Fruit Syrup
1/2 oz Cinnamon Syrup
1 dash Angostura Bitters
10 drop St. George Absinthe
Shake with ice, strain into a Collins glass, fill with crushed ice, garnish with a mint sprig and a grapefruit twist, and add a straw.

Kentucky Shuffle, Spoke

Kid McCoy

Palmer Matthews tinkered with the classic Deshler at Drink in 2013 to make this variation dubbed after another famous turn of the century boxer.

1 3/4 oz Rittenhouse Rye
1 oz Cocchi Americano Rosa
1/4 oz Bigallet China China
1 dash Peychaud's Bitters
Stir with ice, strain into a rocks glass, and garnish with orange oil from a twist.

Killing Floor

Sean Maher crafted this straight spirits delight at the Barrel House in Beverly for a Whistle Pig-sponsored dinner in 2014.

1 1/2 oz Whistle Pig Rye
1/2 oz Cocchi Sweet Vermouth
1/2 oz Bonal Gentiane-Quina
1/2 oz Bigallet China China
Stir with ice, strain into a rocks glass, and garnish with an orange twist.

KI

King's Mistress

Fred Yarm at Loyal Nine riffed on the 1934 rhum agricole-based Pompadour to craft this tribute to the Madame de Pompadour in 2015.

1 1/4 oz Chinaco Blanco Tequila
1 1/4 oz Pineau des Charentes
1/2 oz Lime Juice
2 dash Regan's Orange Bitters
Shake with ice and strain into a cocktail glass.

Kingston Cup

Sean Frederick and staff opened the Townsman in 2015 with this Pimm's Cup variation on their menu.

1 1/2 oz Pimm's No. 1
1/2 oz Smith & Cross Rum
1/2 oz Ginger Syrup
1/2 oz Five Spice Syrup
1/2 oz Lime Juice
Shake with ice, strain into a Collins glass, and fill with crushed ice. Garnish with a cucumber wheel and 3 dashes aromatic bitters, and add a straw.

Kingston Shuffle

Ran Duan of Sichuan Garden II won the Boston Campari cocktail competition in 2013 with this tropical libation.

1 oz Campari
3/4 oz Appleton V/X Rum
1/2 oz Lime Juice
1/2 oz Grapefruit Juice
1/2 oz Pineapple Syrup
2 dash Bittermens Tiki Bitters
Shake with ice, strain into a Julep cup or rocks glass, and fill with crushed ice. Garnish with a grapefruit twist and a cherry, and add a straw.

(The) Kirby

Juan Mederos crafted this herbal Margarita of sorts at Firebrand Saints circa 2016.

1 1/2 oz Olmeca Altos Blanco Tequila
3/4 oz Green Chartreuse
1/2 oz Combier Pamplemousse Liqueur
3/4 oz Lime Juice
Shake with ice, strain into a Collins glass, fill with crushed ice, garnish with 3 dashes Peychaud's Bitters and a paper parasol, and add a straw.

188

Kitty Leroy

For a 2013 Whiskey & Amari night at the Blue Room with a Women of the Wild West theme, Fred Yarm and Katie Emmerson of the Hawthorne offered a choose your own (or bartender's choice) Amaro Fix named after one of the more promiscuous gunslingers in the old West.

2 oz Choose Your Own Amaro
3/4 oz Pineapple Syrup
1/2 oz Lemon Juice
Shake with ice, strain into a rocks glass, fill with crushed ice, add a straw, and garnish with berries in season.

Kodiak Island

A 2012 cross between an Alaska and a South Side created by Joe Cammarata and Alex Homans at Backbar.

1 1/2 oz Beefeater Gin
1/2 oz Yellow Chartreuse
1/2 oz Lemon Juice
1/2 oz Simple Syrup
1 dash Angostura Orange Bitters
4 leaf Mint
Shake with ice, strain into a cocktail glass, and garnish with a short mint sprig.

Kokomo

Mick Kellogg crafted this Mai Tai-inspired number in 2016 at the Baldwin Bar at Sichuan Garden II.

1 1/2 oz Avua Cachaça
3/4 oz Lime Juice
1/2 oz Orgeat
1/2 oz Cinnamon Syrup
1/2 oz Absinthe
Shake with ice, strain into a double Old Fashioned glass, and fill with crushed ice. Garnish with mint sprigs, a smouldering cinnamon stick, and 3-4 dashes Peychaud's Bitters, and add straws.

KO

Kongo Jungle,
A4cade

Kongo Jungle

*An adaptation of one of the drinks
on the Tiki section of A4cade's
opening 2017 menu; the original
called for a banana syrup.*

1 oz Blackwell Jamaican Rum
1 oz JM Rhum Agricole Gold
3/4 oz Demerara Syrup
1/2 oz Allspice Dram
1/2 oz Grapefruit Juice
1/2 oz Lime Juice
1 inch piece Banana
*Muddle the banana in the syrup,
add the rest of the ingredients,
shake with ice, and strain into a Tiki
mug. Fill with crushed ice, garnish
with Tiki intent, and add a straw.*

Kon'Nichiwa!!!

*Brick & Mortar's tropical-flavored
Japanese Black Manhattan in
2016.*

1 1/2 oz Iwai Japanese Whiskey
1/2 oz Meletti Amaro
1/4 oz Giffard Banane du Bresil
1/4 oz Crème de Cacao
2 dash Teapot Bitters
*Stir with ice, strain into a rocks
glass, fill with ice, and add a straw.*

Krakatoa

In 2008 for the Jewish Festival of Lights, John Gertsen at Drink added to the flaming drink collection a tribute to the volcano whose threats make Batavia Arrack all the more precious.

2 oz Batavia Arrack
1/2 oz Fernet Branca
1/2 oz Demerara Syrup
1/4 oz Green Chartreuse
1 Orange Twist
Stir the Batavia Arrack, Fernet, and demerara syrup with ice. Add the Chartreuse to a cocktail coupe, ignite, and flame the orange oils from a twist. After a few moments of burning, strain the cocktail into the glass to extinguish the flame, and garnish with the original orange twist.

Kuula Hina

Fred Yarm created this Tiki libation at Russell House Tavern for a sherry-loving guest facing academic woes in 2014.

1 1/2 oz Privateer Silver Rum
1/2 oz Lustau Amontillado Sherry
3/4 oz Pineapple Juice
1/2 oz Lime Juice
3/8 oz Vanilla Syrup
3/8 oz Allspice Dram
1 dash Angostura Bitters
Shake with ice, strain into a Collins glass, fill with crushed ice, and float 1/2 oz Cruzan Black Strap Rum. Garnish with a pineapple wedge and add a straw.

Lady Midnight

For a Loyal Nine drink of the day in 2016, Fred Yarm riffed on the Marconi Wireless to create this autumnal Leonard Cohen tribute.

1 1/2 oz Morin Selection Calvados
1 oz Cinzano Sweet Vermouth
3/8 oz Benedictine
1/8 oz Green Chartreuse
1 dash Bittermens Mole Bitters
Stir with ice, strain into a cocktail coupe, and garnish with a cherry.

Lagunas Get Away

Barrel House in Beverly's tropical get-away Sour for Summer 2016.

2 oz Peloton de la Muerte Mezcal
1 oz Passion Fruit Syrup
1/2 oz Lemon Juice
1 Egg White
Shake once without ice and once with ice, strain into a snifter glass, fill with ice, and add straws.

LA

La Joya

Brother Cleve's jewel of a drink, a Pisco Bijou, that he served at his cocktail series at the Think Tank in 2011.

1 1/2 oz Macchu Pisco
3/4 oz Green Chartreuse
3/4 oz Sweet Vermouth
2 dash Angostura Orange Bitters
Stir with ice, strain into a cocktail glass, and garnish with an orange twist.

Lake Union

Mike Fleming created this tribute to Seattle circa 2014 at West Bridge.

1 1/4 oz Rittenhouse Rye
3/4 oz Old Monk Rum
1/2 oz Cynar
1/2 oz Caffè Borghetti
1 dash Angostura Bitters
Stir with ice, strain into a rocks glass, and garnish with lemon oil from a twist.

Land Shark

For A4cade's inaugural 2017 menu, the bartenders were inspired by the Fog Cutter to create this tribute to the Saturday Night Live character.

3/4 oz Privateer Tiki Gin
3/4 oz Maison Rouge Cognac
3/4 oz Angostura 7 Year Rum
3/4 oz Amontillado Sherry
1/4 oz Giffard Blue Curaçao
3/4 oz Passion Fruit Syrup
1/2 oz Lime Juice
Shake with ice, strain into a shark or other Tiki mug, fill with crushed ice, garnish with a paper umbrella, and add a straw.

L'Année du Mexique

Tyler Wang at No. 9 Park circa 2013 honored the attempted year-long French celebration of Mexican culture.

2 oz Siete Leguas Reposado Tequila
1/2 oz Amontillado Sherry
1/2 oz Salers Gentian Liqueur
1+ bsp Crème de Mûre (or Cassis)
1 dash Orange Bitters
Stir with ice, strain into a cocktail glass, and garnish with orange oil from a twist.

La Nuez de Jerez

One of Sahil Mehta's Scaffa masterpieces at Estragon circa 2015.

1 1/2 oz Lustau Amontillado Sherry
1 oz Bonal Gentiane-Quina
1/2 oz Nocino Walnut Liqueur
1 dash Fee's Walnut Bitters
1 dash Regan's Orange Bitters
Build in a white wine (or rocks) glass, and briefly stir to mix __without__ ice. Note: This is a room temperature cocktail.

La Pagerie

Scott Holiday paid tribute to Napoleon's wife right before Rendezvous closed its doors in 2014.

1 1/2 oz JM Rhum Agricole Gold
3/4 oz Lime Juice
3/4 oz Orgeat
Shake with ice, strain into a Collins glass containing 2 oz soda water, fill with ice, garnish with a lime wedge, and add a straw.

La Passeggiata

Tyler Wang was inspired by Carrie Cole's use of salt in cocktails, and he crafted this bitter sparkler at No. 9 Park in 2012.

1 oz Campari
1/4 oz Luxardo Amaretto
1/4 oz Anchor Junipero Gin
1/4 oz Combier Triple Sec
1 pinch Salt
Stir with ice and strain into a flute glass containing 2 1/2 oz Bisol Prosecco.

La Perla de Oaxaca

Tyler Wang at No. 9 Park fell in love with the combination of coffee and Campari which came together beautifully in this 2013 creation.

1 oz Del Maguey Mezcal Vida
1 oz Campari
1 oz Cynar
1/4 oz Simple Syrup
1 Whole Egg
Shake once without ice and once with ice, strain into a rocks glass, and garnish with freshly grated coffee bean.

LA

Lapsang Souchong Buck

Ben Sandrof took a smoky tea Old Fashioned on the menu at the Sunday Salon one step further in 2010.

1 oz Old Monk Rum
3/4 oz Lapsang Souchong Tea Syrup
3/4 oz Lemon Juice
1/2 oz Hartley & Gibson Amontillado Sherry

Shake with ice, strain into a Collins glass with 2 oz ginger beer, fill with ice, garnish with a lemon twist and a dash of aromatic bitters, and add a straw.

Last Nights of Paris

Fred Yarm crafted this for the ShakeStir's 2013 Avèze competition and named it after a book written around the same time of the liqueur's creation.

1 oz Rittenhouse Rye
1 oz Cocchi Sweet Vermouth
1 oz Avèze Gentian Liqueur
1 bsp Luxardo Maraschino
1 bsp Lemon Juice
2 Blackberries

Muddle 2 blackberries with Maraschino and lemon juice. Add rest of the ingredients, stir with ice, strain into a rocks glass, fill with ice, garnish with an orange peel-blackberry flag, and add straws.

Laughing Boy (Deep Ellum variation)

A 2014 expansion of Oliver La Farge's 1935 Laughing Boy into a complex cocktail at Deep Ellum that takes a page from the Little Guiseppe playbook.

1 1/2 oz Plantation Barbados Rum
1/2 oz Carpano Sweet Vermouth
1/2 oz Fernet Branca
1/2 oz Meletti Amaro
1 dash Aromatic Bitters
1 dash Orange Bitters

Stir with ice, strain into a rocks glass with a large cube, add a pinch of salt to the top of the ice cube, and garnish with a lemon twist.

Lauren and Orange

Todd Maul invented this Margarita variation in 2012 for a Clio regular with an unusually colored shirt.

2 oz Chinaco Añejo Tequila
1 oz Carpano Sweet Vermouth
1/2 oz Creole Shrubb Orange Liqueur
1/2 oz Lime Juice

Shake with ice and strain into a cocktail glass.

Lavender Menace

Ben Sandrof at the Sunday Salon perhaps riffed on Misty Kalkofen's 1820 with this floral-sherry number in 2010.

1 3/4 oz Bols Genever
1/2 oz Lemon Juice
1/2 oz Lavender Syrup
1/4 oz Hartley & Gibson
  Amontillado Sherry
2 dash Jerry Thomas Decanter
  Bitters
Shake with ice and strain into a cocktail glass.

La Verdad

Armsby Abbey in Worcester promised "No lies, deception, or misdirection, just the promise that Spring is here" for their 2011 menu.

1 1/2 oz Tru Organic Gin
1 oz Blandy's Bual Madeira
1/2 oz Rosemary Syrup
1/2 oz Lime Juice
Shake with ice and strain into a rocks glass.

Laughing Boy,
Deep Ellum

Law Harbor

Tyler Wang riffed on one of his favorite drinks, the Lawhill, by taking it in a rum direction at Audubon Boston in 2015.

1 1/2 oz Privateer Amber Rum
3/4 oz Dolin Dry Vermouth
1/4 oz Luxardo Maraschino
1 dash Absinthe
1 dash Angostura Bitters
Stir with ice, strain into a rocks glass, and garnish with an orange twist.

Leaf Peeper

Matty Durgin crafted this Pimm's Cup variation at Brick & Mortar in 2016.

1 oz Plantation Barbados Rum
1 oz Pimm's No. 1
3/4 oz Cinnamon Syrup
3/4 oz Lime Juice
1 dash Angostura Bitters
Shake with ice and strain into a Collins glass containing 2 oz ginger ale. Fill with ice, garnish with a lime wedge, and add a straw.

Left Hand of Darkness

Kat Lamper's 2017 Boulevardier riff tribute to Ursula Le Guin at Backbar.

1 1/2 oz Jim Beam Black Bourbon
3/4 oz Carpano Sweet Vermouth
1/2 oz Campari
1/4 oz Cynar
Stir with ice, strain into a rocks glass, and add ice.

Left Turn at Alburquerque

Trina's Starlite Lounge paid homage to Bugs Bunny in 2012 with this carrot juice Sour.

2 oz Macchu Pisco
3/4 oz Cocchi Americano
1 oz Carrot Juice
1/2 oz Lemon Juice
1/2 oz Agave Nectar
1 Egg White
Shake once without ice and once with ice, and strain into a rocks glass.

Leonetto

A Manhattan-like cocktail by Ryan Lotz at Hawthorne in 2012 named after the Italian-born artist who painted the iconic Maurin Quina label.

2 oz Old Weller 7 Year Bourbon
3/4 oz Maurin Quina
1/2 oz Cardamaro
1 dash Angostura Bitters
Stir with ice, strain into a cocktail coupe, and garnish with a cherry and orange oil from a twist.

Let's Go Crazy

Kobie Ali's 2015 Prince-inspired drink of the day at Backbar.

1 oz El Buho Mezcal
1 oz Reposado Tequila
1/2 oz Bonal Gentiane-Quina
1/4 oz Crème de Cacao
1/4 oz Amontillado Sherry
Stir with ice, strain into a cocktail glass, and garnish with an orange twist.

Libertine

The Barrel House merged the Army Navy with a gin Mai Tai circa 2013.

1 1/2 oz Ransom Old Tom Gin
1/2 oz Creole Shrubb Orange
    Liqueur
1/2 oz Orgeat
1/2 oz Lemon Juice
Shake with ice and strain into a cocktail coupe.

Life on Mars

Fred Yarm's 2016 David Bowie tribute at Loyal Nine in the form of an elegant fruit-driven Negroni variation.

1 oz Berkshire Greylock Gin
1 oz Lillet Blanc
1/2 oz St. George Spiced Pear
    Liqueur
1/2 oz Campari
Stir with ice, strain into a cocktail coupe, and garnish with a floated lemon peel lightning bolt.

Lifting the Fog

Jon Theris crafted this riff on the Fog Cutter for a Loyal Nine drink of the Day. While the original also included 1/2 oz Batavia Arrack, it was removed when it hit the Fall 2016 menu.

1 1/2 oz Privateer Silver Rum
3/4 oz Lustau Brandy
1/2 oz Passion Fruit Syrup
1/2 oz Velvet Falernum
1/2 oz Demerara Syrup
1/2 oz Lemon Juice
Shake with ice and strain into a tall glass. Fill with crushed ice almost to the top, float 1/2 oz Blandy's Sercial Madeira, garnish with an orange peel-cherry flag, and add a straw.

Linden Park

Bobby McCoy at Eastern Standard created this Manhattan variation in 2013, and he named it after the neighborhood in Malden, MA, where his father grew up.

1 1/2 oz Rye Whiskey
1 oz Carpano Sweet Vermouth
1/2 oz Amaro Nonino
1/2 oz Aperol
1 dash Bittermens Mole Bitters
Stir with ice, strain into a cocktail coupe, and garnish with a cherry and orange oil from a twist.

Lionheart

At Steel & Rye in 2013, Ted Gallagher focused on French apple brandy and paid tribute to the Duke of Normandy in Old Fashioned style.

1 1/2 oz Dupont Calvados
1/2 oz Rittenhouse Rye
1 bsp Maple Syrup
1 dash St. Elizabeth Allspice Dram
1 dash Angostura Bitters
Stir with ice, strain into a rocks glass with a large ice cube, and garnish with lemon oil from a twist.

Little Branch

Deep Ellum's 2010 tribute to Sam Ross' Penicillin Cocktail was named after one of the New York City bars Sam worked in.

2 oz Lunazul Reposado Tequila
1/2 oz Lemon Juice
1/4 oz Ginger Syrup
1/4 oz Honey Syrup
1 dash Aromatic Bitters
Shake with ice and strain into a rocks glass pre-rinsed with Del Maguey Mezcal Vida.

Little Camillo,
Belly Wine Bar

CRE5OEOCRCRE5OEOCRCRE5OEOCRCRE5OEOCRCRE5OEOCRCRE5OEOCRCRE5OEOCRCR

Little Buddy

Backbar's rum addition to the Little Giuseppe concept (minus the pinch of salt) for one of their drinks of the day in 2016.

3/4 oz Privateer Navy Yard Rum
3/4 oz Bacardi 8 Year Rum
3/4 oz Punt e Mes
3/4 oz Cynar
1 bsp Falernum
1 bsp Lime Juice
Stir with ice, strain into a rocks glass with a large ice cube, and garnish with a lime twist.

Little Camillo

Ryan Connelly used the gin-based Pimm's cordial to craft a low proof Negroni variation at Belly Wine Bar in 2013.

1 1/4 oz Pimm's No. 1
1 oz La Garracha Fino Sherry
3/4 oz Campari
Stir with ice, strain into a rocks glass, and fill with ice. Garnish with a grapefruit twist, add a pinch of salt over the ice, and add straws.

Little Giuseppe

Misty Kalkofen at Drink crafted this in parallel with the Violet Hour's Stephen Cole who in turn came up with a similar cocktail, the Bitter Giuseppe, circa 2009.

2 oz Cynar
2 oz Punt e Mes
1 bsp Lemon Juice
6 dash Angostura Orange Bitters
Build in a rocks glass, add a large ice cube, and stir to mix and chill. Garnish the ice cube with a pinch of salt.

Little Grey Lady

Jackson Cannon of the Hawthorne offered this tribute to Nantucket at the Bartenders' Breakfast at Tales of the Cocktail 2016; the drink also appeared on the Island Creek Oyster Bar menu.

3/4 oz Plymouth Gin
3/4 oz Cocchi Americano
3/4 oz St. Germain
3/4 oz Lemon Juice
1 dash Peychaud's Bitters
Shake with ice and strain into a cocktail coupe.

Little Ronnie

Kevin Martin's 2012 variation at Eastern Standard on the Cynar-based Little Giuseppe.

1 oz Zacapa Rum
1 oz Punt e Mes
1/2 oz Zwack (sub Averna)
1 bsp Lemon Juice
1 pinch Salt
Stir with ice, strain into a rocks glass, and garnish with orange oil from a twist.

Little Sinner

A light but complex aperitif crafted by Sahil Mehta at Estragon in 2014.

2 oz Amontillado Sherry
1 1/2 oz Bonal Gentiane-Quina
1/2 oz Avèze Gentian Liqueur
2 dash Orange Bitters
1 pinch Salt
Stir with ice, strain into a rocks glass pre-rinsed with absinthe, and garnish with an orange twist.

Little Valiant

Will Thompson at Drink named his 2012 creation after the first Salers cattle, a bull named Valiant, to be shipped to North America.

2 oz Salers Gentian Liqueur
2 oz Cocchi Americano
1 bsp Lemon Juice
3 dash Orange Bitters
Build in a rocks glass, add a large ice cube, and stir to mix and chill. Garnish the ice cube with a pinch of salt.

Lohengrin

Sahil Mehta was looking for an escape from the Winter weather in 2017, and he dubbed this tropical number after King Ludwig II whose Wagnerian escapism garnered him the nickname Lohengrin in a caricature.

1 1/2 oz Angostura White Oak Rum
1 oz Lustau Amontillado Sherry
1/2 oz Luxardo Apricot Liqueur
1/2 oz Orgeat
1/2 oz Lime Juice
1 bsp St. Elizabeth Allspice Dram
Shake with ice, strain into a rocks glass, fill with ice, garnish with 2 dashes Angostura Bitters and a mint sprig, and add straws.

London Calling

Dale Murphy created this sparkler for the Tanqueray Bloomsbury launch event at the Sinclair in 2015.

1 1/2 oz Tanqueray Bloomsbury Gin
1/2 oz Aperol
1/2 oz Grapefruit Juice
Shake with ice, strain into a flute glass containing 2 oz sparkling wine, and garnish with grapefruit oil from a twist.

Loneliest Monk

An adaptation of one of Backbar's drinks of the day in 2013.

1 1/2 oz Laird's Bonded Apple Brandy
1/2 oz Yellow Chartreuse
1/2 oz Benedictine
1/2 oz Lemon Juice
1 bsp Absinthe
Shake with ice and strain into a cocktail glass.

Lonely Dark

Sam Cronin crossed the Widow's Kiss with a Kiss in the Dark at Backbar to create the Lonely Dark in 2016.

3/4 oz Beefeater Gin
3/4 oz GrandTen Apple Brandy
1/2 oz Dolin Dry Vermouth
1/4 oz Cherry Heering
1/4 oz Benedictine
1/4 oz Yellow Chartreuse
1/4 oz Ginger Liqueur
1 dash Bitter Truth Creole Bitters
Stir with ice and strain into a cocktail coupe.

Long Eclipse

A great nightcap on the Tiger Mama opening 2016 menu.

1 oz El Dorado 12 Year Rum
1 oz Zucca Rabarbaro Amaro
1/2 oz Carpano Sweet Vermouth
1/2 oz Amontillado Sherry
1 bsp Apricot Liqueur
Stir with ice, strain into a rocks glass, and garnish with an orange twist.

LO

Lost in Laos

Ran Duan at Sichuan Garden II was influenced by the White Buddha, a tequila-cucumber Ramos-like Fizz from Luc-Lac in Portland, OR, in 2013.

1 1/2 oz Plantation Barbados Rum
1/2 oz Green Chartreuse
1/2 oz Lime Juice
1/2 oz Simple Syrup
3 oz Coconut Milk
4 slice Cucumber
Muddle the cucumber slices. Add the rest of the ingredients, shake with ice, and strain into a Collins glass. Fill with ice, garnish with cucumber slice-cherry flag, and add a straw.

Lost U-Boat

Fred Yarm crafted this Jet Pilot riff in response to a reporter's request for a Jägermeister recipe in 2016.

2 oz Plantation Dark Rum
1/2 oz Jägermeister
1/2 oz St. Elder Elderflower
   Liqueur
1/2 oz Lime Juice
1/2 oz Grapefruit Juice
2 dash Angostura Bitters
4 drop Orange Blossom Water
Shake with ice, strain into a Tiki mug, fill with crushed ice, garnish with mint sprigs, and add a straw.

Love & Fear

A fruity gin drink at West Bridge circa 2012 that gains a bit of complexity from a hint of Fernet.

1 1/2 oz Plymouth Gin
3/4 oz Pineapple Syrup
1/2 oz Aperol
1/2 oz Lemon Juice
1 bsp Fernet Branca
Shake with ice, strain into a cocktail glass, and garnish with lemon oil from a twist.

Love in an Elevator

Matt Whitney's nightcap-worthy creation at Local 149 in 2013.

2 oz Zacapa Rum
1/2 oz Pedro Romero Oloroso
   Sherry
1/2 oz Punt e Mes
1/2 oz Benedictine
1 dash Angostura Orange Bitters
Stir with ice, strain into a rocks glass, and garnish with flamed orange oil from a twist.

Love & Fear, West Bridge

Lovely Bunch of Coconuts

Kat Lamper celebrates the mid-century song in 2016 with this tropical number at Backbar.

1 1/2 oz Mezcal
1/2 oz Punt e Mes
1/2 oz Coconut Cream
1/2 oz Demerara Syrup
1/2 oz Lime Juice
Shake with ice and strain into a coconut-shaped Tiki mug. Fill with crushed ice, garnish with a paper parasol and a lime wheel dashed with Angostura Bitters, and add a straw.

Lower Mills

An adaptation of a cocktail created by Ted Gallagher at Steel & Rye in 2013 to honor the restaurant's neighborhood.

1 1/2 oz Ransom Old Tom Gin
3/4 oz Lustau Amontillado Sherry
1/2 oz Suze Gentian Liqueur
1/2 oz Pierre Ferrand Dry Curaçao
Stir with ice, strain into a rocks glass containing an orange wheel, fill with crushed ice, and add straws.

Madame Mustache

A curious drink named after a curious woman; created by Fred Yarm for a Whiskey & Amari night at the Blue Room in 2013.

1 1/2 oz Aged Rhum Agricole
1 oz Drambuie
1/2 oz Cynar
1 dash Angostura Bitters
Build in a rocks glass, briefly stir to mix <u>without</u> ice, and garnish with grapefruit oil from a twist. Note: This is a room temperature cocktail.

Magical Mezcal Mystery Cure

Kat Lamper's 2016 smoky Beatles tribute at Backbar.

1 1/2 oz El Buho Mezcal
1/2 oz Amaro Montenegro
1/2 oz Orgeat
1/2 oz Lemon Juice
1 bsp Allspice Dram
Shake with ice, strain into a rocks glass containing 1 oz ginger beer, fill with ice, and add straws.

Maitalia

Charles Koykendall launched the cocktail menu at Benedetto in 2016 with this Italian-inspired Mai Tai riff.

1 oz Appleton Reserve Rum
3/4 oz Borducan Orange Liqueur
1/2 oz Galliano l'Autentico
1/4 oz Orgeat
3/4 oz Lime Juice
Shake with ice, strain into a rocks glass, fill with crushed ice, garnish with 2-3 dashes Angostura Bitters and a mint sprig, and add straws.

Man About Town

Victor Pelegrin's Boulevardier-like tribute to worldly and sophisticated gentlemen created at Russell House Tavern in 2013.

1 1/2 oz Rittenhouse Rye
1 oz Aperol
3/4 oz Amaro Montenegro
1/2 oz Dolin Dry Vermouth
1 dash Regan's Orange Bitters
Stir with ice, strain into a rocks glass, fill with ice, garnish with an orange twist, and add straws.

Maneater

Fred Yarm crafted this Jasmine-like "Cosmo on the Riviera" for Loyal Nine's Yacht Rock Sundays in 2015.

1 1/2 oz Privateer Silver Rum
1/2 oz Grapefruit Juice
1/2 oz Lime Juice
1/2 oz Creole Shrubb Orange
  Liqueur
1/4 oz Campari
Shake with ice, strain into a cocktail coupe, and garnish with grapefruit oil from a twist.

Mansion in the Sky

At Estragon in 2013, a guest asked Sahil Mehta to make a variation on their Delta Dawn, a whiskey drink with a peach-ginger shrub.

1 1/2 oz Diabolique Bourbon
3/4 oz Lemon Juice
1/2 oz Rothman & Winter Apricot
  Liqueur
1/4 oz Velvet Falernum
1/4 oz Combier Kümmel
1 dash Angostura Bitters
Shake with ice and strain into a snifter glass.

Man Who Left Town

Russell House Tavern's tribute to bartender Victor Pelegrin as a successor to his Man About Town after Vic left for the West Coast in 2014. Originally, the drink was served with Amaro Nonino in the same format as the Man About Town before a shortage led bartenders to switch to Braulio and the down serving style.

2 oz Bulleit Bourbon
3/4 oz Amaro Braulio or Nonino
3/4 oz Byrrh Quinquina
5 dash Orange Bitters
1 dash Bitter Truth Creole Bitters
Stir with ice and strain into a rocks glass. If using Amaro Nonino, fill with ice, garnish with an orange twist, and add straws.

Marigny Cocktail

Fred Yarm paid tribute to one of the funkier and music-driven neighborhoods in New Orleans after his first visit in 2009.

1 oz Apple Brandy or Calvados
1 oz Gin
1 oz Blanc Vermouth
1 bsp Benedictine
1 dash Peychaud's Bitters
Stir with ice, strain into a cocktail glass, and garnish with an orange twist.

Marshall Island Swizzle,
The Hawthorne

Maritime Out

*Ted Gallagher's 2013 addition at
Steel & Rye to the Daiquiri Time
Out legacy.*

3/4 oz Clement Rhum Agricole
1 oz Bonal Gentiane-Quina
3/4 oz Lime Juice
3/4 oz Simple Syrup
*Shake with ice and strain into a
cocktail glass.*

Marksman

*An adaptation of Ted Gallagher's
2010 cocktail at Craigie on Main
that called for rosemary-infused
tequila and housemade pear
bitters; this is how I make the
drink for guests at Loyal Nine.*

1 1/4 oz Blanco Tequila
1 oz Pineau des Charentes
1/2 oz Averna
1/4 oz Pear Eau de Vie
2 dash Orange Bitters
*Stir with ice and strain into a
cocktail glass.*

Maroon Beret

Sahil Mehta crafted this complex herbal number at Estragon in 2014.

1 1/2 oz Diabolique Bourbon
3/4 oz Avèze Gentian Liqueur
1/2 oz Green Chartreuse
1/4 oz Angostura Bitters
1 sprig Rosemary
Shake with ice and strain into a cocktail coupe.

Marshall Islands Swizzle

Scott Marshall named his Swizzle at the Hawthorne in 2012 after his namesake islands in the Pacific.

2 oz Plantation Barbados Rum
1/2 oz Ginger Syrup
1/2 oz Honey Syrup
1 oz Lime Juice
Build in a Collins glass, fill with crushed ice, and swizzle to mix and chill. Garnish with 5-6 dashes Angostura Bitters and add a straw.

Mata Va'ha

Fred Yarm's 2011 Tiki tribute to intrigue on Nuku Hiva in the South Pacific.

3/4 oz Amber Rum
3/4 oz White Rum
3/4 oz Helbing Kümmel
3/4 oz Pineapple Juice
1/2 oz Lime Juice
1/2 oz Passion Fruit Syrup
Shake with ice, strain into a rocks glass, and fill with crushed ice. Carefully ignite 1/4 oz 151 proof rum and pour Blue Blazer style to float on the drink's surface.

Maurizio

Tyler Wang crafted this inverse Palmetto at Audobon in 2014 for a restaurant on the Cape. It was served to me with Lemon Hart 151 and Meletti at the Kirkland Tap & Trotter but would appear on the menu as written.

1 3/4 oz Cinzano Sweet Vermouth
3/4 oz Plantation Overproof Dark Rum
1/2 oz Amaro Ramazzotti
1 pinch Salt
Stir with ice, strain into a rocks glass, and garnish with orange oil from a twist.

Maximo Blue

William Weston's 2014 tribute to Weber Blue Agave at Bronwyn.

2 oz Lunazul Reposado Tequila
3/4 oz Salers Gentian Liqueur
1/4 oz Benedictine
1/2 oz Pineapple Juice
Shake with ice and strain into a single Old Fashioned glass.

Me & My Grandfather

Steven Shellenberger's split spirit Sour at Pomodoro in 2013 that contrasts young and aged spirits; the structure also works well with other spirit pairings such as rums.

3/4 oz Pisco
3/4 oz Cognac
3/4 oz Lemon Juice
3/4 oz Simple Syrup
Shake with ice and strain into a cocktail glass.

Medeiné

Estragon's Sahil Mehta crafted this tribute to the Lithuanian goddess of the forest for Craft by Under My Host magazine in 2014.

1 oz Hayman's Old Tom Gin
1 oz Lustau Oloroso Sherry
1/2 oz Benedictine
1/2 oz Lemon Juice
Shake with ice, strain into a cocktail coupe, and garnish with a dried chamomile flower if available.

Mela Rose

Hugh Fiore's embittered egg white Sour at Eastern Standard circa 2014.

1 oz Laird's Bonded Apple Brandy
1 oz Campari
3/4 oz Lemon Juice
1/2 oz Cointreau
1/2 oz Simple Syrup
1 Egg White
6 drop Pernod Absinthe
Shake once without ice and once with ice, strain into a single Old Fashioned glass, and garnish with freshly grated cinnamon.

Mellow Yellow

At Craigie on Main, Rob Ficks crafted this spiced Green Point-like number in 2013.

1 1/2 oz W.L. Weller Bourbon
1/2 oz Yellow Chartreuse
1/2 oz Becherovka
1/4 oz Rothman & Winter Apricot Liqueur
1 dash Regan's Orange Bitters
Stir with ice, strain into a rocks glass, and garnish with orange oil from a twist.

Melting Pot

One of Sahil Mehta's drinks of the day at Estragon in 2016 that came across much like a Manhattan.

1 1/2 oz Rittenhouse Rye
3/4 oz Fidencio Mezcal
3/4 oz Lustau Palo Cortado Sherry
1/2 oz Chai Tea Syrup
Stir with ice, strain into a rocks glass, fill with ice, garnish with a lemon twist, and add straws.

Mercado

California Gold's creation at the Blue Room in Kendall Square circa 2012.

2 oz Del Maguey Mezcal Vida
1/2 oz Lustau Pedro Ximenez Sherry
1/2 oz Amaro Montenegro
1 dash Bittermens Mole Bitters
Stir with ice, strain into a rocks glass, and garnish with grapefruit oil from a twist.

Merchants Exchange Manhattan

Fred Yarm in 2015 thought about his two favorite rye drinks, the Manhattan and the Sazerac, and thought why can't we have both?

2 oz Rye Whiskey
1 oz Sweet Vermouth
3 dash Peychaud's Bitters
Stir with ice, strain into a rocks glass pre-rinsed with absinthe, and garnish with lemon oil from a twist.

Merchant's Fog Cutter

Sarma's 2016 riff on the classic Fog Cutter Tiki drink.

3/4 oz Lustau Brandy
3/4 oz Lehment Aquavit
1 oz Falernum
1 oz Lime Juice
1/2 oz Orange Juice
Shake with ice, strain into a Collins glass, and fill with crushed ice. Float 1/2 oz Blandy's Malmsey Madeira, garnish with freshly grated nutmeg and a mint sprig, and add a straw.

Messenger

One of Ryan Connelly's contributions to the "Let's Get Fortified" vermouth section of the 2013 Belly Wine Bar cocktail list.

1 1/2 oz Bonal Gentiane-Quina
1/2 oz Cocchi Sweet Vermouth
1/2 oz Calvados
1/2 oz Pierre Ferrand Dry Curaçao
1 dash Bittermens Mole Bitters
1 dash Angostura Orange Bitters
Stir with ice, strain into a rocks glass, and garnish with an orange twist.

Midnight Runner

Sam Olivari crafted this in 2012 at No. 9 Park in response to a request for a really twisted Vieux Carré.

1 1/4 oz Smith & Cross Rum
1 oz Pierre Ferrand 1840 Cognac
1 oz Cocchi Sweet Vermouth
1/4 oz Vanilla Syrup
1 dash Jerry Thomas Decanter Bitters
Stir with ice, strain into a rocks glass, and garnish with orange oil from a twist.

Midtown

Sean Maher's New England in Autumn-themed Manhattan at the Barrel House in Beverly; it won ShakeStir's sherry cocktail competition in 2013.

2 oz Old Fitzgerald Bonded Bourbon
1 oz Lustau East India Sherry
1 bsp Maple Syrup
4 dash Fee's Walnut Bitters
Stir with ice and strain into a rocks glass.

Mighty Aphrodite

A fruity and floral beer cocktail at Park Restaurant circa 2013.

1 1/2 oz Berkshire Ethereal Gin
3/4 oz Grapefruit Juice
1/2 oz Aperol
1/2 oz St. Germain
Shake with ice, strain into a flute glass containing 1 1/2 oz High & Mighty Beer of the Gods blonde ale, and garnish with a grapefruit twist.

Mind the Gap

Eastern Standard's tribute to the London subway warning for the No. 3 Gin launch in 2011.

1 1/2 oz No. 3 Gin
3/4 oz Grapefruit Juice
3/4 oz Martini & Rossi Sweet
  Vermouth
1/2 oz Cardamom Syrup
2 dash Angostura Bitters
Shake with ice and strain into a cocktail coupe.

Merchant's Fog Cutter, Sarma

MI

Mint Fizz

A funky, herbal Fizz crafted by Tom Schlesinger-Guidelli at Eastern Standard in 2008.

1 1/2 oz Grappa
3/4 oz Lemon Juice
3/4 oz Mint Syrup
1 Egg White
Shake once without ice and once with ice, strain into a Highball glass containing 1 1/2 oz soda water, and garnish with a few drops of orange blossom water and a mint sprig.

Missing Link

Greg Thornton at Backbar paid tribute in 2014 to a lost style of cocktail -- the room temperature variety.

1 1/4 oz Laphroaig Scotch
1/2 oz Punt e Mes
1/2 oz Dolin Dry Vermouth
1/2 oz Benedictine
1/4 oz Herbsaint
1/2 oz Water
1 dash Angostura Orange Bitters
1 dash Angostura Bitters
Build in a rocks glass, briefly stir to mix __without__ ice, and garnish with lemon oil from a twist. Note: This is a room temperature cocktail.

Mistaken for Strangers
(Brick & Mortar)

Misty Kalkofen first named this The Grinch for Brick & Mortar's Holiday menu in 2012, but soon renamed it for the 2013 menu to a less seasonal name reflecting the unusual pairing of grappa and Chartreuse.

1 oz Nardini Grappa Bianca
1 oz Green Chartreuse
1/2 oz Lime Juice
1/2 oz Simple Syrup
Shake with ice and strain into a rocks glass.

Cઉୄୠઉୄୠૣ૱ઉୄୠૣ૱ઉૣ૱ૣ૱ઉૣ૱ૣ૱ઉૣ૱

Mistaken for Strangers
(Spoke)

Chris Danforth took sipping-style rums in 2015 and mixed them at Spoke in ways many people do not expect.

1 1/2 oz Aged Rum
1/2 oz Pineapple Syrup
1/2 oz Aperol
1/2 oz Lemon Juice
1 dash Angostura Bitters
1 dash Regan's Orange Bitters
Shake with ice and strain into a cocktail coupe.

M.N. Roy

Sahil Mehta at Estragon was inspired by the Mexican spirit and Communist red color of the drink in 2016 and dubbed this after an Indian revolutionary and founder of the Mexican Communist Party.

1 1/2 oz Milagro Blanco Tequila
1/2 oz Campari
1/2 oz Passion Fruit Syrup
1/2 oz Lime Juice
1/4 oz St. Elizabeth Allspice Dram
Shake with ice and strain into a cocktail coupe.

Monk Ate Lunch

This fruity-herbal libation was crafted at Bergamot and named after a Doors song circa 2013. Bergamot also makes a Cognac version called the Monk Got Crunked.

1 1/2 oz Luksusowa Vodka
1/2 oz Rothman & Winter Apricot
   Liqueur
1/2 oz Benedictine
1/2 oz Lemon Juice
Shake with ice and strain into a cocktail glass.

Monkey Paw

Barrel House in Beverly's tropical twist on the classic Monkey Gland in 2016.

2 oz Dry Gin
1 oz Orange Juice
1/4 oz Giffard Banane du Bresil
1/4 oz Grenadine
1 dash Absinthe
Shake with ice and strain into a cocktail glass.

Mon Sherry Amour

A savory and smoky chocolate creation of Sahil Mehta at Estragon circa 2013.

1 oz Del Maguey Mezcal Vida
1 oz Lustau Manzanilla Sherry
1/2 oz Campari
1/2 oz Crème de Cacao
2 dash Scrappy's Chocolate Bitters
Stir with ice and strain into a single Old Fashioned glass.

Monte Cassino

Paul Manzelli's 2013 Cognac and citrus-herbal riff on the Negroni at Bergamot.

1 oz Pierre Ferrand Amber Cognac
1 oz Campari
1 oz Amaro Montenegro
1 dash Fee's Peach Bitters
Stir with ice and strain into a rocks glass containing a large ice cube.

Montenegroni

Bergamont's Negroni variation in 2014 crafted by Paul Manzelli.

1 oz Citadelle Reserve Gin
1 oz Campari
1 oz Amaro Montenegro
Stir with ice, strain into a rocks glass, fill with with ice, and garnish with an orange twist.

Montenegroni, Bergamot

Montesco

Katie Emmerson's Mamie Taylor-like Highball that she created for the La Diablada Pisco event at the Hawthorne in 2013.

1 1/2 oz Macchu Pisco La Diablada
1/2 oz Benedictine
1/2 oz Ginger Syrup
1/2 oz Lime Juice
Shake with ice, strain into a Highball glass containing 2 oz ginger ale, fill with ice, and add a straw.

Monument Valley

Peter Nelson Jr. at State Park in 2015 modeled the drink after a park in the Four Corners region (as well as the name of one of his favorite video games).

3/4 oz Del Maguey Mezcal Vida
1/2 oz Chinaco Blanco Tequila
1 1/4 oz Avèze Gentian Liqueur
1/2 oz St. Germain
1/4 oz Cynar
Stir with ice and strain into a rocks glass.

More Scotch Than Sincerity

Tony Iamunno created this recipe at Stoddard's in 2013 and he named it after a phrase he spotted in a friend's LiveJournal.

2 oz Cutty Sark Scotch
3/4 oz Cinnamon Syrup
3/4 oz Lemon Juice
1/2 oz Cherry Heering
2 dash Angostura Bitters
Shake with ice, strain into a cocktail glass, and garnish with a lemon twist.

More Than Classic

Matthew Schrage of Brick & Mortar crafted this libation in 2013 for their downstairs neighbor, Central Kitchen.

1 oz La Favorite Rhum Agricole Amber
1 oz Aperol
1 oz Amaro Braulio
1 bsp St. Germain
1 dash Angostura Bitters
Stir with ice, strain into a rocks glass, fill with ice, garnish with an orange twist, and add straws.

Mother of Turin

Ran Duan crossed Old World and New World flavors in this refreshing take on Rome with a View at Sichuan Garden II in 2014.

1 oz Dolin Dry Vermouth
3/4 oz Gran Classico
3/4 oz Guava Syrup
1 oz Lime Juice
Shake with ice, strain into a Collins glass containing 2 oz soda water, and fill with ice. Garnish with an orange twist–cherry flag, and add a straw.

Mount Pelée

For a drink of the day at Loyal Nine in 2016, Fred Yarm was inspired by Smuggler's Cove's Abricot Vieux and John Gertsen's Rhum Agricot and named the combination after Martinique's active volcano.

1 1/2 oz JM Rhum Agricole Blanc
1/2 oz Rothman & Winter Apricot Liqueur
1/2 oz Velvet Falernum
1/2 oz Dolin Dry Vermouth
2 dash Regan's Orange Bitters
1 dash Angostura Bitters
Stir with ice, strain into a cocktail coupe, and garnish with an orange twist.

Movin' to the Country

Tony Iamunno tapped into the great combination of peach and Campari at Trina's Starlight Lounge in 2016.

2 oz Campari
1 oz Punt e Mes
1/2 oz Crème de Peche
1/2 oz Lemon Juice
1 Egg White
Shake once without ice and once with ice, strain into a large cocktail coupe, and garnish with a grapefruit twist.

Murder of Dutch Schultz

Tony Iamunno was inspired during an insomnia-driven Wikipedia fest in 2014 to craft this recipe at Stoddard's.

1 1/2 oz Bols Genever
1 oz Lustau Amontillado Sherry
1 oz Pierre Ferrand Dry Curaçao
1/2 oz Bols Crème de Cacao
Stir with ice, strain into a cocktail coupe, and garnish with an orange twist.

My Dark Heart

Russell House Tavern's Winter 2013-2014 Fernet cocktail.

1 1/2 oz Fernet Branca
3/4 oz Pampero Anniversario Rum
3/4 oz Cinnamon Syrup
3/4 oz Lemon Juice
Shake with ice, strain into a rocks glass, fill with ice, and add straws.

My Leathers So Soft

Ran Duan's complex Tiki-like libation at Sichuan Garden II in 2013.

3/4 oz St. George Agricole Rum
3/4 oz Bigallet China China
3/4 oz Cinnamon Syrup
3/4 oz Pineapple Juice
3/4 oz Lemon Juice
Shake with ice, strain into a footed water or double Old Fashioned glass, fill with ice, garnish with mint sprigs and a lemon twist, and add straws.

Mytoi Gardens

Fred Yarm's Tikism added to Russell House Tavern's Daiquiri Time Out section of the 2014 brunch cocktail menu before moving to the main list of drinks.

1 1/2 oz Old Monk Rum
1 oz Pineapple Juice
3/4 oz Lime Juice
1/2 oz St. Elizabeth Allspice Dram
1/2 oz Vanilla Syrup
1 dash Angostura Bitters
Shake with ice, strain into a rocks glass, and fill with crushed ice. Garnish with 2-3 dashes Angostura Bitters and a pineapple wedge, and add straws.

My Triumphs, My Mistakes

Sam Gabrielli paid tribute to Gaius Baltar's manifesto in Battlestar Galactica with this 2013 riff on the Godfather at Russell House Tavern.

2 oz Great King Street Scotch
3/4 oz Russo Nocino Walnut Liqueur
1/2 oz Cynar
1/2 oz Batavia Arrack
1 dash Orange Bitters
Stir with ice, strain into a rocks glass, and garnish with orange oil from a twist.

My Word is Gold

Steve Shur crafted this modern mixology take on the Last Word in 2012 at the Boston College Club.

3/4 oz Fernet Branca
3/4 oz Green Chartreuse
3/4 oz St. Germain
3/4 oz Lime Juice
Shake with ice and strain into a rocks glass.

Nana's Rocker

John McElroy crafted this herbal apple number for the Fall 2012 Russell House Tavern menu.

2 oz Laird's Bonded Apple Brandy
3/4 oz Pedro Ximenez Sherry
1/2 oz Amaro Montenegro
1/2 oz Lime Juice
1 dash Peychaud's Bitters
Shake with ice, strain into a rocks glass, fill with ice, and add straws.

Navigator

Fred Yarm's low proof Madeira take on the Test Pilot in 2016 named after Peter the Navigator who claimed the island of Madeira for Portugal.

1 1/2 oz Blandy's Sercial Madeira
1/2 oz St. Elder Elderflower
   Liqueur
1/2 oz Velvet Falernum
1/2 oz Lime Juice
2 dash Angostura Bitters
10 drop St. George Absinthe
Shake with ice, strain into a double Old Fashioned glass, fill with crushed ice, garnish with a lime twist, and add straws.

Nebbia Di Garda

At the Blue Room, Matthew Schrage paid homage in 2012 to Lake Garda where S. Maria al Monte is made.

1 1/2 oz Meletti Amaro
3/4 oz Amaro S. Maria al Monte
1/2 oz Lemon Juice
1/2 oz Simple Syrup
Shake with ice, strain into a Highball glass, fill with crushed ice, garnish with a mint sprig and freshly grated nutmeg, and add a straw.

Navigator,
Loyal Nine

Necromancer

Chad Arnholt's gin Tiki drink at the Citizen Public House in 2012.

1 1/2 oz St. George Terrior Gin
1/2 oz Banks 5 Island Rum
3/4 oz Lime Juice
3/4 oz Orgeat
1/4 oz Cinnamon Syrup
4 drop St. George Absinthe
Shake with ice, strain into a rocks glass, fill with crushed ice, garnish with mint, and add straws.

Negrimlet

Scott Holliday of Rendezvous presented this drink at Gertstravaganza, John Gertsen's going away event in 2014 at the Hawthorne; the two of them created this recipe hybrid when they were roommates years back.

2 oz Citadelle Gin
3/4 oz Campari
1/2 oz Lime Juice
1/2 oz Lime Cordial Syrup
Shake with ice and strain into a cocktail coupe. Substitute Rose's or equal parts lime juice and simple syrup for the cordial.

Newmarket Swizzle

A Swizzle created by Katie Emmerson at the Hawthorne in 2012 and named after the Boston neighborhood where the Bully Boy Distillery resides.

2 oz Bully Boy White Rum
1/2 oz Pineapple Juice
1/2 oz Lime Juice
1/2 oz Cinnamon Syrup
Build in a Collins glass, fill with crushed ice, and swizzle to mix and chill. Garnish with 3-4 dashes Fee's Whiskey Barrel Bitters and add a straw.

New Stone Wall

Citizen Public House's modern take on the classic rum and apple cider libation in 2012.

1 1/2 oz Laird's Bonded Apple Brandy
1/2 oz Banks 5 Island Rum
1/2 oz Amaro Montenegro
1/2 oz Cinnamon Syrup
1/2 oz Lime Juice
Shake with ice and strain into a cocktail coupe.

Noah Calhoun

John Mayer and Spencer at Local 149 came up with this drink in 2013 to sooth a guest's breakup, and they named it after a character from The Notebook.

1 oz Booker's Bourbon
1 oz Pierre Ferrand Ambre Cognac
1 oz Amaro Montenegro
1 dash Bitter Cube Vanilla Cherry Bitters
Stir with ice and strain into a rocks glass.

Noble Order

Created by Katie Emmerson for the Scotch cocktail section of the 2013 Hawthorne menu.

1 1/2 oz Famous Grouse Scotch
3/4 oz Dolin Dry Vermouth
1/2 oz Amaro Nonino
1/4 oz Marie Brizard Apricot Liqueur
Stir with ice, strain into a cocktail coupe, and garnish with grapefruit oil from a twist.

CRSDKRCRSDKRCRSDKRCRSDKRCRSDKRCRSDKRCRCRS

Nonesuch Scaffa

A room temperature drink created by Fred Yarm in 2011 and influenced by PDT's Newark.

1 1/4 oz Laird's Bonded Apple Brandy
1 1/4 oz Lustau East India Sherry
1/4 oz Crème de Cacao
1 bsp Fernet Branca
Build in a rocks glass, briefly stir to mix __without__ ice, and garnish with orange oil from a twist. Note: This is a room temperature cocktail.

Nose Dive

Ran Duan created this Sling in 2016 for the Baldwin & Sons Trading Co. at Sichuan Garden II.

1 oz Angel's Envy Bourbon
1 oz Pineapple Juice
1/2 oz Cherry Heering
1/2 oz Gran Classico
3/4 oz Lemon Juice
1/2 oz Demerara Syrup
Shake with ice, strain into a Collins glass, fill with crushed ice, garnish with 2-3 dashes Angostura Bitters, a mint sprig, an orchid, and a paper airplane (elevated on a cocktail pick), and add a straw.

No Sleep Till Brookline

Patrick Gaggiano's 2014 tribute to Fairsted Kitchen's Brookline location.

1 1/2 oz Four Roses Bourbon
1 oz Amaro Montenegro
1/2 oz Lemon Juice
1/2 oz Simple Syrup
1 dash Angostura Bitters
Shake with ice, strain into a rocks glass, fill with ice, garnish with a lemon twist, and add straws.

No Stone Unturned

Ran Duan's herbal discovery at Sichuan Garden II in 2013 as perhaps a continuation of the Little Giuseppe lineage or an expansion of the Appetizer L'Italienne.

1 1/2 oz Carpano Sweet Vermouth
1/2 oz Lustau Pedro Ximenez Sherry
1/2 oz Fernet Branca
1/2 oz St. George Absinthe
Stir with ice, strain into a rocks glass containing a large ice cube, and garnish the ice cube with a pinch of salt.

❧❧❧❧❧❧❧❧❧❧❧❧❧❧❧❧❧❧❧❧❧❧❧

Oaxacan Dead,
Deep Ellum

Not the First Cyn

Taso Paptsoris' bitter, earthy, and fruity libation found its genesis at Casa B in 2013.

1 1/2 oz Bulleit Bourbon
1 oz Cynar
1/2 oz Cherry Heering
2 dash Fee's Rhubarb Bitters
Stir with ice, strain into a rocks glass, fill with ice, garnish with an orange twist, and add straws.

Novara Fresco

One of Vikram Hedge's food friendly libations at Sarma circa 2013 that is a reference to where Campari was invented in Italy in 1860.

1/2 oz Campari
1/2 oz Cardamaro
1/2 oz Pineapple Juice
1/2 oz Lemon Juice
Shake with ice, strain into a cocktail coupe containing 2 oz Casteller Cava, and garnish with lemon oil from a twist.

Oaxacan Dead

Ethan Armstrong at Deep Ellum thought up the name in 2013 and figured that a Zombie riff would fit the "Walkin' Dead" pun; when it finally hit the menu, it was closer to the 1934 classic than this mid-century variation.

1 1/2 oz Sombra Mezcal
1/2 oz Falernum
1/2 oz Rothman & Winter Apricot Liqueur
1/2 oz Lime Juice
2 dash Peychaud's Bitters
2 dash Orange Bitters
Shake with ice, strain into a rocks glass, fill with crushed ice, garnish with mint sprigs, and add straws.

Oaxacan Fix

Sam Treadway at Backbar riffed on Phil Ward's Oaxacan Old Fashioned in 2013.

1 1/2 oz Añejo Tequila
1/2 oz Mezcal
1/2 oz Lemon Juice
1/4 oz Curaçao
1/4 oz Agave Syrup
1 dash Bittermens Mole Bitters
Shake with ice, strain into a rocks glass, fill with crushed ice, garnish with an orange twist, and add straws.

Oaxacan Punch

Patrick Clark's smoky and spiced Daisy at the Citizen Public House in 2016.

1 1/2 oz Del Maguey Mezcal Vida
1/2 oz Kronan Swedish Punsch
1/2 oz Cinnamon Syrup
1/2 oz Lime Juice
Shake with ice, strain into a rocks glass, fill with ice, garnish with a grapefruit twist, and add straws.

Oaxacan Rose

Deep Ellum's smoky and grapefruity 2012 Margarita riff.

1 1/2 oz Fidencio Mezcal
3/4 oz Combier Pamplemousse Liqueur
1/2 oz Lemon Juice
1/4 oz Grapefruit Juice
2 dash Peychaud's Bitters
1 dash Orange Bitters
Shake with ice, strain into a cocktail coupe, and garnish with a grapefruit twist.

Oaxacan Standoff

Ryan McGrale's sherry and mezcal number at Tavern Road circa 2014.

1 1/2 oz El Buho Mezcal
1/2 oz Aperol
1/2 oz Lustau Amontillado Sherry
1/4 oz Agave Syrup
1/2 oz Lime Juice
Shake with ice, strain into a rocks glass, and garnish with a grapefruit twist.

Of Lambs and Lions

Sahil Mehta at Estragon was inspired by Spring to craft this herbal and floral Daisy in 2014.

1 oz Martin Miller Gin
1/2 oz Green Chartreuse
1/2 oz Avèze Gentian Liqueur
1/4 oz Rothman & Winter Crème de Violette
3/4 oz Lemon Juice
Shake with ice, strain into a cocktail glass, and garnish with a lemon twist.

Of Shoes and Ships

Fred Yarm riffed on the Pegu Club in Swizzle format for Loyal Nine's The Walrus and The Carpenter event in 2015.

1 1/2 oz Berkshire Greylock Gin
1/2 oz Creole Shrubb Orange Liqueur
1/2 oz Aperol
1/2 oz Lime Juice
2 dash Angostura Bitters
Build in a Collins glass, add crushed ice, and swizzle to mix and chill. Garnish with a mint sprig and freshly grated nutmeg, and add a straw.

Old (Barbara) West

Backbar's Sam Treadway riffed on the classic Barbara West for a 2013 Spaghetti Western-themed Whiskey & Amari Night at the Blue Room.

1 oz Ransom Old Tom Gin
3/4 oz Lustau Amontillado Sherry
3/4 oz Lemon Juice
1/2 oz Meletti Amaro
2 dash Angostura Bitters
1 pinch Salt
Shake with ice, strain into a cocktail glass, and garnish with a lemon twist.

Old Man Winter

A warming nightcap created by Ryan Connelly at Belly Wine Bar in 2013. The drink was originally created with Averna, and during a shortage, it was switched to S. Maria al Monte.

1 oz Old Fitzgerald Bourbon
1 oz Old Monk Rum
1/2 oz Pedro Ximenez Sherry
1/2 oz Averna or S. Maria al Monte
1 dash Mole Bitters
Stir with ice and strain into a rocks glass.

One Night in Bangkok

For Yacht Rock Sundays at Loyal Nine, Fred Yarm crafted this Peruvian Honeymoon in 2015.

1 1/2 oz Barsol Pisco
1/2 oz Benedictine
1/2 oz Creole Shrubb Orange Liqueur
1/2 oz Lime Juice
Shake with ice and strain into a cocktail coupe.

One One Thousand

Paul Yem's fruity-herbal Last Word at Brick & Mortar in 2015.

3/4 oz Henry McKenna Bourbon
3/4 oz Cynar
3/4 oz Apricot Liqueur
3/4 oz Lemon Juice
Shake with ice and strain into a cocktail coupe.

(The) Onset

Will Thompson riffed on the Negroni at Drink in 2012 on a night he could not watch the band The Onset perform in concert.

1 oz Bols Genever
1 oz Gran Classico
1 oz Dolin Blanc Vermouth
Stir with ice, strain into a rocks glass, and garnish with grapefruit oil from a twist.

Orana Maria

Sahil Mehta's 2016 banana and spice Mai Tai riff at Estragon; the drink was named after a Paul Gaugin painting featuring Tahitian fe'i bananas.

2 oz Hamilton's Guyana Rum
3/4 oz Lime Juice
1/2 oz Giffard Banane du Bresil
1/4 oz Velvet Falernum
1/4 oz Orgeat
1 dash Angostura Bitters
Shake with ice and strain into a cocktail coupe.

Orange & Essex

Fred Yarm was inspired by Loyal Nine's Revoluton-era theme in 2015 and dubbed this Madeira drink after the site of the Liberty Tree in Boston.

1 oz Brandy
1 oz Verdelho or Sercial Madeira
1/2 oz Campari
1/2 oz Maraschino Liqueur
2 dash Peychaud's Bitters
Stir with ice, strain into a cocktail glass, and garnish with an orange twist.

Organized Noize

Ted Kilpatrick won the Appleton Remixology competition in 2012 with this tribute to the producers of TLC's Waterfalls. He also made a rye version with Old Overholt at No. 9 Park called The Son of Chico Dusty.

2 oz Appleton Estate Reserve Rum
3/4 oz Lime Juice
3/4 oz Grenadine
3/4 oz Angostura Bitters
2 dash Chalula Hot Sauce
Build in a water goblet or Collins glass, fill with crushed ice, and swizzle to mix and chill. Garnish with a wide lime twist and add a straw.

Otoño

Naomi Levi's Fall-themed drink on Eastern Standard's 2013 "Sherry Baby" section of the menu.

1 1/2 oz Lustau East India Sherry
1/2 oz Ron Bermudez Aged Rum
3/4 oz Lime Juice
1/2 oz Vanilla Syrup
1/4 oz Cinnamon Syrup
Shake with ice, strain into a Highball glass, fill with ice, garnish with a lime slice, and add a straw.

Oude Negroni

Joel Atlas' 2015 Negroni variation at the Baldwin Bar at Sichuan Garden II.

1 1/2 oz Diep 9 Aged Genever
1 oz Zucca Rabarbaro Amaro
1 oz Carpano Sweet Vermouth
Stir with ice, strain into a rocks glass, and garnish with an orange twist.

(The) Outlaw

Brick & Mortar's rich agave nightcap circa 2015.

2 oz Lunazul Añejo Tequila
3/4 oz Yellow Chartreuse
1/4 oz St. George Coffee Liqueur
2 dash Bittermens Mole Bitters
Stir with ice, strain into a rocks glass, fill with ice, garnish with orange oil from a twist, and add straws.

Pair of Queens

Ran Duan crafted this whiskey libation at Sichuan Garden II, and it propelled him into the Diageo World Class finals in 2014.

1 1/2 oz Bulleit Rye
3/4 oz Amaro Ramazzotti
1/2 oz Lustau Amontillado Sherry
1/4 oz Fraise de Bois (or Strawberry Syrup)
Stir with ice, strain into a cocktail glass, and garnish with an orange twist-cherry flag.

Pair of Queens,
Sichuan Garden II

Palace of the Dead

Ran Duan's 2015 gaming tribute at the Baldwin Bar at Sichuan Garden II.

1 oz Del Maguey Mezcal Vida
1/2 oz Ancho Reyes Chile Liqueur
1/2 oz Brovo 14 Amaro
1 oz Carpano Sweet Vermouth
Stir with ice, strain into a rocks glass, and garnish with a lime twist.

Palaver

Enough of this idle talk, it is time for a 2012 drink by Nick Korn at the Citizen Public House.

1 1/2 oz Beefeater Gin
1/2 oz Fernet Branca
1/2 oz Punt e Mes
1/2 oz Demerara Syrup
1 dash Angostura Orange Bitters
Stir with ice, strain into a rocks glass, and garnish with an orange twist.

Palazzo

Sam Gabrielli created this at Russell House Tavern for Negroni Week 2014; an overproof Bourbon is essential to balance this drink out.

1 oz Beefeater Gin
1 oz Campari
1/2 oz St. George Raspberry Liqueur
1/2 oz Booker's Bourbon
Stir with ice, strain into a cocktail coupe, and garnish with an orange twist.

Palenque

A complex bitter tequila drink from Sahil Mehta at Estragon in 2015.

1 oz Milagro Blanco Tequila
1 oz Lustau Oloroso Sherry
1/2 oz Campari
1/2 oz King's Ginger Liqueur
2 dash Cocktail Kingdom Coffee Bitters
Stir with ice and strain into a rocks glass.

Palmetto Bug

Riffing on a mezcal Paloma served at Sylvain in New Orleans, Jen Harvey crafted the Palmetto Bug at Zócalo in 2012.

1 1/2 oz Del Maguey Mezcal Vida
3/4 oz Drambuie
1 1/2 oz Grapefruit Juice
1/2 oz Lime Juice
Shake with ice and strain into a Collins glass with a salt rim and containing 2 oz soda water. Fill with ice and add a straw.

Palomino Sling

Trevor LeBlanc's refreshing sherry-laden offering at Stoddard's in 2016.

1 1/2 oz Amontillado Sherry
1 oz Cruzan Dark Rum
1/2 oz Orgeat
1/2 oz Cinnamon Syrup
1/2 oz Lime Juice
1 dash Angostura Bitters
Shake with ice, strain into a tulip glass, and fill with crushed ice. Garnish with fruits of the season such as berries, lime wedge, pineapple chunk, and mint sprig, and add a straw.

Pancho Villa

A flavorful tequila drink crafted by John Mayer in 2013 at the Citizen Public House and named after the Mexican Revolutionary.

2 oz Tequila Ocho Plata
1/2 oz Lustau Oloroso Sherry
1/2 oz Luxardo Maraschino
1/2 oz Lime Juice
Shake with ice and strain into a cocktail coupe.

Pan-European Pandemonium

Sahil Mehta's 2014 complex, herbal, and savory sipper at Estragon.

1 oz Drambuie
1/2 oz Del Maguey Mezcal Vida
1/2 oz Cynar
1/2 oz Manzanilla Sherry
Stir with ice, strain into a cocktail coupe, and garnish with lemon oil from a twist.

Pantomimist

Sahil Mehta of Estragon's offering for a 2015 ShakeStir Negroni variation competition.

1 oz Bourbon
1 oz Campari
1/2 oz Mezcal
1/2 oz Crème de Cacao
Stir with ice, strain into a cocktail coupe, and garnish with an orange twist.

PA

Paper Aviator

Kat Lamper mashed up the Paper Plane with the Aviation for a 2016 drink of the day at Backbar.

1 oz Four Roses Bourbon
1/2 oz Lemon Juice
1/2 oz Aperol
1/2 oz Luxardo Maraschino
1/2 oz Tempus Fugit Crème de Violette
Shake with ice and strain into a cocktail glass.

Paper Schooner

At Island Creek Oyster Bar, Vikram Hedge and Tom Schlesinger-Guidelli crafted this variation on Sam Ross' Paper Plane in 2012.

3/4 oz Rittenhouse Rye
3/4 oz Becherovka
3/4 oz Aperol
3/8 oz Lemon Juice
3/8 oz Simple Syrup
Shake with ice, strain into a cocktail coupe, and garnish with a lemon twist.

Passport Painkiller, Backbar

Paraiso

Fairsted Kitchen's Will Isaza won Boston's Bacardi Legacy competition in 2015 with his version of paradise.

1 oz Bacardi Gold Rum
1/2 oz Cynar
1/2 oz Grenadine
1 oz Lime Juice
2 dash Angostura Bitters
Shake with ice and strain into a cocktail glass.

Passaggio

Jared Sadoian's gateway to bitter drinks at Craigie on Main in 2013.

1 oz Batavia Arrack
1 oz Cocchi Americano
3/4 oz Amaro Nonino
1 dash Angostura Bitters
Stir with ice, strain into a cocktail coupe, and garnish with an orange twist.

Passport Painkiller

Sam Cronin's ticket to relief from 2016 election stress at Backbar.

1 oz Dewar's Scotch
1/4 oz Laphroaig Scotch
1/2 oz Blackwell Jamaican Rum
1/4 oz St. Elizabeth Allspice Dram
2 oz Pineapple Juice
1 oz Orange Juice
1 oz Coconut Cream
Shake with ice, strain into a Tiki mug, fill with crushed ice, garnish with a pineapple fruit leaf, orange twist, and freshly grated nutmeg, and add a straw.

Pastis Fizz

Eastern Standard's 2013 twist on a Sloe Gin Fizz.

1 1/2 oz Plymouth Sloe Gin
1/2 oz Lemon Juice
1/2 oz Ricard Pastis
1/4 oz Simple Syrup
1 Egg White
Shake once without ice and once with ice, and strain into a Fizz glass containing 1 oz soda water.

PA-PE

Pastry War

Rob Ficks at Craigie on Main paid tribute to one of the early French-Mexican conflicts with this 2016 chocolate-herbal mezcal libation.

1 1/2 oz Peloton de la Muerte Mezcal
1/2 oz Tempus Fugit Crème de Cacao
1/2 oz Averna
1/2 oz Lemon Juice
2 dash Bitter Truth Mole Bitters
Shake with ice, strain into a cocktail coupe, and garnish with a lemon twist.

Patriot Sling

Kit Paschal created this for Eastern Standard's DrinkOne charity menu item in 2013 to support the victims of the Boston Marathon bombing.

1 1/2 oz Plantation Barbados Rum
3/4 oz Lemon Juice
3/4 oz Honey Syrup
2 dash Angostura Bitters
Shake with ice, strain into a Collins glass containing 2 oz ginger beer, fill with ice, garnish with a lemon twist, and add a straw.

Payaso de Rodeo

Sahil Mehta created this earthy and smoky aperitif at Estragon in 2015.

1 oz Xicaru Mezcal
1 oz Lustau Oloroso Sherry
3/4 oz Bonal Gentiane-Quina
1/4 oz Avèze Gentian Liqueur
2 dash Angostura Bitters
Stir with ice and strain into a cocktail coupe.

Peacefield

Townshend's 2015 tribute to the 18th century home and farmstead of John Adams and later John Quincy Adams located not too far from the restaurant.

1 oz Plantation 3 Star White Rum
3/4 oz Pineapple Juice
1/2 oz Green Chartreuse
1/2 oz Lime Juice
1/4 oz Simple Syrup
Shake with ice, strain into a double Old Fashioned glass, fill with crushed ice, garnish with mint leaves, and add straws.

❦❧❦❧❦❧❦❧❦❧❦❧❦❧❦❧❦❧❦❧❦❧❦❧❦❧❦

Pearl de Vere

A tribute to the Soiled Dove of Crippled Creek created by Fred Yarm for a Women of the Wild West night at the Blue Room in 2013.

1 oz Reposado Tequila
1 oz Cocchi Americano
1/2 oz Lime Juice
1/2 oz Benedictine
1 dash Angostura Bitters
Shake with ice, strain into a cocktail glass, and garnish with an orange twist.

Peat's Kiss

For a drink of the day in 2017, Carlo Caroscio at Backbar riffed on Phil Ward's Shruff's End and combined it with the Widow's Kiss.

1 1/4 oz Laird's Bonded Apple Brandy
3/4 oz Laphroaig Scotch
1/2 oz Amaro Nonino
1/2 oz Yellow Chartreuse
1 dash Angostura Bitters
Stir with ice, strain into a cocktail glass, and garnish with lemon oil from a twist.

Peloni

Chris Danforth crafted this Toronto-like libation in 2013 using Braulio mellowed by Maraschino at the Blue Room.

2 oz Old Overholt Rye
1/2 oz Amaro Braulio
1/4 oz Maraschino Liqueur
1/4 oz Demerara Syrup
1 dash Angostura Orange Bitters
Stir with ice, strain into a rocks glass, and garnish with orange oil from a twist.

Penn

A recipe Brick & Mortar needed to create to fill in the gap in their Ivy League Cocktails menu in Fall 2012.

1 1/2 oz Rittenhouse Rye
3/4 oz Punt e Mes
1/2 oz Nux Alpina Walnut Liqueur
1/4 oz Avèze Gentian Liqueur
Stir with ice and strain into a rocks glass.

Perfect Bamboo

Ryan McGrale at Tavern Road updated the classic aperitif in 2013.

1 1/2 oz Lustau Amontillado Sherry
3/4 oz Cinzano Sweet Vermouth
3/4 oz Noilly Prat Dry Vermouth
1 dash Angostura Bitters
1 dash Regan's Orange Bitters
Stir with ice, strain into a cocktail glass, and garnish with an olive and lemon oil from a twist.

Persecuted Gentleman

A complex brown, bitter, and stirred drink created in 2013 by Ramona Shah at Stoddard's.

1 1/2 oz Old Overholt Rye
1/2 oz Brandy
1/2 oz Fernet Branca
1/2 oz Cynar
1/4 oz Agave Nectar
2 dash Orange Bitters
Stir with ice, strain into a cocktail coupe, and garnish with a cherry.

Peru Négro

Brother Cleve created this Pisco Negroni riff that appeared in a 2016 book entitled Peru: A World of Cocktails. The Bittermens site provided the recipe with Amaro Nonino.

1 oz Pisco
1 oz Campari
1 oz Sweet Vermouth
1/2 oz Amaro Montenegro (or Nonino)
1 dash Bittermens Mole Bitters
Stir with ice, strain into a rocks glass, and garnish with an orange twist.

Peruvian Necktie

For a drink of the day at Loyal Nine in 2016, Fred Yarm was inspired by the name of grappling chokehold and took it in a fruity-herbal direction.

1 1/2 oz Encanto Pisco
1/2 oz Benedictine
1/2 oz Rothman & Winter Apricot Liqueur
1/2 oz Lime Juice
10 drop St. George Absinthe
Shake with ice, strain into a cocktail coupe, and garnish with a knotted orange twist.

Piazza Vecchia

Scott Holliday riffed on the Vieux Carré in 2012 using mostly clear ingredients at Rendezvous.

1 oz Chinaco Blanco Tequila
1 oz Nardini Bassano Grappa
1 oz Dolin Dry Vermouth
1/3 oz Yellow Chartreuse
1 dash Scrappy's Celery Bitters
1 dash Angostura Orange Bitters
Stir with ice and strain into a rocks glass.

Pimm's Up

Saloon's take on the classic Summer pleaser, the Pimm's Cup, circa 2012.

3/4 oz Pimm's No. 1
1/2 oz Gin
1/2 oz Lime Juice
1/2 oz Mint Syrup
Shake with ice, strain into a cocktail coupe containing 1 oz dry sparkling wine, and garnish with a mint sprig.

Persecuted
Gentleman,
Stoddard's

Pineapple Project

Kyle Powell created this spin on the Laphroaig Project at Russell House Tavern circa 2012, and Ames Street Deli adapted the recipe slightly by adding absinthe for their 2014 menu.

1 oz Pineapple Juice
1/2 oz Green Chartreuse
1/2 oz Yellow Chartreuse
1/2 oz Laphroaig Scotch
1/4 oz Maraschino Liqueur
1/2 oz Lemon Juice
1 dash Absinthe (or omit)
Shake with ice and strain into a cocktail coupe.

Pink Penelope

Barrel House in Beverly's rose-colored sparkler in 2015.

3/4 oz Campari
3/4 oz St. Germain
3/4 oz Grapefruit Juice
Shake with ice and strain into a cocktail glass containing 1 oz Louis de Grenelle sparkling rosé wine.

PI

Pinky Ring

Kenny Belanger's 2013 aperitif at Kirkland Tap & Trotter that reminded him of the classic Chrysanthemum.

1 1/2 oz Pineau des Charentes
1 oz Dolin Dry Vermouth
1/2 oz Yellow Chartreuse
1 dash Regan's Orange Bitters
Stir with ice and strain into a cocktail coupe.

Pinwheel Swizzle

Dan Braganca crafted this complex Caribbean-inspired number in 2016 at Backbar.

1 1/2 oz Blackwell Jamaican Rum
3/4 oz Orgeat
3/4 oz Lime Juice
1/2 oz Campari
2 dash Fee's Peach Bitters
Build in a Collins glass, fill with crushed ice, and swizzle to mix and chill. Garnish with a rosemary sprig and a pinwheel straw (or a pinwheel and add a straw).

Pipe Dream

Sahil Mehta's mezcal Martinez-like creation at Estragon in 2013.

1 oz Del Maguey Mezcal Vida
1 oz Bonal Gentiane-Quina
1 oz Lustau Oloroso Sherry
1/4 oz Luxardo Maraschino
2 dash Regan's Orange Bitters
Stir with ice, strain into a cocktail coupe, and garnish with an orange twist.

Pirate's Revenge

The result of Vikram Hedge and Tom Schlesinger-Guidelli tinkering with St. Germain in 2013 at Island Creek Oyster Bar.

3/4 oz Sailor Jerry Spiced Rum
3/4 oz St. Germain
3/4 oz Pimm's No. 1
3/4 oz Lemon Juice
1 bsp Cinnamon Syrup
1 dash Bittermens Tiki Bitters
Shake with ice, strain into a cocktail coupe, and garnish with grated nutmeg.

ഗ്രജ്ഞാഗ്രജ്ഞാഗ്രജ്ഞാഗ്രജ്ഞാഗ്രജ്ഞാഗ്രജ്ഞാഗ്ര

Pizarro's Voyage

At Eastern Standard, Seth Freidus riffed on the classic Pisco Punch in 2013.

1 1/2 oz Macchu Pisco La Diablada
1/2 oz Plantation Barbados Rum
3/4 oz Lime Juice
1/2 oz Pineapple Juice
1/2 oz Grenadine
1/4 oz Vanilla Syrup
Shake with ice, strain into a Highball glass, fill with ice, garnish with a lime wedge and cherry, and add a straw.

Plateau Cocktail

A lighter, bitter herbal libation at Deep Ellum created in 2013.

1 oz Dry Gin
1 oz Lillet Rose
1/2 oz Meletti Amaro
1/2 oz Avèze Gentian Liqueur
2 dash Peychaud's Bitters
Stir with ice, strain into a rocks glass with a large ice cube, and garnish with an orange twist.

Plaza Vieja

Sam Treadway and Joe Cammarata at Backbar came up with this smoky, bitter riff of the Vieux Carré in 2013.

1 oz Pierre Ferrand 1840 Cognac
1 oz El Buho Mezcal
1 oz Amaro Braulio
1 bsp Benedictine
1 dash Angostura Bitters
1 pinch Salt
Stir with ice, strain into a rocks glass, and garnish with orange oil from a twist.

Pliny the Elder

Ran Duan crafted this herbal Negroni-like Julep in 2012 at Sichuan Garden II.

1 oz Genever
1 oz Punt e Mes
1 oz Campari
1/2 oz St. George Absinthe
1 cube Sugar
2 leaf Mint
Muddle the mint, sugar cube, and Campari in the bottom of a Julep cup. Add the rest of the ingredients, fill with crushed ice, and stir to mix and chill. Garnish with mint sprigs and add straws.

Poppin' Tags,
Russell House Tavern

Ploughman Poet

Stephen Shellenberger tweaked a Bobbie Burns recipe he crafted at Dante for the Pomodoro menu in 2012.

2 oz Great King Street Scotch
1 oz Vergano Americano
1 bsp Honey
Stir with ice and strain into a rocks glass.

Plymouth Street Harvest

Seth Corliss was inspired by the 1919 Cocktail formula to craft an autumnal tribute at Little Donkey in 2016.

3/4 oz Rittenhouse Rye
3/4 oz Laird's Bonded Apple
  Brandy
1 oz Punt e Mes
1/2 oz Lustau Pedro Ximenez
  Sherry
Stir with ice, strain into a rocks glass, and garnish with orange oil from a twist.

CB✿✿CB✿✿CB✿✿CB✿✿CB✿✿CB✿✿CB✿✿CB✿✿CB

Polymorphous Perversity

Created by Scott Holliday at Rendezvous in 2012 to make Freud proud.

2 oz Morin Selection Calvados
1/2 oz Yellow Chartreuse
1/2 oz Cocchi Americano
1 dash Angostura Orange Bitters
Stir with ice, strain into a cocktail glass, and garnish with lemon oil from a twist.

Poppin' Tags

Caleb Linton's easy drinking punch-like variation on the Negroni at Russell House Tavern in 2014. Not his choice of names, and certainly don't mention that he looks like Macklemore...

1 oz Beefeater Gin
1 oz Campari
1 oz Kronan Swedish Punsch
1 oz Orange Juice
Shake with ice and strain into a Collins glass containing 2 oz soda water. Top with ice, garnish with an orange twist, and add a straw.

Port of Call

Alden & Harlow's Tiki meets Autumn in a glass in 2014.

1 oz Daron Calvados
1 oz Plantation Barbados Rum
3/4 oz Sercial Madeira
1/4 oz Falernum
2 dash Peychaud's Bitters
Stir with ice and strain into a rocks glass.

(A) Postcard to Nina

Matt Schrage at Brick & Mortar named his complex libation in 2013 after a Jens Lekman song.

1 oz Meletti Amaro
1/2 oz Cinzano Sweet Vermouth
1/2 oz Aperol
1/2 oz Lime Juice
1/2 oz Pineapple Juice
2 dash Peychaud's Bitters
Shake with ice, strain into a Collins glass containing 2 oz soda water, fill with ice, and add a straw.

Power, Corruption, & Lies

Josh Childs 2014 tribute to New Order at Trina's Starlite Lounge.

1 1/2 oz Pierre Ferrand Ambre Cognac
3/4 oz Aperol
1/2 oz Velvet Falernum
1/2 oz Lime Juice
1 pinch Salt
Shake with ice and strain into a cocktail coupe.

ငဒၵၵၚၕၵၵၵၓၚၕၵၵၵၓၚၕၵၵၵၓၚၕၵၵၵၓၚၕၵၵၵၓၚၕၵၵၵ

Private Shandy

A great beer cocktail with flavors complementary to the hops' resiny and grapefruit notes; it was created in 2013 by Sam Gabrielli at Russell House Tavern.

1 1/2 oz Privateer Gin
3/4 oz Cinnamon Syrup
1/2 oz Pamplemousse Liqueur
1/2 oz Lemon Juice
Shake with ice, and strain into a beer tulip or Collins glass containing 3 oz of Blatant (or other West Coast-style) IPA, fill with ice, garnish with a grapefruit twist, and add a straw.

Proclaimer

Bobby McCoy's 2012 smoky Bee's Knees at Eastern Standard is worth walking 500 miles for.

3/4 oz Del Maguey Mezcal Vida
3/4 oz Drambuie 15 Year
3/4 oz Honey Syrup
3/4 oz Lemon Juice
1 dash Angostura Bitters
Shake with ice, strain into a cocktail glass, and garnish with lemon oil from a twist.

Prosecutor

Created by Josey Packard at Drink and named by Rachel Maddow, the Prosecutor started out as a Last Word variation that worked best as a non-equal parts recipe.

1 1/2 oz Old Overholt Rye
1/2 oz Yellow Chartreuse
1/2 oz St. Germain
1/2 oz Lemon Juice
Shake with ice and strain into a rocks glass.

Pua Lani

Misty Kalkofen originally created this drink with the 86 Co. Tequila Cabeza for the spirits line's launch party at Brick & Mortar in 2013 as the Sufrimiento de Simon in honor of Simon Ford; she later served this as a mezcal drink as the Pua Lani at Tales of the Cocktail's Drive Through Daquiri event held at New Orleans' Cane & Table in 2015.

2 oz Del Maguey Mezcal Vida
3/4 oz Plymouth Sloe Gin
1/2 oz Falernum
1/4 oz Galliano Ristretto
3/4 oz Pineapple Juice
1/2 oz Lemon Juice
Shake with ice, strain into a Collins glass, fill with crushed ice, and add a straw. Tiki-style garnishes such as a paper umbrella would not be out of place here.

Pugilist

Vikram Hedge's 2014 variation at Sarma of Nick Jarrett's Prize-fighter.

1 oz Cardamaro
1/2 oz Punt e Mes
1/2 oz Fernet Branca
1/2 oz Cardamom Syrup
6-8 leaf Mint
2 wedge Lemon
Muddle lemon wedges and mint, add the rest of ingredients, and shake with ice. Strain into a rocks glass, fill with crushed ice, garnish with mint sprigs, and add straws.

Purple Princess

No. 9 bartender Tyler Wang and Pavement barista Wolfie Barn teamed up to craft this cocktail at the Bartender-Barista Exchange competition held at Backbar in 2013.

1 1/2 oz Wireworks Aged Gin
1 1/2 oz El Puente Coffee (cooled)
3/4 oz Crème Yvette
1/2 oz Dolin Blanc Vermouth
1 dash Jerry Thomas Decanter Bitters
Stir with ice and strain into a cocktail coupe.

Queen's Slipper

Ran Duan crafted this rum funk-laden earthy sip at Sichuan Garden II in 2014.

1 oz Smith & Cross Rum
1 oz Carpano Sweet Vermouth
1/2 oz Nux Alpina Walnut Liqueur
1/2 oz Averna
Stir with ice, strain into a cocktail glass, and garnish with orange oil from a twist.

Quick & the Bitter

No. 9 Park's Tyler Wang created this Wild West tribute for one of the Blue Room's Whiskey & Amari nights in 2013.

3/4 oz Rittenhouse Rye
3/4 oz Carpano Antica Vermouth
3/4 oz Amaro S. Maria al Monte
1/2 oz Lemon Juice
1/4 oz Cinnamon Syrup
Shake with ice and strain into a cocktail coupe.

RA-RE

Rainy Dayz

Bar manager Patrick Dole created this complex rum libation at The Independent in 2014.

1 1/2 oz Old Monk Rum
3/4 oz Cardamaro
1/2 oz Honey Syrup
1/4 oz Lime Juice
2 dash Angostura Bitters
Shake with ice and strain into a cocktail coupe.

Razor Ramon

Ryan Connelly at Belly Wine Bar paid tribute in 2013 to his favorite professional wrestler via discovering how well coffee and Campari pair up.

1 3/4 oz Siete Leguas Reposado
   Tequila
3/4 oz Punt e Mes
1/2 oz Coffee Syrup (or Liqueur)
1/2 oz Campari
1 dash Mole Bitters
Stir with ice, strain into a cocktail glass, and garnish with flamed orange oil from a twist.

Real Fancy

One of Backbar's 2014 drink of the day offerings was a gussied up Julep with the 19th century "fancy" aspect of curaçao.

1 1/2 oz Pierre Ferrand Ambre
   Cognac
1 oz La Garrocha Amontillado
   Sherry
1/4 oz Pierre Ferrand Dry Curaçao
1/4 oz Raspberry Syrup
6-8 leaf Mint
Muddle the mint leaves in the bottom of a Julep cup, add the rest of the ingredients and crushed ice, and stir to mix and chill. Garnish with a strawberry, mint sprigs, and a lemon twist, and add straws.

Red Dragon

Fred Yarm was inspired by the Dame en Rouge at the Baldwin Bar and by his Safety Dance at Loyal Nine to create this low octane delight in 2016.

2 oz Cinzano Sweet Vermouth
1/2 oz Chai Tea Syrup
1/2 oz Lime Juice
2 dash Peychaud's Bitters
Shake with ice, strain into a cocktail coupe containing 1 oz soda water, and garnish with a floated lemon twist.

Red Duster Swizzle

Matt Schrage's 2014 Negroni-inspired tribute at Brick & Mortar to the flag of the Royal British Merchant Navy.

1 oz Plymouth Navy Strength Gin
1 oz Malmsey Madeira
3/4 oz Lime Juice
1/2 oz Velvet Falernum
1/2 oz Campari
Build in a Collins glass, fill with crushed ice, swizzle to mix and chill, garnish with 2 dashes Angostura Bitters, and add a straw.

Red Dwarf

At Rendezvous, Scott Holiday took the essences of the Cocktail à la Louisiane, Sazerac, and Boulevardier in 2013 and constructed this New Orleans-inspired libation.

2 oz Rye
1 oz Campari
1/2 bsp Henri Bardouin Pastis
2 dash Peychaud's Bitters
Stir with ice, strain into a cocktail glass, and garnish with orange oil from a twist.

Real Fancy,
Backbar

Red Line Book Club

Todd Maul in 2012 tinkered around with his Dwight Street Book Club at Clio.

1 1/2 oz El Dorado 3 Year Rum
3/4 oz El Maestro Sierra
  Amontillado Sherry
3/4 oz Lime Juice
1/2 oz Carpano Sweet Vermouth
1/2 oz Cinnamon Syrup
Shake with ice, strain into a cocktail glass, and garnish with a lime twist.

Red Maple Swizzle

The Hawthorne demonstrated in 2012 that not every Swizzle needs to be tropical in theme.

2 oz Smith & Cross Rum
1 oz Lemon Juice
1 oz Maple Syrup
2 dash Peychaud's Bitters
Build in a Collins glass, fill with crushed ice, swizzle to mix and chill, and add a straw.

Red Nose

Adam Hockman's 2013 Last Word variation created at Russell House Tavern.

1 oz Beefeater Gin
1 oz Lemon Juice
1 oz Luxardo Maraschino
1 oz Jelinek Fernet
1 dash Peychaud's Bitters
Shake with ice, strain into a cocktail glass, and garnish with a cherry.

Red Right Hook

Boston cocktail enthusiast Eric Witz created this mashup of the Manhattan variation the Red Hook with the Rum Negroni variation the Right Hand in 2013.

1 oz Rittenhouse Rye
1 oz Scarlet Ibis Rum
3/4 oz Cocchi Sweet Vermouth
1/4 oz Luxardo Maraschino
1/4 oz Campari
2 dash Chocolate Bitters
Stir with ice, strain into a cocktail glass, and garnish with an orange twist.

Remedios Varo

One of Sahil Mehta's 2015 drink of the day offerings at Estragon.

1 oz Del Maguey Mezcal Vida
3/4 oz Palo Cortado Sherry
3/4 oz Amaro Ramazzotti
1/2 oz Ancho Reyes Chile Liqueur
1 dash Regan's Orange Bitters
1 dash Scrappy's Chocolate Bitters
Stir with ice, strain into a cocktail glass, and garnish with an orange twist.

René Barbier

At Gary Regan's Cocktails in the Country 2015, Fred Yarm was inspired by the Lucien Gaudin and Phil Ward's Cornwall Negroni – the latter of which was created a decade before at that same retreat.

1 oz Camus VS Cognac
1 oz Punt e Mes
1/2 oz Pierre Ferrand Dry Curaçao
1/2 oz Campari
2 dash Jerry Thomas Decanter Bitters
Stir with ice, strain into a cocktail glass, and garnish with lemon oil from a twist.

Revision #3

A richly flavored Manhattan variation from Ran Duan at the Baldwin Bar at Sichuan Garden II circa 2014.

1 1/2 oz Rittenhouse Rye
1/2 oz Nux Alpina Walnut Liqueur
1/2 oz Zucca Rabarbaro Amaro
1/2 oz Byrrh Quinquina
Stir with ice, strain into a cocktail glass, and garnish with a cherry.

Rhum Agricot

A delightful tropical number crafted by John Gertsen at Drink in 2008.

1 1/2 oz JM Rhum Agricole Blanc
3/4 oz Boissiere Dry Vermouth
3/4 oz Rothman & Winter Apricot Liqueur
Stir with ice, strain into a cocktail glass, and garnish with a mint leaf.

River Queen

An adaptation of Alex Homan's 2015 Pimm's Cup variation that utilized a cucumber-infused Pimm's at The Frogmore.

1 1/2 oz Pimm's No. 1
1/2 oz Ginger Syrup
1/2 oz Campari
1/2 oz Lemon Juice
3 slice Cucumber
Muddle 3 slices of cucumber in the ginger syrup, add the rest of the ingredients, shake with ice, and strain into a Collins glass containing 2 oz soda water. Fill with ice and add a straw.

Riviera di Ponente

Part of Ryan Lotz's Italian Tiki series at No. 9 Park; this one was the first that he got on the menu in 2015.

1 1/2 oz Plantation Barbados Rum
1/2 oz Lemon Hart 151 Rum
1/2 oz Amaro Ramazzotti
1/2 oz St. Elder Elderflower
  Liqueur
1/2 oz Cinnamon Syrup
1/2 oz Lime Juice
6 drop Absinthe
2 dash Angostura Bitters
Shake with ice, strain into a tulip glass, and fill with crushed ice. Garnish with a paper umbrella, cherry, lime wheel, and mint sprigs, and add straws.

Roger That, Estragon

Roberta Roy

Thomas Tietjen crafted his take on the Rob Roy at Trina's Starlite Lounge in 2012.

2 oz Cutty Sark Scotch
3/4 oz Noilly Prat Dry Vermouth
1/2 oz Luxardo Maraschino
Stir with ice, strain into a cocktail glass, and garnish with a cherry.

Rock Beats Scissors

Ran Duan crossed a Brooklyn with a Bensonhurst in 2016 to win the battle of the trio.

2 oz Old Overholt Rye
1/2 oz Cynar
1/2 oz Bigallet China China
2 dash Angostura Bitters
Stir with ice, strain into a cocktail glass, and garnish with a cherry.

Roger That

Sahil Mehta created this whiskey Aviation riff for Roger, one of his regulars at Estragon, in 2015.

1 1/2 oz The Knot Irish Whiskey
1 oz Lustau Amontillado Sherry
1/2 oz Punt e Mes
1/4 oz Rothman & Winter Crème de Violette
1/4 oz Lemon Juice
Shake with ice, strain into a single Old Fashioned glass, and garnish with 2 dashes Barkeep's Lavender Bitters.

Rome with a Slight View

At Sichuan Garden II in 2013, Ran Duan riffed on Michael McIlroy's Rome with a View from Milk & Honey.

1 oz Kina L'Avion d'Or
1 oz Aperol
1 oz Lime Juice
1/2 oz Passion Fruit Syrup
Shake with ice, strain into a Collins glass containing 2 oz soda water, fill with ice, garnish with a grapefruit twist, and add a straw.

Rooftop Cooler

A light session libation crafted at Brick & Mortar for Summer 2013.

2 oz Dolin Dry Vermouth
1 oz Lime Juice
1/2 oz Simple Syrup
2 dash Peychaud's Bitters
Shake with ice, strain into a Collins glass containing 2 oz ginger ale, fill with ice, and add a straw.

Root and the Flower

Sahil Mehta crafted this libation at Estragon for Misty Kalkofen of Del Maguey Mezcal in 2014.

1 1/2 oz Del Maguey Mezcal Vida
1 oz Avèze Gentian Liqueur
1/2 oz St. Germain
1 dash Absinthe
Stir with ice, strain into a cocktail glass, and garnish with a lemon twist.

Root of All Evil

Jeff Grdinich's riff on Chuck Taggart's Hoskins Cocktail for a Grand Marnier event at Drink in 2009. Jeff was at the White Mountain Cider Company at the time before he started working at Drink.

2 oz Eagle Rare Bourbon
3/4 oz Grand Marnier
1/2 oz Fernet Branca
1/2 oz Luxardo Maraschino
2 dash Regan's Orange Bitters
Stir with ice and strain into a cocktail glass.

Royal Cadiz Yacht Club

Palmer Matthews at Drink concocted a sherry riff in 2013 on the classic Royal Bermuda Yacht Club.

1 3/4 oz Lustau Palo Cortado Sherry
3/4 oz Lime Juice
1/4 oz Pierre Ferrand Dry Curaçao
1/4 oz Falernum
Shake with ice and strain into a cocktail glass.

Royal Flush

In 2013, Ran Duan riffed on the Appetizer l'Italienne at Sichuan Garden II.

2 oz Carpano Sweet Vermouth
3/4 oz Crème de Cacao
3/4 oz Fernet Branca
1/2 oz St. George Absinthe
Stir with ice, strain into a cocktail glass, and garnish with a cherry.

Royal Jubilee

Bergamot's tribute in 2012 to Queen Elizabeth's 60th anniversary on England's throne.

1/2 oz Apple Brandy
1/2 oz Becherovka
1/2 oz Grenadine
1/2 oz Lemon Juice
3 dash Peychaud's Bitters
Shake with ice and strain into a flute glass containing 2 1/2 oz dry sparkling wine.

Rubberband Man

An adaptation of Shaher Misif's circa 2013 tribute to The Spinners at the Highball Lounge.

1 oz Caña Brava Rum
1 oz Pierre Ferrand Cognac
3/4 oz Cardamaro
1/4 oz Benedictine
1 dash Angostura Bitters
Stir with ice, strain into a rocks glass with a large ice cube, and garnish with a cherry and flamed orange oil from a twist.

Rue Morgue

John Henderson paid tribute in 2013 to an Iron Maiden song with this Chancellor-like drink at Tavern Road.

2 oz Old Pulteney Scotch
3/4 oz Ruby Port
1/2 oz Benedictine
1/4 oz Crème de Cacao
Stir with ice and strain into a cocktail coupe.

Rugg Road

Jace Sheehan served up his Swizzle tribute to his motorcycle repair shop at Tavern Road's inaugural Tiki Tuesday in 2017.

1 1/2 oz Privateer Amber Rum
3/4 oz Lime Juice
1/2 oz Falernum
1/4 oz Honey Syrup
2 dash Herbsaint
Build in a tulip glass, fill with crushed ice, and swizzle to mix and chill. Garnish with a mint sprig and add a straw.

Rumble Bee

Nika Orlovsky's 2016 creation at the Baldwin Bar at Sichuan Garden II that appears to expand on Trader Vic's Arawak.

1 oz El Dorado 12 Year Rum
1 oz Old Monk Rum
1/2 oz Amontillado Sherry
1/2 oz Pedro Ximenez Sherry
2 dash Fee's Whiskey Barrel Bitters
Stir with ice, strain into a double Old Fashioned glass, fill with ice, and garnish with lemon oil from a twist.

Rum Fizz Tropical

Ran Duan's 2015 cross of a Ramos Gin Fizz and a Painkiller at the Baldwin Room at Sichuan Garden II.

1 1/2 oz Old Monk Rum
1 oz Coconut Cream
1 oz Pineapple Juice
3/4 oz Lime Juice
1 1/2 oz Heavy Cream
1 Egg White
Shake once without ice and once with ice, strain into a Collins glass containing 2 oz soda water, garnish with an edible orchid (if available) and freshly grated nutmeg, and add a straw.

Rusty Cadillac

A Flip that Ryan Lotz created at the Hawthorne and later served at a guest shift at No. 9 Park in 2012.

1 1/2 oz Barbancourt 8 Year Rhum
1/2 oz Galliano l'Autentico
1/2 oz Crème de Cacao
1/2 oz Angostura Bitters
1 Whole Egg
Shake once without ice and once with ice, strain into a rocks glass, and garnish with a few drops of Angostura Bitters.

Rusty Shakleford

At the Hawthorne, Scott Marshall combined his love of Chartreuse and blender drinks in 2012 and named it after his alias that he borrowed from King of the Hill.

1 3/4 oz Ron Matusalem Platino Rum
1 1/4 oz Green Chartreuse
1 oz White Crème de Cacao
3/4 oz Coconut Cream
Blend with 6 oz ice for 10 seconds, pour into a water goblet, and add a straw. Optional: garnish with cocktail monkeys or other plastic ornaments.

Rye Rising

Ted Gallagher's brunch cocktail at Steel & Rye in 2012 also makes for an elegant dessert one as well.

1 oz Old Overholt Rye
1 oz Galliano Ristretto
1/2 oz Boston Bual Madeira
1/2 oz Simple Syrup
1 dash Mole Bitters
1 Egg
Shake once without ice and once with ice, strain into a rocks glass, and garnish with freshly grated coffee bean.

Saber & Foil,
Spoke Wine Bar

Saber & Foil

*At Spoke Wine Bar in 2013,
California Gold was influenced by
Scott Holiday's Defensio, a rhum
agricole variation of the Lucien
Gaudin Cocktail.*

1 oz Neisson Rhum Agricole Blanc
1 oz Dolin Dry Vermouth
1/2 oz Gran Classico
1/2 oz Lustau Amontillado Sherry
*Stir with ice, strain into a cocktail
glass, and garnish with grapefruit
oil from a twist.*

Sacré Coeur

*Sahil Mehta at Estragon found a
middle ground in 2015 of a
Brandy Manhattan and a
Champs-Élysées riff using all
French ingredients.*

1 1/2 oz Cerbois VSOP Armagnac
1 oz Dry Vermouth
1/2 oz Benedictine
1 bsp Green Chartreuse
*Stir with ice, strain into a cocktail
coupe, and garnish with lemon oil
from a twist.*

SA

Sad Waltz of Pietro Crespi

Sean Sullivan's 2015 tribute at Straight Law to the tragic love triangle in One Hundred Years of Solitude.

1 1/4 oz Lustau Brandy
3/4 oz Zucca Rabarbaro Amaro
1/2 oz Punt e Mes
1/2 oz Pedro Ximenez Sherry
5 drop Sherry Vinegar
Stir with ice, strain into a double Old Fashioned glass with a large ice cube, and garnish the ice cube with a pinch of salt.

Safety Dance

Fred Yarm crafted this low proof number in 2015 for Loyal Nine's Yacht Rock Sundays that got subtitled "So You Can Dance Later."

1 oz Dolin Blanc Vermouth
1 oz Dolin Dry Vermouth
1/2 oz Blossom Oolong Tea Syrup
1/2 oz Lemon Juice
2 dash Peychaud's Bitters
Shake with ice, strain into a cocktail coupe containing 1 oz soda water, and garnish with a floated lemon twist. Note: Blossom oolong is a hibiscus-black tea blend.

Sagarno Scaffa

Sahil Mehta paid tribute in 2014 to the long history of Basque cider making with this room temperature number at Estragon.

1 oz Daron Calvados
1 oz Amontillado Sherry
3/4 oz Strega
1/4 oz Domaine de Canton Ginger Liqueur
Build in a rocks glass, briefly stir to mix <u>without</u> ice, and garnish with lemon oil from a twist. Note: This is a room temperature cocktail.

Sailor's Delight
(Backbar)

At Backbar in 2016, Dan Braganca riffed on the classic Fog Cutter and added a sunrise effect with Cherry Heering that settles down like the liqueur in a Bramble.

3/4 oz Laird's Applejack
3/4 oz Beefeater Gin
1/2 oz Orange Juice
1/2 oz Lemon Juice
1/4 oz Lustau Amontillado Sherry
1/4 oz Orgeat
1 dash Angostura Bitters
Shake with ice, strain into a Collins glass, fill with crushed ice, "float" 1/4 oz Cherry Heering, garnish with a paper parasol and a cherry, and add a straw.

Sailor's Delight
(No. 9 Park)

At No. 9 Park, Tyler Wang riffed in 2012 on the classic Widow's Kiss.

1 oz Laird's Bonded Apple Brandy
1 oz Del Maguey Mezcal Vida
3/4 oz Benedictine
3/4 oz Yellow Chartreuse
1 dash Angostura Bitters
Stir with ice, strain into a cocktail glass, and garnish with lemon oil from a twist.

Saint Bernard's Pass

Drink's Jan Andrew Brown did a guest bartending shift at the Hawthorne in 2015, and he named his drink after the Alpine pass that connects Switzerland and Italy not too far from where Braulio is made.

1 1/2 oz Pierre Ferrand 1840 Cognac
1 1/2 oz Amaro Braulio
1 dash Angostura Bitters
1 dash Angostura Orange Bitters
Stir with ice, strain into a rocks glass with a large ice cube, and garnish with orange oil from a twist.

Sainted Devil

Fred Yarm's 2012 Blood & Sand variation named after another one of Rudolph Valentino's films.

3/4 oz Blanco Tequila or Mezcal
3/4 oz Cherry Heering
3/4 oz Fernet Branca
3/4 oz Orange Juice
Shake with ice and strain into a cocktail glass.

Salt & Stone

In 2014, Tyler Wang at Kirkland Tap & Trotter mellowed this Fancuilli-like cocktail into an Inverse Manhattan-like drink with a pinch of salt.

1 3/4 oz Cinzano Sweet Vermouth
1 oz McKenna Bourbon
1/4 oz Amaro Braulio
1 pinch Salt
Stir with ice and strain into a rocks glass.

Santiago Squall,
Ames Street Deli

Sandpiper

*The Franklin Southie's 2013
coffee-flavored riff on a classic
Painkiller.*

2 oz Zaya 12 Year Rum
1/2 oz Luxardo Espresso Liqueur
2 oz Pineapple Juice
1/2 oz Coconut Cream
*Shake with ice, strain into a Collins
glass, fill with ice, and add a straw.*

Sanlucar Sling

*Sahil Mehta's entry to the Heering
Sling competition in 2015 that he
crafted at Estragon.*

2 oz Lustau Amontillado Sherry
1 oz Cherry Heering
1/2 oz Nocino Walnut Liqueur
1/2 oz Lemon Juice
*Shake with ice, strain into a Collins
glass, and fill with ice. Garnish with
a lemon twist, 2 dashes Fee's
Walnut Bitters, and 1 dash
Angostura Bitters, and add a straw.*

Santa Rosa
(Audubon)

One of the offerings at the 2016 Tequila Interchange Project charity night at Audubon; sub Campari, Aperol, or a mix of the two for the Contratto.

1 1/2 oz The 86 Co. Tequila Cabeza
1/2 oz Lemon Juice
1/2 oz Combier Crème de Peche
1/4 oz Contratto Bitter
1/4 oz Agave Syrup
Shake with ice and strain into a cocktail coupe.

Santa Rosa
(Estragon)

At Estragon, Sahil Mehta was intrigued by the flavors in Mexican molé sauce and named this 2015 recipe after the convent where the sauce is believed to have been invented.

1 1/2 oz Mezcal
1/2 oz Ancho Reyes Chile Liqueur
1/4 oz Crème de Cacao
1/4 oz Angostura Bitters
Stir with ice, strain into a single Old Fashioned glass, and garnish with orange oil from a twist.

Santiago Squall

Ames Street Deli in 2016 crossed an Old Cuban with a Dark and Stormy.

2 oz Aged Rum
1/2 oz Lime Juice
1/2 oz Demerara Syrup
6 leaf Mint
Shake with ice, strain into a Collins glass containing 1 1/2 oz Gosling's Ginger Beer, fill with crushed ice, garnish with 2 dashes Angostura Bitters and a mint sprig, and add a straw.

Sargasso Sea

Matt Schrage crafted this dark, grassy Tiki-like drink at Brick & Mortar in 2014.

1 oz Cruzan Black Strap Rum
3/4 oz Cynar
3/4 oz Pineapple Juice
1/2 oz Lime Juice
1/2 oz Raspberry Liqueur or Syrup
Shake with ice, strain into a Collins glass containing 2 oz soda water, fill with ice, and add a straw.

Sass Mouth

A vodka drink created by Andrew Keefe at Kirkland Tap & Trotter circa 2014 that works really well with gin.

1 1/2 oz Vodka or Beefeater Gin
1/2 oz Rothman & Winter Apricot Liqueur
1/2 oz Aperol
1/2 oz Lemon Juice
1 bsp St. Elizbeth Allspice Dram
Shake with ice, strain into a rocks glass, fill with crushed ice, garnish with 2-3 dashes Peychaud's Bitters, and add straws.

Savannah Unknown

An adaptation of a 2012 Craigie on Main drink that originally called for a grapefruit cordial.

1 1/2 oz Appleton Rum
1/2 oz Averna
1/2 oz Punt e Mes
1/2 oz Grapefruit Juice
1 dash Bittermens Grapefruit Bitters
Stir with ice, strain into a cocktail coupe, and garnish with a grapefruit twist.

Sawbuck

A rich, spiced beer cocktail at Kirkland Tap & Trotter circa 2014.

1 oz Rittenhouse Rye
1/2 oz Cinnamon Syrup
1/2 oz Lemon Juice
1/4 oz Nux Alpina Walnut Liqueur
Shake with ice, strain into a tulip glass containing 3 oz Sierra Nevada Ruthless Rye IPA, fill with ice, and add straws.

Sazerac Toddy

John McElroy transformed his favorite chilled drink into a Hot Toddy at Russell House Tavern in 2012.

3 oz Old Overholt Rye
1/2 oz Simple Syrup
7 dash Peychaud's Bitters
Build in a pre-heated Irish coffee mug, fill with boiling water (~4-5 oz) leaving some space at the top, and stir to mix. Top with ~1 oz Herbsaint whipped cream and garnish with a lemon twist. Prepare the Herbsaint whipped cream in advance by mixing 2 1/2 oz heavy cream, 1 oz Herbsaint, and 1/2 oz simple syrup and either shaking with a balled up spring from a Hawthorne strainer until stiff or aerating in an iSi charger with nitrous.

Scarecrow

At Backbar in 2015, Sam Treadway crafted this inverse Manhattan variation for a bartender at Rhode Island's Dorrance, and Sam dubbed it after that bartender's nickname.

1 1/2 oz Amaro Montenegro
1 1/4 oz Four Roses Bourbon
1/4 oz Fernet Branca
1 dash Orange Bitters
Stir with ice, strain into a cocktail coupe, and garnish with orange oil from a twist.

Scarlet Letter

Scholars pays tribute in 2012 to Nathaniel Hawthorne with this deep red drink.

1 1/2 oz Bacardi 8 Year Rum
1/2 oz Pimm's No. 1
3/4 oz Drambuie
1/4 oz Balsamic Vinegar
1 dash Bittermens Mole Bitters
Stir with ice, strain into a cocktail glass, and garnish with a lemon twist.

Schiphol

Sahil Mehta was inspired by Sam Ross' Paper Plane and crafted a Dutch-inspired riff in 2011.

3/4 oz Bols Barrel-Aged Genever
3/4 oz Amaro Montenegro
3/4 oz Aperol
3/4 oz Lemon Juice
Shake with ice and strain into a cocktail glass.

Search for the Cure

At Drink, Will Thompson riffed on the Cure's Search for Deliciousness from Beta Cocktails in 2013.

1 oz Zucca Rabarbaro Amaro
1/2 oz Dolin Blanc Vermouth
1/2 oz Palo Cortado Sherry
3/4 oz Punt e Mes
1 bsp Lemon Juice
1 bsp Grenadine
3 dash Orange Bitters
Stir with ice, strain into rocks glass partially rimmed with salt and containing a large ice cube, garnish with lemon oil from 6 twists, and include one twist in the drink.

Seaward

An adaptation of Jared Sadoian's 2014 nautical-themed drink at Kirkland Tap & Trotter.

1 1/2 oz Appleton V/X Rum
1/2 oz Privateer Silver Rum
3/4 oz Amaro Montenegro
1/4 oz Luxardo Maraschino
2 large swath Lemon Peel
2 dash Regan's Orange Bitters
Express oil from lemon peels into mixing glass, add the peels and the rest of the ingredients, stir with ice, and strain into a cocktail coupe.

Sebastian

Sahil Mehta created this one night at Estragon in 2014 for one of his regulars.

1 1/2 oz Palo Cortado Sherry
1/2 oz Xicaru Mezcal
1/2 oz Zucca Rabarbaro Amaro
1/2 oz Drambuie
Stir with ice, strain into a cocktail coupe, and garnish with 2 drops of Regan's Orange Bitters.

Second Wife

At Local 149, be careful asking for this around your spouse; crafted circa 2012-2013.

1 1/2 oz Power's Irish Whiskey
1 oz Carpano Sweet Vermouth
3/4 oz Suze Gentian Liqueur
Stir with ice and strain into a cocktail glass.

Secret Weapon

California Gold's 2013 floral pisco variation on the French 75 at Spoke Wine Bar.

1 oz Macchu Pisco
1/2 oz Lavender Syrup
1/2 oz Lemon Juice
Shake with ice, strain into a cocktail coupe containing 1 oz Dibon Cava, and garnish with a lemon twist.

Señor Elmo's Fire

A cocktail created at Scholars in Boston in 2012 that was subtitled, "smoke not fire, with a taste of Fall spices."

1 1/2 oz Del Maguey Mezcal Vida
1/2 oz St. Elizabeth Allspice Dram
1/2 oz Luxardo Maraschino
1/2 oz Lemon Juice
Shake with ice and strain into a cocktail glass.

Señor Mucho Pronto

At Brick & Mortar, Rob Hoover's 2016 menu item came across like a blend of an agave Toronto and an Oaxacan Old Fashioned.

1 oz Tequila Ocho Reposado
1 oz Del Maguey Mezcal Vida
1/2 oz Cinnamon Syrup
1/2 oz Amaro S. Maria al Monte
1 dash Regan's Orange Bitters
1 dash Angostura Bitters
1 dash Bittermens Mole Bitters
Stir with ice, strain into a double Old Fashioned glass, fill with ice, garnish with an orange twist, and add straws.

Search for the Cure, Drink

SH

Shadows & Tall Trees

At Russell House Tavern in 2013, Fred Yarm made this for a guest wanting Fall in a glass when their request for the Wigglesworth was denied since the bar stopped preparing cinnamon cider syrup.

2 oz Four Roses Bourbon
1 oz Cocchi Sweet Vermouth
1/2 oz Cynar
1/4 oz Nocino Walnut Liqueur
1/4 oz Cinnamon Syrup
1 dash Angostura Bitters
Stir with ice, strain into a double Old Fashioned glass, fill with ice cubes, garnish with an orange twist, and add straws.

Shepherd's Secret

A complex bitter herbal Scotch drink crafted by John Drew at Blue Dragon in 2013.

1 1/2 oz Sheep Dip Scotch
3/4 oz Luxardo Amaro Abano
3/4 oz Punt e Mes
1 bsp Green Chartreuse
Stir with ice, strain into a rocks glass, and garnish with an orange twist.

Sherry Colada

The Baldwin Room at Sichuan Garden II added their own creation to the tapestry of sherry Tiki in 2015. Other blends of dry sherries would probably work well here too.

1 1/2 oz Palo Cortado Sherry
3/4 oz Manzanilla Sherry
1/4 oz Amontillado Sherry
3/4 oz Pineapple Juice
1 oz Coconut Cream
3/4 oz Lemon Juice
Shake with ice, strain into a Collins glass, fill with crushed ice, garnish with two cherries on a pick, and add a straw.

Sherry Jungle Bird

Will Thompson crafted this Tiki variation at Drink in response to a 2013 discussion about the Sherry Mai Tai.

1 1/2 oz Lustau Palo Cortado
  Sherry
2 1/2 oz Pineapple Juice
3/4 oz Lime Juice
3/4 oz Campari
1/2 oz Simple Syrup
Shake with ice, strain into a large glass, fill with crushed ice, garnish with a mint sprig, an orange twist, and a cherry, and add a straw.

❧❦❧❦❧❦❧❦❧❦❧❦❧❦❧❦❧❦❧❦

Sherry Mai Tai

Influenced by Belly's sherry-centric cocktail menu, Fred Yarm crafted this Mai Tai variation in 2013. Subbing 2 oz of a medium-dry cream sherry such as Lustau East India Solera for the two sherries might work here.

1 1/2 oz Amontillado Sherry
1/2 oz Pedro Ximenez Sherry
1 oz Lemon Juice
1/2 oz Orgeat
1/2 oz Curaçao
Shake with ice, strain into a rocks glass, fill with crushed ice, garnish with mint sprigs, and add straws.

Sherry Painkiller

No. 9 Park's 2015 fortified wine take on the classic Tiki libation.

1 oz Lustau Amontillado Sherry
1/2 oz Lustau East India Sherry
1/2 oz Lemon Hart 151 Rum
1 oz Pineapple Juice
1 oz Orange Juice
1 oz Coconut Cream
Shake with ice, strain into a snifter glass, fill with crushed ice, float 1/4 oz Hamilton's Black Strap Rum, garnish with freshly grated nutmeg and a paper parasol, and add straws.

Shining on the Sea

Fred Yarm created this recipe inspired by the West Indies Punch for Loyal Nine's The Walrus and The Carpenter party in 2015.

2 oz Privateer Silver Rum
1/2 oz Green Tea Syrup
1/2 oz Lime Juice
1 heaping bsp Guava Paste
Shake without ice to integrate the guava paste, add ice and shake again, strain into a cocktail glass, and garnish with a sun-shaped orange twist. Melting the guava (especially if it is heavily pectinized) in an equal part hot water allows for better integration; in which case, double the volume to 1/4 oz.

ᘓᘔᘖᘕᘓᘔᘖᘕᘓᘔᘖᘕᘓᘔᘖᘕᘓᘔᘖᘕᘓᘔᘖᘕᘓ

Shipwrecked in Paradise

At Stoddard's, Tony Iamunno crafted this Tiki number in 2016 that reminded me of a mid-century Zombie recipe.

1 oz Cruzan Dark Rum
1 oz Cruzan Light Rum
3/4 oz Apricot Liqueur
1/2 oz Dry Curaçao
1/2 oz Orgeat
3/4 oz Lime Juice
1 oz Pineapple Juice
Shake with ice, strain into a Collins glass or Tiki mug, fill with crushed ice, garnish with 3-4 dashes Angostura Bitters, and add a straw.

Shirley Temple Black

Silvertone's 2012 adult take on the classic children's mocktail originally created in the 1930s.

2 oz Old Overholt Rye
1/2 oz Maurin Quina
1/2 oz Ginger Syrup
1 dash Lemon Juice
Shake with ice, strain into a Collins glass containing 2 oz Barritts Ginger Beer, fill with ice, garnish a cherry, and add a straw.

Sid & Nancy,
Eastern Standard

Shot in the Dark

A beer cocktail crafted at Deep Ellum in Allston circa 2012.

1 1/2 oz Lustau East India Sherry
1/2 oz Cognac
10 oz O'Hara's Irish Stout
Build in a Highball glass, top with the stout, and garnish with freshly grated nutmeg.

Sid & Nancy

Bobby McCoy's hot punk rock tribute at Eastern Standard for Winter 2012-2013.

3/4 oz Plantation Barbados Rum
3/4 oz Pierre Ferrand 1840 Cognac
3/4 oz Spiced Syrup
Build in a preheated coffee mug, top with 4 oz steamed Half & Half, and garnish with grated nutmeg.

Silent X

Jordan Runion's smoky Sherry Cobbler on The Automatic's opening 2016 menu.

1 1/2 oz Lustau Amontillado Sherry
3/4 oz Del Maguey Mezcal Vida
1/2 oz Cinnamon Syrup
1/4 oz Agave Syrup
1/2 oz Lemon Juice
1/4 oz Lime Juice
Shake with ice, strain into a Collins glass, fill with crushed ice, garnish with 7 dashes Regan's Orange Bitters and an orange twist, and add a straw.

Sin Agua

Tyler Wang's worked some room temperature magic in 2012 at No. 9 Park.

1 1/2 oz Milagro Blanco Tequila
1 oz La Gitana Manzanilla Sherry
1/2 oz Velvet Falernum
Briefly stir without ice and pour into a rocks glass pre-rinsed with 3 flamed spritzes of Angostura Bitters. Note: This is a room temperature cocktail.

Sinister Street

Rob Ficks created this 2015 Bobby Burns variation at Craigie on Main.

1 1/2 oz Grant's Scotch
3/4 oz Bonal Gentiane-Quina
1/2 oz Amaro Nonino
1/4 oz Benedictine
Stir with ice, strain into a cocktail coupe, and garnish with 2 spritzes Angostura Bitters.

Sinking Ship Swizzle

Fred Yarm merged the idea of a rhum agricole Corpse Reviver #2 with a Royal Bermuda Yacht Club in 2016 at Loyal Nine.

1 oz JM Rhum Agricole Blanc
1 oz Lillet Blanc
1/2 oz Creole Shrubb Orange Liqueur
1/2 oz Velvet Falernum
1/2 oz Lime Juice
10 drop St. George Absinthe
Build in a Collins glass, fill with crushed ice, swizzle to mix and chill, garnish with 3-4 dashes Peychaud's Bitters and a floated pirate ship made out of citrus peels and toothpicks, and add a straw.

Sinnerman

An herbal and spiced aperitif at West Bridge crafted by Mike Fleming in 2014.

2 oz Cocchi Sweet Vermouth
1/2 oz Suze Gentian Liqueur
1/2 oz St. Elizabeth Allspice Dram
Stir with ice, strain into a rocks glass, fill with ice, garnish with an orange twist, and add straws.

Sinnerman Swizzle

Fred Yarm was impressed by the flavor profiles in Mike Fleming's Sinnerman and applied the Death & Co. Swizzle formula to the combination at Russell House Tavern in 2014.

1 oz Bombay Dry Gin
1 oz Cocchi Sweet Vermouth
1/2 oz Suze Gentian Liqueur
1/2 oz St. Elizabeth Allspice Dram
3/4 oz Lemon Juice
Build in a Collins glass, fill with crushed ice, swizzle to mix and chill, garnish with 3-4 dashes Angostura Bitters and mint sprigs, and add a straw.

Skeptic and the Believer

Kat Lamper at Backbar was inspired to create this drink as she caught up on old X-Files shows in 2016 before the new season came out.

1 oz Olmeca Altos Tequila
1/2 oz El Buho Mezcal
1/2 oz Pierre Ferrand Dry Curaçao
1/2 oz Green Chartreuse
1/2 oz Lime Juice
1 dash Bittermens Boston Bittahs
Shake with ice and strain into a cocktail glass.

Sky's the Limit

Jared Sadoian crafted this spiced sherry drink for Kirkland Tap & Trotter's Winter 2014-2015 menu.

1 oz Hochstadter's Rock & Rye
1 oz Lustau Amontillado Sherry
1/2 oz Cinnamon Syrup
1/2 oz Lemon Juice
Shake with ice, strain into a rocks glass, fill with ice, garnish with an orange twist, and add straws.

Sling & Arrow

Ran Duan's created this fruit and bitter Bourbon Sling at Sichuan Garden II in 2012; he later switched the whiskey to Four Roses Bourbon and renamed it the Offshore Account for the 2014 menu.

1 oz Larceny Bourbon
1/2 oz Gran Classico
1/2 oz Cherry Heering
1 oz Pineapple Juice
1/2 oz Lemon Juice
Shake with ice, strain into a Collins glass, fill with ice, garnish with a mint sprig, 2 dashes Angostura Bitters, and a cherry, and add a straw.

Sloe Ryed

After a regular requested a drink at No. 9 Park with this name, Tyler Wang crafted this sloe gin and rye whiskey number in 2013.

1 1/2 oz Rittenhouse Rye
1 oz Plymouth Sloe Gin
3/4 oz Dolin Dry Vermouth
1/4+ oz Apricot Liqueur
7 leaf Mint
Stir with ice and strain into a cocktail glass.

Slow Dance with Pedro Infante

Misty Kalkofen at Brick & Mortar paid tribute in 2013 to one of the most famous actors and singers of the Golden Age of Mexican cinema.

1 3/4 oz Del Maguey Crema de Mezcal
3/4 oz Gran Classico
1/2 oz Averna
Stir with ice and strain into a rocks glass. Substitute a 9 part mezcal to 1 part agave nectar blend for the crema de mezcal.

Slurred Word

One of the variations on Trina's Starlite Lounge's Last Word section of their menu back in 2012.

1 oz Smith & Cross Rum
1/2 oz Green Chartreuse
1/2 oz Maraschino Liqueur
1/2 oz Lime Juice
1 oz Pineapple Juice
Shake with ice and strain into a single Old Fashioned glass.

Smoke & Mirrors

A smoky and fruity down drink at the Citizen Public House circa 2015.

1 1/2 oz Del Maguey Mezcal Vida
1/2 oz Oloroso Sherry
1/2 oz Rothman & Winter Apricot
 Liqueur
1/2 oz Punt e Mes
2 dash Jerry Thomas Decanter
 Bitters
Stir with ice and strain into a rocks glass.

Smoke n' Bols

Kenny Belanger had the name and Jared Sadoian developed the drink at Kirkland Tap & Trotter in 2014.

1 1/2 oz Bols Genever
1/4 oz Ardbeg Scotch
3/4 oz Lemon Juice
1/2 oz Maple Syrup
2 dash Angostura Bitters
Shake with ice, strain into a cocktail coupe, and garnish with a lemon twist.

Smoky The Pear

An adaptation of Greg Neises' creation at Mooo for a Bols Genever-sponsored bar crawl on Prohibition Repeal Day 2016; the original called for a honey-ginger syrup.

1 1/2 oz Bols Genever
3/4 oz Del Maguey Mezcal Vida
3/4 oz Belle de Brillet Pear
 Liqueur
3/4 oz Lemon Juice
1/4 oz Honey Syrup
Shake with ice, strain into a cocktail glass, and garnish with a dehydrated pear slice on a pick if available and a spritz of mezcal.

Smoking Fanny,
Blue Room

Smokin' Fanny

Matthew Schrage created this number at Saloon but named it at the Blue Room in 2012 after neighboring Belly Wine Bar's bar manager Fanny Katz.

1 1/2 oz Laphroaig Scotch
1/2 oz Amaro Montenegro
1/2 oz Honey Syrup
3/4 oz Lemon Juice
1 Egg White
Shake once without ice and once with ice, strain into a rocks or wine-glass, and garnish with a few drops of Angostura Bitters.

Smuggler

Dan Berestsky's concept was made into a drink by Beau Sturm in 2013 at Trina's Starlight Lounge.

2 oz Zaya 12 Year Rum
3/4 oz Contrabandista
    Amontillado Sherry
1/2 oz Pierre Ferrand Dry Curaçao
4 dash Angostura Bitters
Stir with ice and strain into a cocktail coupe.

SN-SO

Snow Day Swizzle

Kat Lamper celebrated the first big snowstorm of 2017 with this escapist Swizzle at Backbar.

1 oz Denizen's Merchant Reserve Rum
1/2 oz Blackwell Jamaican Rum
1/2 oz Diplomatico Reserva Rum
1/2 oz Cinnamon Syrup
1/2 oz Grenadine
1/2 oz Lime Juice
Build in a Collins glass, fill with crushed ice, and swizzle to mix and chill. Garnish with 1 dash Angostura Bitters and add a straw.

Sock Drawer Sexuality

At Local 149, John Mayer's naming convention is sometimes influenced by his wife's job as a sexuality teacher such as with this 2013 creation.

1 1/2 oz Luxardo Amaretto
3/4 oz Siete Leguas Añejo Tequila
3/4 oz Lemon Juice
1/2 oz Angostura Bitters
Shake with ice and strain into a cocktail glass.

Somerville 75

An adaptation of The Independent's 2013 riff on a French 75.

1 oz Gin
1/2 oz Lime Juice
1/2 oz Green Chartreuse
Shake with ice, strain into a flute glass containing 2 1/2 oz sparkling wine, and garnish with a lime slice.

Son of Dad

Originally created by Kenny Belanger for a Backlash Brewery Spin the Bottle night at Brick and Mortar in 2013 using their saison in a drink called Delayed Apocalypse.

1 oz Old Overholt Rye
3/4 oz St. Germain
1/4 oz Campari
3/4 oz Lemon Juice
1 dash Angostura Orange Bitters
Shake with ice, strain into a rocks glass containing 2 oz Notch Session Ale, fill with ice, and add straws.

Son of Man

Matthew Schrage paid tribute to a Magritte painting with this apple-forward 2012 drink at the Blue Room.

1 1/2 oz Calvados
1/2 oz Amaro Montenegro
1/2 oz Galliano l'Autentico
1/2 oz Cynar
1 dash Bittermens Boston Bitters
Stir with ice and strain into a cocktail glass.

Soul Patch

A funky creation from Ran Duan at Sichuan Garden II in Woburn for their Ugly Sweater Party on Christmas Day 2012.

1 1/2 oz Weller 12 Year Bourbon
1/2 oz St. George Agricole Rum
1/2 oz Dry Vermouth
1/4 oz Syrup from a Luxardo Cherry Jar
1/4 oz Vinegar
2 dash Angostura Bitters
Stir with ice, strain into a rocks glass, and garnish with orange oil from a twist.

South Congress

John Mayer pays homage in 2012 to an Austin neighborhood in this Red Hook-like cocktail at Local 149.

2 oz Del Maguey Crema de Mezcal
1/2 oz Punt e Mes
1/2 oz Maraschino Liqueur
1 dash Angostura Bitters
1 dash Mole Bitters
Stir with ice, strain into a cocktail glass, and garnish with a cherry. Substitute a 9 part mezcal to 1 part agave nectar blend for the crema de mezcal.

South End Sling

Sahil Mehta became a finalist in the 2012 Heering Sling competition with this tribute to Estragon's neighborhood in Boston.

1 oz Cherry Heering
1 oz Del Maguey Crema de Mezcal
1 oz Fernet Branca
1 oz Lime Juice
Shake with ice, strain into a Highball glass containing 1 1/2 oz ginger beer, fill with ice, garnish with a mint sprig, and add a straw. Substitute a 9 part mezcal to 1 part agave nectar blend for the crema de mezcal.

Southern Belle,
Sichuan Garden II

Southern Belle

*Vannaluck Hongthong created
this entry to Bombay Sapphire's
Most Imaginative Bartender 2015
competition at the Baldwin Bar in
Sichuan Garden II.*

1 1/2 oz Bombay Sapphire Gin
1 oz Cinnamon Syrup
1 oz Lime Juice
1/2 oz Giffard Apricot Liqueur
1 Egg White
*Shake once without ice and once
with ice, strain into a cocktail
coupe, and garnish with a mint
sprig and lemon oil from a twist.*

Spanish Union

*A light offering crafted by Vikram
Hedge at Island Creek Oyster Bar
in 2013.*

3/4 oz Milagro Blanco Tequila
3/4 oz Lustau East India Sherry
3/4 oz Lime Juice
3/4 oz Cinnamon Syrup
1 dash Bittermens Mole Bitters
*Shake with ice and strain into a
cocktail coupe.*

Spice & Wine

Tyler Wang at No. 9 Park was inspired in 2013 by Sahil Mehta's Butchertown at Estragon.

2 1/2 oz La Gitana Manzanilla Sherry
1/2 oz Krogstad Aquavit
1/2 oz Yellow Chartreuse
1 dash Berg & Hauck's Celery Bitters
Stir with ice, strain into a rocks glass, and garnish with lemon oil from a twist.

Spice Trade

At Sichuan Garden II in 2012, Ran Duan honored the Dutch's rich history of gathering spices from around the world.

1 oz Bols Barrel-Aged Genever
1 oz Zacapa Rum
1/2 oz Bonal Gentiane-Quina
1/2 oz Lustau Pedro Ximenez Sherry
2 dash Bittermens Tiki Bitters
Stir with ice, strain into a cocktail coupe, and garnish with a cherry and an orange twist.

Stack Banana

The Baldwin Bar at Sichuan Garden II paid tribute to Harry Belafonte's Day'O with this 2016 banana and rum libation.

1 1/2 oz Plantation Pineapple Rum
1 oz Lime Juice
3/4 oz Demerara Syrup
1/2 oz Giffard Banane du Bresil
2 dash Bittermens Mole Bitters
Shake with ice, strain into a cocktail glass, and garnish with an edible orchid and dehydrated banana chips on a pick if available.

Stagecoach Mary

For the Blue Room's Women of the Wild West night in 2013, Fred Yarm honored the first African American U.S. postal service worker.

1 1/2 oz Macchu Pisco
1/2 oz Campari
1/2 oz Crème de Cacao
1/2 oz Dry Vermouth
1 pinch Salt
Stir with ice, strain into a cocktail coupe, and garnish with a lemon twist.

Stagecoach Traveler

A great split spirits drink crafted by Ted Gallagher at Steel & Rye in 2013.

3/4 oz Pierre Ferrand 1840 Cognac
3/4 oz Rye Whiskey
1 oz Aperol
1/2 oz Amaro S. Maria al Monte
Stir with ice and strain into a rocks glass pre-rinsed with Lucid Absinthe.

Steady As She Goes

One of the soda fountain-style libations at Merrill & Company in 2014.

1 3/4 oz Cocchi Sweet Vermouth
1 1/4 oz Averna
2 dash Mole Bitters
Stir with ice, strain into a rocks glass with 3 oz soda water, fill with ice, garnish with an orange wedge, and add straws.

Stinger Snowcone

A modernization of the classic Stinger at the Citizen Public House in Boston circa 2012.

1 1/2 oz Pierre Ferrand Cognac
1 1/2 oz Coconut Cream
1/4 oz Fernet Branca Menta
Shake with ice, strain into a snifter or rocks glass, fill with crushed ice, and add straws.

Stitzle Flip

An adaptation Art Bar's autumnal Flip in 2012 with a tip of the hat to Bulleit's spot on the Bourbon Trail.

2 oz Bulleit Bourbon
1 oz Bonal Gentiane-Quina
1/2 oz Vanilla Syrup
1/2 oz Velvet Falernum
1 Whole Egg
2 dash Fee's Cherry Bitters
Shake once without ice and once with ice, strain into a cocktail coupe, and garnish with 5 drops of Fee's Whiskey Barrel Bitters.

Storm Cloud

On the opening 2013 menu of Kirkland Tap & Trotter, Tyler Wang crafted this aperitif tribute to old friends whose nicknames are Lightning, Thunder, Boom, and [Thunder] Clap.

1 1/2 oz Cocchi Americano
1/2 oz Fernet Branca
1 oz Grapefruit Juice
1/4 oz Simple Syrup
Shake with ice, strain into a Collins glass containing 2 oz soda water, fill with ice, garnish with a grapefruit twist, and add a straw.

Streets of San Miguel

A 1794 variation crafted by John Henderson of Scholars for one of the Blue Room's 2013 Whiskey & Amari nights.

1 oz Old Overholt Rye
1 oz Bonal Gentiane-Quina
1 oz Campari
Stir with ice, strain into a rocks glass, and garnish with an orange twist.

Suhm Heering Float

Tyler Wang paid homage at No. 9 Park in 2012 to the Danish merchant who created the famous cherry liqueur in the 19th century.

2 oz Cherry Heering
1/2 oz Old Monk Rum
1/2 oz Bitter Science Mole Bitters
1 Egg Yolk
Shake once without ice and once with ice, strain into a Highball glass containing 4 oz of Maine Root's Root Beer, and add a straw.

Summertime Sling

Mick Kellogg and Vannaluck Hongthong's fruity and floral thirst quencher for Summer 2016 at the Baldwin Bar at Sichuan Garden II.

2 oz Bombay Sapphire Gin
1/2 oz St. Germain
1 1/2 oz Watermelon Juice
1/2 oz Lemon Juice
1/2 oz Simple Syrup
10 drop Orange Blossom Water
Shake with ice, strain into a Collins glass containing 1 1/2 oz soda water, fill with ice, garnish with mint sprigs, and add a straw.

Sun City

Alex Homan's 2015 tribute at Frogmore to Charleston being a major importer of Madeira back in the Colonial era.

1 1/4 oz Bar Hill Gin
3/4 oz Pineapple Juice
1/2 oz Blandy's Malmsey Madeira
1/2 oz Lime Juice
1 pinch Black Pepper
Shake with ice, strain into a cocktail coupe, and garnish with an additional pinch of black pepper.

SU-TA

Sunday Disco

One of the champagne cocktails at Local 149 circa 2013.

1 oz Aperol
1/2 oz Peychaud's Bitters
1/2 oz Grenadine
1/2 oz Lemon Juice
Shake with ice, strain into a tulip glass containing 2 oz prosecco, fill with crushed ice, garnish with an orange twist, and add straws.

Suze-E-Q

A fruity and complex beer cocktail crafted in 2013 by Beau Sturm at Trina's Starlite Lounge.

3/4 oz Suze Gentian Liqueur
3/4 oz Lazzaroni Amaretto
1/2 oz Lemon Juice
1/2 oz Orange Juice
Shake with ice, strain into a rocks glass containing 3 oz of Harpoon IPA beer, fill with ice, garnish with an orange slice, and add straws.

Swinney Park

Nic Mansur at Brick & Mortar paid tribute in 2013 to Johnny Appleseed.

2 oz Laird's Bonded Apple Brandy
1/2 oz Cinnamon Syrup
1/2 oz Lemon Juice
3 dash Peychaud's Bitters
Shake with ice and strain into a cocktail coupe.

Tainted Love

Fred Yarm created this riff on the Havana Cocktail for Loyal Nine's Yacht Rock Sundays in 2015. A tequila version called Monopoly Money made the main menu later that year using Chinaco Blanco and an orange oil garnish.

1 oz Mezcal Amaras
1 oz Kronan Swedish Punsch
1/2 oz Rothman & Winter Apricot Liqueur
1/2 oz Lime Juice
Shake with ice, strain into a cocktail glass, and garnish with an orange twist.

Take a Minute

Alex Homans returned to Backbar for a guest shift in 2015 and offered this low proof, re-calibrating cocktail as the drink of the day shortly before he opened the Frogmore.

1 1/2 oz Cocchi Americano
3/4 oz Pimm's No. 1
1/2 oz Cynar
1/4 oz Pierre Ferrand Dry Curaçao
Stir with ice, strain into a cocktail coupe, and garnish with a lemon twist.

Take on Me

For Loyal Nine's Yacht Rock Sundays in 2015, Fred Yarm riffed on Michael McIlroy's Rome with a View after being inspired by a request earlier in the week for a Zucca Spritz.

1 oz Zucca Rabarbaro Amaro
1 oz Dolin Dry Vermouth
1/2 oz Creole Shrubb Orange
  Liqueur
1/2 oz Lemon Juice
Shake with ice, strain into a Collins glass containing 2 oz soda water, fill with ice, garnish with an orange twist, and add a straw.

Take the Long Way Home

Fred Yarm was inspired by the Seventh Heaven and Sensation cocktails, and he crafted this refresher in 2015 for Loyal Nine's Yacht Rock Sundays.

1 oz Angostura 5 Year Rum
3/4 oz Blandy's Sercial Madeira
3/4 oz Grapefruit Juice
1/2 oz Luxardo Maraschino
4 leaf Mint
Shake with ice, strain into a cocktail glass, garnish with a mint leaf.

Suze-E-Q,
Trina's Starlite
Lounge

TA

Tale of Two Kitties

Tyler Wang at Kirkland Tap & Trotter paid tribute in 2013 to a long lost cat and said owner's love of rum Lion's Tails.

1 3/4 oz Plantation Dark Rum
3/8 oz Orgeat
3/8 oz Allspice Dram
1/2 oz Lime Juice
Spent 1/2 Lime Shell
Shake with ice, strain into a rocks glass, fill with crushed ice, garnish with the retrieved lime shell, and add straws.

Tartini Sling

Will Tomlinson at Tavern Road created this riff on the Singapore Sling in 2013.

3/4 oz Dry Gin
3/4 oz Cherry Heering
3/4 oz Cynar
1/2 oz Benedictine
3/4 oz Lime Juice
Shake with ice, strain into a Highball glass containing 2 oz High & Mighty Beer Of The Gods blonde ale, fill with ice, and add a straw.

Tarzan Boy

Fred Yarm's tropical Negroni riff created originally in 2015 for Yacht Rock Sundays at Loyal Nine.

1 oz JM Rhum Agricole Blanc
1/2 oz Dolin Dry Vermouth
1/2 oz Dolin Blanc Vermouth
1/2 oz Campari
1/2 oz Passion Fruit Syrup
Stir with ice, strain into a rocks glass, fill with ice, garnish with an orange twist, and add straws.

Taylor Rain

Sam Gabrielli's 2012 riff on a Mamie Taylor and a Dark & Stormy that was named in tribute to the American film actress; Sam created this at Russell House Tavern as a companion piece to J.M. Curley's Jenna Haze.

1 1/2 oz Bacardi 8 Year Rum
3/4 oz Drambuie
1/2 oz St. Elizabeth Allspice Dram
1 oz Lime Juice
Shake with ice, strain into a Collins glass containing 2 oz ginger beer, fill with ice, and add a straw.

Tea Punch

A punch that appeared on the Backbar's Tradesman section of their 2013 menu that was perhaps a play on the classic 'Ti Punch.

1/2 oz Clement VSOP Rhum Agricole
1/2 oz Plantation Barbados Rum
1 oz Amontillado Sherry
1/2 oz Lemon Juice
1/2 oz Black Tea Syrup
Stir with ice, strain into a punch cup containing an ice cube, and garnish with a lemon wheel topped with a dash of Angostura Bitters.

Ted's Tiki Hut

One of Ted Gallagher's more theatrical creations at Craigie on Main in 2010. A fire-safe version can be accomplished by subbing a lemon twist and a floated dash of Angostura Bitters.

1 oz Smith & Cross Rum
1 oz Barbancourt 15 Year Rhum
1/2 oz Fee's Falernum
1/2 oz Lime Juice
1 bsp St. Elizabeth Allspice Dram
1 dash Bittermens Tiki Bitters
Trim the fruit away from a lemon wedge, score the pith side of the peel with a few lines using a knife, place the peel in a plate, add a few dashes of Angostura Bitters and a dash of Lemon Hart 151 Rum, and set afire. As the peel is burning, shake the drink ingredients above with ice and strain into a rocks glass. Twist the extinguished peel over drink to express the oils and drop in the glass.

Telenovela

Michelle Harrington's dramatic Mexican-themed Swizzle on the Loyal Nine Fall 2016 menu.

1 1/2 oz Mezcal Amaras
1/2 oz Green Chartreuse
1/2 oz Velvet Falernum
1/2 oz Lime Juice
Build in a Collins or tulip glass, fill with crushed ice, and swizzle to mix and chill. Garnish with 3-4 dashes Angostura Bitters and a mint sprig, and add a straw.

Tempest

Sahil Mehta's 2014 amaro-tinged Hurricane riff at Estragon.

1 1/2 oz Ron Abuelo Rum
3/4 oz Meletti Amaro
1/2 oz Passion Fruit Syrup
1 oz Lime Juice
Shake with ice, strain into a rocks glass containing 1 oz soda water, fill with ice, garnish with a lime wedge, and add straws.

The Matic

Fanny Katz crafted this herbal libation for Belly Wine Bar's sherry section of their 2013 cocktail menu.

1 oz Fino Sherry
1 oz Ford's Gin
3/4 oz Meletti Amaro
1/2 oz Lemon Juice
1/4 oz Simple Syrup
Shake with ice and strain into a cocktail glass pre-rinsed with Green Chartreuse.

The Sun Also Rises, Estragon

The Sun Also Rises

At Estragon, Sahil Mehta crafted this aperitif for the 2013 Avèze competition.

2 oz Fino Sherry
1 oz Avèze Gentian Liqueur
1 oz Cocchi Americano
2 dash Orange Bitters
Stir with ice, strain into a rocks glass, fill with ice, garnish with an orange twist, and add straws.

Thief of My Heart

A complex sipper from the Baldwin Room at Sichuan Garden II circa 2015.

1 oz Great King Street Scotch
1/2 oz Hamilton's Black Strap Rum
3/4 oz Amaro Sibona (or Nardini)
3/4 oz Byrrh Quinquina
2 dash Fee's Rhubarb Bitters
Stir with ice, strain into a rocks glass, and garnish with lemon oil from a twist.

Tidbit

Kenny Belanger's elegant Tiki number at Kirkland Tap & Trotter in 2014.

1 1/2 oz Plantation 3 Star White Rum
1/2 oz Dolin Genepy des Alpes
1/2 oz Velvet Falernum
1/2 oz Lime Juice
1 dash Kübler Absinthe
Shake with ice and strain into a rocks glass.

Tigress of Forli

Sahil Mehta of Estragon won ShakeStir's flash mixology competition in 2014 with this tribute to Caterina Sforza, Countess of Forli.

2 oz Carpano Bianco Vermouth
1/2 oz Cynar
1/4 oz St. Germain
1/4 oz Lemon Juice
1 pinch Salt
Shake with ice, strain into a rocks glass, fill with ice, garnish with a lemon twist, and add straws.

Time Traveler

For the Brick & Mortar's first anniversary of the Spin the Bottle Monday nights menu in 2013, this equal parter was named after a character in the Castlevania video game series.

3/4 oz Citadelle Gin
3/4 oz Luxardo Maraschino
3/4 oz St. Germain
3/4 oz Lemon Juice
Shake with ice and strain into a rocks glass.

Tin Can Telephone

At Russell House Tavern, Fred Yarm riffed on the Marconi Wireless in 2013.

1 1/4 oz Laird's Bonded Apple Brandy
1 1/4 oz Sweet Vermouth
1 1/4 oz Salers Gentian Liqueur
1/4 oz Benedictine
2 dash Orange Bitters
Stir with ice, strain into a cocktail glass, and garnish with a lemon twist.

Titania

Sahil Mehta at Estragon made reference to A Midsummer Night's Dream to pay tribute to the two epic distilleries making the liqueurs for this 2016 creation.

3/4 oz Green Chartreuse
3/4 oz Amaro di Angostura
3/4 oz Pineapple Shrub
3/4 oz Lime Juice
Shake with ice and strain into a cocktail coupe.

To Become Small Again

Tony Iamunno's magical 2015 creation at Stoddard's.

2 oz Kronan Swedish Punsch
1/2 oz Lillet Blanc
1/2 oz Suze Gentian Liqueur
2 dash Lemon Bitters
Stir with ice and strain into a cocktail glass.

Tomb of the Caribs

Fred Yarm paid tribute at Loyal Nine in 2017 to the cliff where the last Caribs jumped instead of surrendering to the Europeans on Martinique just as in classic 'Ti Punch service where ingredients are provided such that "each can prepare their own death."

1 1/2 oz JM Rhum Agricole Blanc
1/2 oz Cynar
1/2 oz Honey Syrup
1/2 oz Lime Juice
Build in a double Old Fashioned glass, add ice, stir, and garnish with a lime wheel inserted along the inside of the glass.

Tombstone Mule

A smoky Western-themed Mule at Bergamot circa 2013.

2 oz Del Maguey Mezcal Vida
1/2 oz Lemon Juice
1/2 oz Honey Syrup
Shake with ice, strain into a rocks glass containing 1 oz ginger beer, fill with ice, garnish with flamed lemon oil from a twist, and add straws.

Torino Highball

Ran Duan and Vannaluck Hongthong's refreshing berry-driven 2015 libation at the Baldwin Bar at Sichuan Garden II.

1 1/2 oz Cocchi Sweet Vermouth
1/2 oz Leopold Blackberry Liqueur
3/4 oz Lime Juice
3/4 oz Simple Syrup
Shake with ice, strain into a Collins glass containing 2 oz of soda water, fill with ice, garnish with a mint sprig and a blackberry-lime slice flag, and add a straw.

Torino Retiree

At No. 9 Park, Sam Olivari pondered in 2014 what old Italian men would drink on the Riviera as their patio pounder.

1 oz Tanqueray 10 Gin
3/4 oz Gran Classico
3/4 oz Cocchi Americano
1/2 oz Pierre Ferrand Dry Curaçao
2 dash Angostura Orange Bitters
Shake with ice, strain into a Collins glass containing 2 oz soda water, fill with ice, and garnish with an orange twist.

Toronto (Yvonne's variation)

The split spirits Toronto variation crafted at Yvonne's library bar in 2015.

1 1/4 oz Calvados
1 oz Old Simon Genever
1/2 oz Amaro S. Maria al Monte
1/4 oz Demerara Syrup
2 dash Angostura Bitters
Stir with ice, strain into a rocks glass with a large ice cube, and garnish with freshly grated nutmeg.

Torpedo Juice

At Eastern Standard, Kit Paschal paid tribute in 2013 to naval sailors' inventiveness in distilling the alcohol out of torpedo fuel.

1 oz Pierre Ferrand Cognac
1/2 oz King's Ginger Liqueur
3/4 oz Lemon Juice
3/4 oz Orgeat
Shake with ice, strain into a rocks glass containing a 2 inch diameter ice cube containing cut up pieces of pineapple frozen inside, and add straws.

Town Crier

Fred Yarm's 2016 tribute to one of the Loyal Nine's neighborhood denizens who occasionally bursts into the restaurant and starts yelling things.

1 oz Morin Selection Calvados
1 oz Barbancourt 8 Year Rhum
1/2 oz Punt e Mes
1/2 oz Benedictine
2 dash Peychaud's Bitters
Stir with ice, strain into a rocks glass, fill with ice, garnish with a lemon twist, and add straws.

Town Meeting

Park Restaurant has the last word at the town meeting with this tropical 2014 creation.

1 1/2 oz Infiniti Rhum Blanc
3/4 oz Green Chartreuse
1/2 oz Maurin Quina
1/2 oz Lemon Juice
1/4 oz Cinnamon Syrup
Shake with ice, strain into a single Old Fashioned Glass, and garnish with lime oil from a twist.

Transatlantic

Citizen's Nick Korn was inspired by drinks he had in London in 2013 using mixed spirit bases and Pedro Ximenez as a sweetener.

1 oz Rittenhouse Rye
1 oz Plantation 3 Star White Rum
3/4 oz Lustau Pedro Ximenez
  Sherry
1 bsp Pierre Ferrand Dry Curaçao
Stir with ice, strain into a cocktail coupe, and garnish with an orange twist.

Transatlantic,
Citizen Public House

Trinidad & Toboggan

Luc Thiers at Backbar combined a guest's interests in the Trinidad Sour and in Amaro Braulio into this riff for the Winter 2014-2015 menu.

3/4 oz Angostura Bitters
1/2 oz Amaro Braulio
1/4 oz Smith & Cross Rum
3/4 oz Orgeat
3/4 oz Lemon Juice
Shake with ice, strain into a cocktail glass, and garnish with freshly grated nutmeg.

Trinidad Medicine

An adaptation of Sam Treadway's 2017 cross of a Trinidad Sour and a Penicillin at Backbar.

1 oz Angostura Bitters
1 oz Laphroaig 10 Year Scotch
1/2 oz Honey Syrup
1/2 oz Ginger Syrup
1/2 oz Lemon Juice
Shake with ice, strain into a cocktail coupe, and garnish with a spritz of Laphroaig Scotch.

Triple Arthrodesis

Dan Braganca at Backbar paid tribute in 2016 to his podiatrist girlfriend by using her favorite ingredients, mezcal and Cherry Heering, and naming it after a surgical procedure.

1 1/2 oz Nuestra Soledad Mezcal
3/4 oz Cherry Heering
3/4 oz Lemon Juice
1/2 oz Clove Syrup (or Falernum)
2 dash Angostura Bitters
Shake with ice, strain into a rocks glass, fill with crushed ice, garnish with a lemon peel pierced with 3 cloves, and add straws.

Triumph of Pompei

No. 9 Park riffed on Milk and Honey's Rome with a View in 2012.

1 1/4 oz Cocchi Americano
3/4 oz Fernet Branca
1 oz Grapefruit Juice
1/2 oz Simple Syrup
Shake with ice, strain into a High-ball glass containing 1 1/2 oz soda water, and fill with ice. Add a pinch of salt to the top ice cube, garnish with a grapefruit twist, and add a straw.

Tropicalia

Sahil Mehta's spiced Daiquiri Time Out at Estragon circa 2015.

1 1/2 oz Leblon Cachaça
3/4 oz Lime Juice
1/2 oz Passion Fruit Syrup
1/4 oz Velvet Falernum
1/4 oz Combier Kümmel
Shake with ice and strain into a cocktail coupe.

Tuxedo Cocktail #3

Eastern Standard added the next variation to the classic Tuxedo series in 2012 by using aged Genever.

1 1/2 oz Bols Barrel-Aged Genever
3/4 oz Tio Pepe Fino Sherry
3/4 oz Martini & Rossi Dry Vermouth
1 bsp Luxardo Maraschino
1 dash Regan's Orange Bitters
Stir with ice, strain into a cocktail glass, and garnish with an orange twist.

Two Caravels

Matt Schrage's 2013 tribute at Brick & Mortar to Christopher Columbus' Niña and Pinta.

1 oz Plantation Dark Rum
1 oz Lustau Amontillado Sherry
1/2 oz Lemon Juice
1/2 oz Simple Syrup
2 dash Peychaud's Bitters
Shake with ice and strain into a cocktail coupe.

Two Stone

A sherry-laden Manhattan variation at Merrill & Co. circa 2014.

2 oz Rittenhouse Rye
1 oz Lustau East India Sherry
1/4 oz Pierre Ferrand Dry Curaçao
2 dash Angostura Bitters
Stir with ice, strain into a rocks glass, and garnish with flamed orange oil from a twist.

Uncosmopolitan

The Citizen's John Mayer crafted this for the Puritan & Co. cocktail menu in 2014.

1 oz Laird's Bonded Apple Brandy
1 oz Lustau Oloroso Sherry
1 oz Amaro Nonino
Stir with ice and strain into a cocktail coupe.

Undercover Angel

Fred Yarm riffed on the Chrysanthemum at Loyal Nine to make this low proof "Improved" cocktail in 2015.

2 oz Blandy's Sercial Madeira
3/4 oz Benedictine
1/4 oz Luxardo Maraschino
10 drop St. George Absinthe
Stir with ice, strain into a cocktail glass, and garnish with a lemon twist.

Under the Gun

Paul Yem crafted this Diablo-inspired drink at Brick & Mortar in 2016.

1 oz Olmeca Altos Tequila
3/4 oz Lime Juice
3/4 oz Falernum
1/2 oz Crème de Cassis
2 dash Chili Bitters (or 1 dash Hot Sauce)
Shake with ice and strain into a cocktail coupe.

Union Dram,
Casa B

Under the Volcano

Katie Emmerson's tribute to the 1947 Malcolm Lowry novel for the Hawthorne's mezcal section of the 2013 menu.

1 oz Del Maguey Chichicapa Mezcal
1 oz Lustau East India Sherry
1 oz Amaro Nonino
1 dash Mole Bitters
Stir with ice, strain into a rocks glass, and garnish with flamed orange oil from a twist.

Unicorn Blood

A magical elixir crafted in 2012 by Patrick Gaggiano at Trina's Starlite Lounge.

1 1/2 oz Patron Añejo Tequila
3/4 oz Cocchi Americano
1/4 oz Benedictine
3 dash Peychaud's Bitters
Stir with ice and strain into a cocktail glass.

Union Dram

Taso Papatsoris's DrinkOne libation at Casa B to benefit the Boston Marathon victims in 2013.

1 1/2 oz Four Roses Bourbon
1 oz Dolin Sweet Vermouth
1/2 oz Drambuie
1 dash Angostura Bitters
1 dash Peychaud's Bitters
1 dash Fee's Orange Bitters
Stir with ice, strain into a cocktail coupe, and garnish with a lemon twist.

Union Mule

Backbar in Union Square, Somerville, crafted this fruity and floral ginger beer drink with a hint of funk for their opening 2010 menu.

1 1/2 oz Beefeater Gin
1/2 oz Laird's Applejack
1/2 oz St. Germain
1/2 oz Lemon Juice
Shake with ice, strain into a rocks glass containing 1 oz ginger beer, add ice, float a barspoon of Batavia Arrack, and add straws.

Upturn Flip

Ryan Connelly's 2013 aromatized wine-driven inverse proportioned Flip at Belly Wine Bar.

1 1/2 oz Punt e Mes
3/4 oz Benedictine
1/2 oz Pierre Ferrand Dry Curaçao
1/4 oz Smith & Cross Rum
1 Whole Egg
Shake once without ice and once with ice, strain into a cocktail glass, and garnish with freshly grated orange zest.

Use Your Words

A drink attributed to Rob Iurilli of Abigail's circa 2011 and served at Sycamore in Newton.

3/4 oz Aged Rum
3/4 oz Maraschino Liqueur
3/4 oz Yellow Chartreuse
3/4 oz Lemon Juice
1 bsp St. Elizabeth Allspice Dram
Shake with ice and strain into a cocktail coupe.

UT-VE

Utrecht-Baden

Sahil Mehta at Estragon in 2012 honored the treaties that ended the War of Spanish Succession.

1 oz Bols Genever
1 oz Aperol
1 oz Cinzano Sweet Vermouth
1 bsp Fernet Branca
1 bsp Mirto
2 dash Regan's Orange Bitters
Stir with ice, strain into a rocks glass, and garnish with orange oil from a twist.

Veldt

Joel Atlas at the Baldwin Bar at Sichuan Garden II riffed on the classic Caipirinha in 2015.

1 oz Novo Fogo Aged Cachaça
1 oz Del Maguey Mezcal Vida
1/2 Lime (quartered)
2 bsp Sugar
Muddle the lime pieces with the sugar. Add the rest of the ingredients, shake with ice, and pour into a rocks glass. Fill with ice, garnish with a lime wheel, and add straws.

Velveteen Rabbit

Ran Duan won a ShakeStir competition in 2014 with this recipe called the Last Cold Night Before Spring using St. George's Bourbon; he later put it on the menu at Sichuan Garden II's Baldwin Bar in 2015 as the Velveteen Rabbit.

1 oz Angel's Envy Bourbon
3/4 oz Lustau Amontillado Sherry
3/4 oz Averna
3/4 oz Water
2 dash Angostura Bitters
Build in a rocks glass, and briefly stir to mix without ice. Note: This is a room temperature cocktail.

Very Old Cow

Created by John Nugent at the Citizen Public House in 2012 as perhaps a smoky variation on the Prospect Park.

1 1/2 oz Del Maguey Mezcal Vida
3/4 oz Aperol
1/2 oz Punt e Mes
1/4 oz Luxardo Maraschino
1 dash Peychaud's Bitters
Stir with ice, strain into a cocktail coupe, and garnish with orange oil from a twist.

Viaduct

Steve Schnelwar crafted this riff on the Aqueduct at the GrandTen distillery's bar in 2017 by substituting in gin and apricot jam for the classic's vodka and apricot liqueur.

1 1/2 oz Wireworks Aged Gin
1/2 oz 383 Curaçao
1/2 oz Lime Juice
1 short tbsp Apricot Jam
Shake with ice and strain into a cocktail coupe.

Vielle Daiquiri

No. 9 Park crafted this flavorful spiced Martinique Daiquiri for their 2015-2016 Winter menu.

2 oz Clement Canne Bleue Rhum
  Agricole
3/8 oz Creole Shrubb Orange
  Liqueur
3/8 oz St. Elizabeth Allspice Dram
3/4 oz Lime Juice
Shake with ice, strain into a cocktail glass, and garnish with freshly grated nutmeg.

Volstead Act

Trade's Tenzin Samdo in 2013 crafted this nod to the act that enforced Prohibition.

2 oz Bulleit Rye
1/2 oz Green Chartreuse
1/2 oz Lillet Blanc
1/2 oz Lemon Juice
2 dash Bitter Truth Orange Bitters
Shake with ice, strain into a cocktail glass, and garnish with a lemon twist.

Voodoo Echo

Fred Yarm's Duran Duran-named follow up at Loyal Nine to Hungry Like a Wolf when a guest wanted the same thing but slightly different in 2016.

1 oz Barbancourt 8 Year Rhum
1 oz Pimm's No. 1
1/2 oz Passion Fruit Syrup
1/2 oz Lime Juice
Shake with ice, strain into a rocks glass containing 2 oz ginger beer, top with crushed ice, garnish with a lime twist, and add straws.

Vow of Silence

Joel Atlas at Sichuan Garden II accidently grabbed the Kina bottle instead of Gran Classico in 2013, and he liked the results.

1 oz Old Monk Rum
1 oz Kina L'Avion d'Or
1 oz Punt e Mes
1 dash Mole Bitters
Stir with ice, strain into a rocks glass, and garnish with an orange twist.

Waking Up Ain't Easy

Richard Fiorillo's 2016 perhaps Mai Tai-inspired riff at the Citizen Public House.

1 oz Milagro Blanco Tequila
1 oz Plantation Dark Rum
3/4 oz Orgeat
1/2 oz Cynar
3/4 oz Lime Juice
Shake with ice and strain into a cocktail coupe.

Waltz of the Flowers

Rob Ficks sparkling tribute to Tchaikovsky at Craigie on Main circa 2015.

3/4 oz JM Rhum Agricole Blanc
1/2 oz St. Germain
1/2 oz Aperol
1/4 oz Lime Juice
2 drop Orange Blossom Water
1 dash Peychaud's Bitters
Shake with ice, strain into a champagne flute containing 2 1/2 oz Cristalino Brut Cava, and garnish with an orange twist.

Ward Eight
(Yvonne's variation)

In 2015, Yvonne's Will Thompson worked with Dave Wondrich to rework the Ward Eight that was originally created over a century ago in that same space. The sherry helps to welcome the orange juice into the equation.

1 1/2 oz Rittenhouse Rye
1/2 oz Lustau Palo Cortado Sherry
1/2 oz Grenadine
1/2 oz Lemon Juice
1/4 oz Orange Juice
Shake with ice and strain into a goblet containing 1 oz soda water. Add a thin pineapple slice garnish inside the glass, fill with crushed ice, and add straws.

CRUSTARRAURUSTARRAURUSTARRAURUSTARRAURUSTARRAURUSTARRAUS

Ward Two

Kobie Ali's tribute to Backbar's Somerville neighborhood voting region in 2015 with the subtitle, "It's where we live; cheers to Union Square with this perfect blend of strong, bitter, and smooth."

1 1/2 oz Old Overholt Rye
1 oz Cocchi Americano
1/2 oz Amaro Braulio
Stir with ice, strain into a rocks glass, and garnish with lemon oil from a twist.

Waterloo Sunset

Toro's Andy McNees named his drink in 2012 after a Kinks' song and included a few symbolic elements from the battle itself.

1 1/2 oz Tanqueray Gin
3/4 oz Martini & Rossi Rosé Vermouth
3/4 oz Pedro Ximenez Sherry
1 dash Bittermens Burlesque Bitters
Stir with ice, strain into a rocks glass pre-rinsed with Lillet Blanc, and garnish with an orange twist.

Ward Eight,
Yvonne's

Water Wings

Franklin Café's Summer-inspired Tiki libation in 2013.

1 1/2 oz Sailor Jerry's Spiced Rum
1/2 oz Smith & Cross Rum
2 oz Pineapple Juice
1/2 oz Pierre Ferrand Dry Curaçao
1/2 oz Velvet Falernum
3 dash Angostura Bitters
Shake with ice, strain into a Highball glass, fill with ice, and add a straw.

Western Passage

Max Toste created this for Imbibe Magazine as well as Deep Ellum's Autumn 2012 menu.

1 1/2 oz Batavia Arrack
1/2 oz Dolin Sweet Vermouth
1/2 oz Dolin Dry Vermouth
1/2 oz Green Chartreuse
1 dash Aromatic Bitters
1 dash Orange Bitters
Stir with ice, strain into a cocktail coupe, and garnish with a cherry and orange oil from a twist.

West of Rome

Sahil Mehta at Estragon in 2015 noticed that his equal part cocktail tasted better after it sat around and warmed up, so he skipped the ice and utilized water as a fourth equal part ingredient.

1 oz Milagro Tequila
1 oz Lustau Oloroso Sherry
1 oz Zucca Rabarbaro Amaro
1 oz Water
Briefly stir <u>without</u> ice, pour into a white wine (or rocks) glass pre-rinsed with absinthe, and garnish with lemon oil from a twist. Note: This is a room temperature cocktail.

What Would Bill Murray Do?

Melissa Filgerleski was inspired by the school teacher scene in the movie Rushmore, and she created this earthy gin drink at the Bancroft in 2015.

1 1/2 oz Boodles Gin
3/4 oz Carrot Juice
1/2 oz Aperol
1/2 oz Falernum
1/4 oz Suze Gentian Liqueur
1/4 oz Lemon Juice
Lemon Oil from a Twist
Shake with ice, strain into a cocktail coupe, and garnish with lemon oil from a second twist.

CR

What You Talkin' 'Bout Willis?

Silvertone's Josh Childs was inspired by his trip to the Bully Boy Distillery in 2012, and he paid homage to the founders, Will and Dave Willis.

1 1/2 oz Bully Boy White Whiskey
3/4 oz Lillet Blanc
3/4 oz Aperol
Stir with ice, strain into a rocks glass, and garnish with an orange twist.

Wheel in the Sky

Fred Yarm took the tequila-based Juschu and riffed on it with the Airmail in mind to create this refresher for Loyal Nine's Yacht Rock Sundays in 2015.

2 oz Chinaco Blanco Tequila
1/2 oz Honey Syrup
1/2 oz Lime Juice
2 dash Angostura Bitters
10 drop St. George Absinthe
Shake with ice, strain into a Collins glass containing 2 oz soda water, fill with ice, garnish with an herb sprig such as rosemary or thyme, and add a straw.

Whispering Pines

Alex Homans took a vague description of a cocktail that a Backbar guest had in Atlanta and later put the successful end result on Fairsted Kitchen's menu.

1 oz Macchu Pisco
1 oz Cocchi Americano
3/4 oz Zirbenz Stone Pine Liqueur
1/4 oz Lemon Juice
Stir with ice, strain into a cocktail coupe containing 1 oz Monte Delle Vigne sparkling wine, and garnish with 5 drops Bittermens Grapefruit Bitters.

White Dahlia

Lea Madda's tribute at Brick & Mortar in 2014 to Spring blooms.

1 1/2 oz La Puritita Mezcal
1/2 oz Combier Pamplemousse Liqueur
1/2 oz Cocchi Americano
1/2 oz Lime Juice
1 dash Angostura Bitters
Shake with ice and strain into a cocktail coupe.

White Giuseppe

Ran Duan at Sichuan Garden II riffed on the Little Giuseppe in 2013.

2 oz Gran Classico
2 oz Lillet Blanc
1 bsp Grapefruit Juice
2 dash Fee's Barrel-Aged Orange Bitters

Build in a rocks glass, add a large ice cube, and stir to chill. Garnish the ice cube with a pinch of salt and garnish the drink with a grapefruit twist.

White Lion
(Deep Ellum's variation)

At Deep Ellum, Max Toste tinkered with the housemade falernum they had just crafted in 2013, and he came up with a Tiki-like drink that was similar to Stan Jones' 1977 White Lion.

2 oz Añejo Rum
1/2 oz Falernum
1/2 oz Grenadine
1/2 oz Lime Juice

Shake with ice, strain into a rocks glass, and fill with crushed ice. Garnish with a mint sprig and 2-3 dashes of aromatic bitters, and add straws.

Wig in a Box, Tremont 647 via the Piccola Italia Event

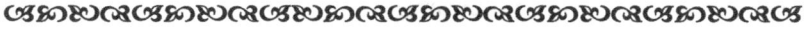

White Rene

Fred Yarm was inspired by the White Devil, Max Toste's riff on the Black Devil, and he riffed on the Black Rene in 2013 from the Pioneers of Mixing at Elite Bars: 1903-1933 cocktail book.

1 1/2 oz Macchu Pisco
1/2 oz Privateer Silver Rum
1/2 oz Maraschino Liqueur
1/2 oz Lime Juice
Shake with ice and strain into a cocktail glass.

Widow's Word

Boston booze collector Eric Witz made a mashup in 2015 of the Last Word and the Widow's Kiss.

3/4 oz Calvados or Apple Brandy
3/4 oz Yellow Chartreuse
3/4 oz Benedictine
3/4 oz Lemon Juice
1 dash Angostura Bitters
Shake with ice and strain into a cocktail glass.

Wight Army

Sahil Mehta's Game of Thrones-themed Zombie riff at Estragon in 2015.

1 oz Rittenhouse Rye
1 oz Amontillado Sherry
1/2 oz Apricot Liqueur
1/2 oz Orgeat
3/4 oz Lemon Juice
1/4 oz Allspice Dram
Shake with ice, strain into a tall glass, fill with crushed ice, and garnish with 1 dash Angostura Bitters and a mint leaf.

Wig in a Box

Kelly Coggins of Tremont 647 was inspired by lyrics from Hedwig and the Angry Inch, and he crafted this vermouth number in 2012 for the Fratelli Branca's Piccola Italia event.

3/4 oz Bombay Dry Gin
3/4 oz Carpano Sweet Vermouth
3/4 oz Rothman & Winter Apricot
    Liqueur
1/4 oz Lemon Juice
Shake with ice, strain into a cocktail coupe, and garnish with a lemon twist.

WI-WO

Winifred Banks

Josey Packard at Drink was too late to make a Banks Rum event recipe submission deadline in 2010, but she was proud of this tribute to an empowering character in Mary Poppins.

2 oz Banks 5 Island Rum
1/2 oz Galliano l'Autentico
1/2 oz Benedictine
2 dash Jerry Thomas Decanter Bitters
2 dash Bittermens Boston Bittahs
Stir with ice and strain into cocktail glass.

Winter Cobbler

Deep Ellum gave a seasonal touch to the classic Cobbler for Winter 2013-2014 with this sherry-laden Penicillin riff.

1 1/2 oz Scotch
1/2 oz Palo Cortado Sherry
1/2 oz Honey Syrup
1/2 oz Ginger Syrup
1/2 oz Lemon Juice
2 dash Aromatic Bitters
Build in a Highball glass, fill with crushed ice, garnish with mint sprigs, and add a straw.

Wit Haven

A delightful Sour at Island Creek Oyster Bar that uses the bottling of the barrel of Genever that Jackson Cannon purchased in 2012.

1 oz Barrel-aged Bols Genever
1 oz Kopke White Port
1/2 oz Lemon Juice
1/2 oz Agave Syrup
1 dash Angostura Bitters
Shake with ice, strain into a cocktail coupe, and garnish with a lemon twist.

Wolfpack

A delightfully light digestif crafted in 2014 at the Baldwin Room at Sichuan Garden II.

1 oz Punt e Mes
3/4 oz Cardamaro
3/4 oz Averna
1/2 oz Nux Alpina Walnut Liqueur
1 dash Angostura Bitters
Stir with ice and strain into a cocktail glass.

꧁ꦧꦤꦕ꧁ꦧꦤꦕ꧁ꦧꦤꦕ꧁ꦧꦤꦕ꧁ꦧꦤꦕ꧁ꦧꦤꦕ꧁ꦧꦤꦕ

Wooden Leg

Tyler Murphy created this stirred Tiki drink at Blue Dragon for the Bacardi Legacy competition in 2015.

2 oz Bacardi 8 Year Rum
3/4 oz Manzanilla Sherry
1/2 oz Velvet Falernum
1/2 oz Demerara Syrup
1 dash Pernod Absinthe
Stir with ice, strain into a cocktail glass, and garnish with a mint leaf.

Wood Word

A recipe created by Scott Woodworth of Catalyst that found its way over to Trina's Starlite Lounge and Silvertone in 2012.

3/4 oz Citadel Gin
3/4 oz Green Chartreuse
3/4 oz Dimmi Liqueur
3/4 oz Lime Juice
1 dash St. George Absinthe
Shake with ice and strain into a cocktail glass.

World's Fair

Vannaluck Hongthong's 2016 Manhattan variation for the Baldwin & Sons Trading Co. at Sichuan Garden II.

1 1/2 oz Willet Rye
3/4 oz Amaro Montenegro
3/4 oz Punt e Mes
1/2 oz Nux Alpina Walnut Liqueur
1 dash Fee's Whiskey Barrel Bitters
Stir with ice, strain into a cocktail coupe, and garnish with a cherry-orange peel flag.

Xocula

For Sarma's 2013 menu, Vikram Hedge riffed on the Negroni and named it after his favorite Count.

1 1/2 oz Amaro Montenegro
1 oz Lustau Amontillado Sherry
1/2 oz Del Maguey Mezcal Vida
1 dash Mole Bitters
Stir with ice, strain into a rocks glass, fill with ice, garnish with an orange twist, and add straws.

YO-ZE

Young Blood

At the Hawthorne in 2012, Katie Emmerson made a musical follow up to a drink from her old co-worker, namely Joaquin Simo's Naked and Famous.

1 1/2 oz Plymouth Gin
3/4 oz Pierre Ferrand Dry Curaçao
3/4 oz Nardini Amaro
Stir with ice and strain into a cocktail coupe.

Zander

A drink created by Isaac Sussman of The Independent and placed on Trina's Starlite Lounge's "Tasty Drinks from Good People" section of their 2013 menu.

2 oz Bols Genever
1 1/2 oz Punt e Mes
1/2 oz Benedictine
1 dash Angostura Bitters
1 dash Regan's Orange Bitters
Stir with ice, strain into a rocks glass, and garnish with a lemon twist.

Zaragoza

Sahil Mehta at Estragon in 2014 symbolized the victory of the smaller Mexican force in a battle in the French-Mexican War.

1 1/2 oz Daron Calvados
1/2 oz Del Maguey Mezcal Vida
1 oz Campari
1/2 oz Crème de Cacao
1 pinch Salt
Stir with ice and strain into a rocks glass.

Zebratail

Fred Yarm's 2015 Bamboo riff for the Loyal Nine "Low Octane" section of the menu.

1 1/2 oz Blandy's Sercial Madeira
1 1/2 oz Dolin Dry Vermouth
1 dash Angostura Bitters
1 dash Angostura Orange Bitters
Stir with ice, strain into a cocktail glass, and garnish with lemon oil from a twist.

Young Blood,
The Hawthorne

Zig Zag Wanderer

Nate at Ames Street Deli's tribute to a Captain Beefheart song circa 2014.

1 3/4 oz Fidencio Clasico Mezcal
3/4 oz Averna
1/2 oz Avèze Gentian Liqueur
1/8 oz Tempus Fugit Crème de Cacao
Stir with ice and strain into a cocktail coupe.

Zucca Hour

Backbar's 2015 creamy and complex spot on the clock.

1 1/2 oz Dewar's Scotch
3/4 oz Zucca Rabarbaro Amaro
3/4 oz Grapefruit Juice
1/4 oz Lime Cordial
1/4 oz Branca Menta
1 pinch Salt
1 Egg White
Shake once without ice and once with ice, strain into a rocks glass, and garnish with a mint leaf and a few drops of Peychaud's Bitters. Lime juice might work well in place of the cordial.

Knickebein

At the end of Leo Engel's 1878 *American & Other Drinks* is a quirky drink called the Knickebein that has become a cult phenomenon in Boston. The Knickebein is a pousse-café (or layered drink) involving an unbroken egg yolk finding its buoyancy in the mix and is taken in a regimented four step process. Leo created this layered cocktail ceremony in the 1870s as a German-American expat working at the American Bar in London's Criterion Hotel. Leo's instructions are as follows:

1. Pass the glass under the *Nostrils* and *Inhale the Flavour* –- Pause.
2. Hold the glass *perpendicularly*, close under your mouth, open it *wide*, and suck the froth by drawing a *Deep Breath*. -- Pause again.
3. *Point* the lips and take *one-third* of the *liquid contents* remaining in the glass without *touching the yolk*. -- Pause once more.
4. Straighten the body, throw the *head backward*, swallow the contents remaining in the glass *all at once*, at the same time *breaking the yolk* in your mouth.

In 2008, I was passively introduced to the Knickebein one night sitting at John Gertsen's bar at No. 9 Park where he took several minutes to assemble the drink in quadruplicate and performed this ceremony with a trio of guests at the other end of the bar replete with each one of the commands intoned. At my next visit to John's bar, I inquired about what had transpired. John described that one of the guests was a major cocktail groupie and he wanted to see how far he could take things with him. Indeed, with one of the steps being taking the egg yolk into the mouth and bursting it, it is not for everyone. But it has found a place here in Boston. Not in a big way, but bigger than in most other cities. I have heard about at least a half dozen bars across town where this ritualized staggered shot has been performed.

My interest in Knickebeins led me to write about them for a Mixology Monday event in January 2009 when I decided to try out the ritual at home. Since Engel's crème de noyeau component in the bottom layer was not available at the time, I went with one from William Boothby circa 1907. That flavor combination with kümmel definitely needed some tweaking, and I began tinkering at home and later by making them for guests at work. Here are two that got published elsewhere, namely in Gaz Regan's 2013 and 2015 *The Negroni* books and in his *101 Best New Cocktails #5* in 2016.

Knickroni

1/2 oz Campari
1/2 oz Sweet Vermouth
1 unbroken Egg Yolk
1/2 oz Gin
Beaten Egg White Meringue
1 dash Orange Bitters
Stir Campari and sweet vermouth with a spoon in a 2 oz sherry glass to mix. Layer an unbroken egg yolk on top. Layer gin on top of that. Beat egg whites in advance until they are stiff (whisk or cobbler shaker with a balled up Hawthorne spring) and cover the gin layer with egg whites. Garnish with a dash of orange bitters. Drink in a ceremonial 4 step process listed on the page before.

Colleen Bawn Knickebein

1/2 oz Benedictine
1/2 oz Yellow Chartreuse
1 unbroken Egg Yolk
1/2 oz Rye Whiskey
Beaten Egg White Meringue
Freshly grated Nutmeg and Cinnamon as a garnish.
Stir Benedictine and Yellow Chartreuse with a spoon in a 2 oz sherry glass to mix. Layer an unbroken egg yolk on top. Layer rye on top of that. Beat egg whites in advance until they are stiff (whisk or cobbler shaker with a balled up Hawthorne spring) and cover the whiskey layer with egg whites. Garnish with freshly grated nutmeg and cinnamon. Drink in a ceremonial 4 step process listed on the page before.

The Knickroni was created when I thought about reformulating the ingredients in a Knickebein to be more modern, and one of the drinks gaining speed with bartenders over the Old Fashioned was the Negroni. I enacted the idea during a Mixoloseum chatroom Thursday Drink Night with the theme of "red and yellow" and nothing said red more than the dye in Campari and egg yolks are rather yellow. When I saw Gaz Regan's call for Negroni recipes, I took a chance, and it was well received. Well, there is no doubt that other recipes in the book were made more, but nothing makes more of a rattle than the absurd. The Colleen Bawn one came by way of a Gaz Regan call for poussé-cafes to see if there could be a revival, and he was going to publish the collection as a separate chapter in his yearly recipe book series. The same day that the call went out, I was also asked by David Wondrich to write an article on the Knickebein for the upcoming *Oxford Companion to Spirits and Cocktails*. The two ideas conjoined and I thought about what delightful Flips might be deconstructed into this odd ritual. With the Colleen Bawn being one of my favorite classic Flips and one that has held its ground since first being published in 1895, I decided to give it a go. Strangely, the only response to Regan's call for poussé-cafes was mine, so he used it as my entry to his best drinks #5 compendium instead.

I am not sure how many of you will try this style of drink, but it is one worth honoring and remembering (even if you are not up to trying). And with this final drink recipe, I am tipping my hat to author Leo Engel and all the others who laid the primordial groundwork for this current wave of cocktail renaissance.

hos·pi·tal·i·ty

ˌhäspəˈtalədē/

noun

1.The reason you go out to drink despite having enough booze to get you & the whole bar wasted at home.

The following essays were written for the Cocktail Virgin and United States Bartender's Guild (USBG) national blogs based on my reading, attending talks, and personal experience. I do not proclaim to have mastered the arts in this section, but merely I have thought enough about them to provide myself and others some ideals to live and work by. Improving on hospitality and bartending skills in general is a life long process. Never stop learning, questioning, and asking how to improve.

Tips for Cocktail Competitions

First published in the CocktailVirgin blog in April 2016 and republished in the USBG blog in May 2016.

Last year, I had the honor to judge a local cocktail competition. The two judges and I made notes as the night progressed on what could be done to improve performances, and I combined that with my experiences judging, competing, and spectating. Neither judging nor competing is an easy task, but they are great tools to improve yourself as a bartender and mentor.

First, view the judges as your bar guests -- your only guests. You do not have to worry about whether seat 4 got their food, if new guests entered the bar that you need to greet, etc. Make them feel comfortable with you in front of them. And do not worry about what they want for you have already chosen the drink(s) that you are preparing for them that you believe will be exactly what they want. Do introduce yourself even if it the information is written on the score sheets and welcome them to your albeit temporary bar even if they were there first. Reclaim the space and greet them.

A lot of the next advice will be about perception of how the drink will taste before the drink hits the judges' mouths. A drink prepared with grace and elegance will be a better experience than the same drink prepared in an awkward way. This includes technique, preparedness, confidence, and knowledge about the ingredients. Also, look like you enjoy bartending and being there. It is usually not just about the ounces and dashes otherwise it would be a web- or email-based competition.

Come to the bar or stage prepared. Have everything on the tray that you need. Before the event, find out what will be available to you. Do you need to bring all or just some of the ingredients? What tools and glassware will be there, and do consider bringing your own. Think of it as an off-site event that you need to cater. If it is a new bar location, ask questions to the bar manager where cubed and crushed ice are, where glasses you might need are kept (and if there is a chilled stash), etc. Make set up time as quick and organized looking as possible. Unscrew and uncork; perhaps have speed pourers already in the bottles. Lay everything out on an attractive towel, mat, or tray. If there are not chilled glasses, fill them with ice and water. Even if they are not perfectly chilled by go time, the intent will be noted.

Keep things tidy. Spills and drips happen. Bring a neat hand towel or two to clean up the station when setting up (many contestants abandon the station after their round and can leave a bit of a mess) and have it handy to clean up drips on jiggers, shaker tins, and bar tops. Pride of workspace and attention to detail help to prepare the judges to think that the same level of detail will go into the drink balance and will believe that it will taste better. Indeed, hygiene is crucial to food service. Also, if you consider muddling, think about where you will put your dirty muddler. If you use a tasting straw, think about where you will put it (and not throw it on the ground).

Have a story to connect to the judges in advance. Why you like the sponsored ingredient but also why each ingredient complements that sponsor and/or why you relate to it. Show the bottles to bring the judges into the process, otherwise it is just a blur of mechanics to get the drink in the glass. Also figure out who your judges are. If that is known in advance, you can cater to their preferences and their hatreds. If last minute, figure out whether they are a brand suit, bartender, journalist, or chef.

Talk while you work. Not always the easiest thing to do, but it will make that often 5 minute window seem like a pleasant wait to the judges before tasting the drink and not just a delay of them getting up to visit the bathroom they so desperately need to use.

Obviously plan out a drink that features the sponsor in a good light by making the ingredient prominent and tasty. However, this goes beyond flavor. What about the name and the story? In one rum competition, I was told that I had the best drink by far but the other contestant was more marketable on a national level. Here in Boston, making reference to the Daiquiri Time Out and the political incidents on Martha's Vineyard that perhaps spawned the phenomenon is normal, but I learned that naming a drink after the gardens off of Martha's (i.e.: Mytoi Gardens, Page 217) and making a connection to the Kennedys' love of the island was enough to make a dark shadow for a conservative liquor brand. Likewise, do not say anything negative even if you think a story about the frustrating people at your bar is part of why you developed a recipe.

Also, when planning out your recipe, re-read the rules several

times. Is there a cap to the number of ingredients? Are infusions or house syrups allowed? Are any of your ingredients from the sponsor's archrival? Can any of them be swapped for ingredients under the sponsor's umbrella. What about maximum and minimum amounts of the sponsor, total alcohol, final volume, etc.? Will the winning recipe be promoted at other bars? If so, a house infusion or syrup or an obscure ingredient like Amer Picon might make the judges shy away.

Are any of the ingredients you are thinking of using a

major allergen or dietary restriction? If you are dead set on orgeat, ask your judges as you are about to prepare your drink if any of them are allergic to nuts. Even if you asked the event promoter in advance, it shows a good deal of sincere hospitality. Similarly, bacon fat-washed spirits might sound tasty unless your judge is a vegetarian or religiously avoidant. Getting the drink into their belly and not pushed aside (or getting them sick or upset) will only help your cause.

Is there a time cap? It was painful watching the Bacardi competition and seeing contestants talk for a few minutes before setting to work with only a fraction of their time allotment left. All of the apologies in the world will make you and the judges feel better, but it may end up with your drink disqualified for being incomplete. Or made less perfectly due to the rush.

Take BarSmarts or read lots of Hess, DeGroff, and others. Know when to shake and when to stir. If you are altering from the norm, mention why. Knowing how to stir and shake well will instill confidence. Fine straining is great for shaken drinks. Do bring or borrow attractive tools (even if house tools are available).

Garnish is always a great touch and should be prepped in advance with all of the cuts made and stuck on a pick already (if you are using one). The less handling of the items in front of the judges that you do, the better. The bartender is part of the drink, but less of the bartender's physicality should enter into the equation.

Practice what you will say and what you will do from set up to clean up. A confident bartender makes it seem like it is not their first rodeo even if it is their first competition or first time behind that workspace.

Remember, it is a combination of recipe, performance, and emotional connection in many cases. Frequently, the best recipe will not win. All too often, I will get emailed recipes from a PR agency, and I will not want to make the winning drink. In fact, if I do make a drink from that collection, it was from someone who did not even place. I am usually surprised when I make the winning drink at home from the competition's collection of recipes.

Finally, network. Sure, the judges are important for reasons that I do not need to mention, but the other contestants can become friends for life. Be pleasant to them. Help them. Speak highly of them. Negativity will reflect poorly on you more than them sometimes. And positive energy will often be returned throughout the night and onward. Definitely go visit their bars in the next few weeks. Friend them on Facebook. You all shared something special and powerful together so make good mileage of that bond.

Do thank the judges afterwards. Be open to what they have to say. Feel free to ask them questions but do not make them feel awkward. Were there 20 contestants and 20 drinks? They might not remember the details without looking at their notes. Ask for general advice to improve your game which might include things that the judges saw but you did not necessarily do wrong.

Keep on trying. Many of the most winningest bartenders here in Boston went through a lot of losses before they worked out what would win. And then it seemed like they could not be defeated.

Top Tips For Bartenders

The 10 comments without explanation were first published on Reddit, and it was expanded upon and published in the Cocktail Virgin and USBG blogs in July 2016.

Recently, there was a thread on Reddit's bartenders forum where an user inquired about "any tips on how to impress my manager behind the bar," and I interpreted the manager as both general and bar. Moreover, I took the ideas from what I gathered as both a bartender and as someone running a bar program. I replied with a list of ten suggestions that was so well received on Reddit, that I decided to repost and expand on them for the USBG blog. While some of the explanatory material was sourced from personal experiences and seminars I attended, many of it was actually written down a century ago in William Boothby's Ten Commandments in his *American Bar-Tender* book.

1. Take initiative. Do things without being asked.

During a talk at Boston's Thirst event, a story was related on a barback asking a bartender, "Why are you mad at me? I do everything you ask." To which the bartender replied, "Because I shouldn't have to ask." Learning to anticipate, being on top of things, and putting out fires before they start will transmit a degree of mastery to any manager more than following through on any series of simple requests will. Some jobs seem thankless like polishing the back bar's bottles on a slow shift, but it will gain a lot more notice than being observed chatting with the servers at the pass or, worse, surfing on your phone.

2. Guest before ego. Hospitality first. Praise and feedback will hit the manager's ear.

At my current restaurant, the owners' described our role as being the guest's advocate and finding out ways to make their night the best for them. Sometimes nothing will make a guest happier than a simple beer or vodka soda and not the latest sour-hoppy beer or recent craft cocktail creation. Some of my most recent vocal praise has come not from beer and cocktail drinkers but from abstainers who were so pleased that I took their mocktail requests with such respect down to the seriousness that I took the garnish.

3. Complain less, offer fixes and improvements more.
This is something that I was horrible at when I first became a bartender and I annoyed my first bar manager to no end. Sometimes I was right in complaining, but many times my timing or tactics in approaching the matter were wrong. Complaining might feel cathartic, but it will cloud your work persona with a bunch of negativity. Coming up with suggestions or solutions to issues will add value though. And it is important to remember that trying not to complain is not the absence of caring.

4. Take shifts, never call out. Consider being on time for a shift as 15+ minutes early. Use the time to read books about booze or hospitality; be available to chat or help out.
Boothby's rule #1 was to be on time if not earlier to make sure that you have used the facilities and set up your station before the shift. I would take it even a step further and be available to help the previous shift, to aide the managers re-arranging the tables for an event, or to talk about the bar program and your days off. If not, read. Or at least be there and relaxing on your last opportunity to use your phone. Not having your phone visible during your shift is actually a great way to impress your managers, and I did not even include it in the original list. And certainly Boothby was not prescient about such matters.

5. Don't do anything shifty. Stay sober. Take responsibility and learn from your mistakes.
My first bar manager when I started to work for him listed a mere handful of rules, one of which was "do not steal from me." Some establishments would consider drinking on the job theft, so the two are linked in my mind. Boothby eloquently had his rule #6 as "Sell all the liquor you can, but use as little as possible yourself." Drinking on the job is obviously nothing new, but if you truly consider bartending not just a job but your occupation, keeping a level head is crucial. The manager on duty can always tell when the bartenders are "a little off" that night even if they do not report them. And even if drinking on the job is part of the bar's accepted culture, many managers report how much more work they have to do when their staff is a bit inebriated (usually

this is mentioned when the drinking instigators move on and the manager now has an easier job).

6. Keep the bar top, wells, bottles, the rest of the bar, and yourself clean. If you have time, clean. Spend out of work time on your hygiene and appearance without going too fancy that is.
About six of Boothby's commandments regard cleanliness ranging from "See that your finger nails are always clean and your person presents a tidy appearance" to concerns regarding bar top, floor, glassware, and tool neatness. Keep in mind that our business is to deliver food and drink that is going into our guests' bodies, and their first view of the establishment's cleanliness and care will be your bar and your person.

7. Don't push an agenda over a guest's desire of a product you sell or can mix up. Managers hear more about unhappy guests than the contented ones.
One of the Redditors commented "On 7 - a rule of thumb is you hear from 10 times as many unhappy guests as happy ones. It even seems conservative based on how quick people are to complain now." Whether or not they speak to the manager, many guests will speak to the Internet on Yelp or other social media outlets to describe a minor slight more frequently than they will a minor good deed; on the flipside, it often takes a lot of hospitality and luck to be namedropped for good service.

8. Respect your co-workers behind the bar. Respect the host, servers, cooks, and the dishwasher (especially the dishwasher). Don't be a dick. These are your family that will have your back if you treat them right and stab you in the back if you treat them wrong.
At Gaz Regan's Cocktails in the Country, he teaches a lot about mindful bartending -- the total awareness of everything around you from what your customers, your fellow staff, and even the kitchen are doing. Set your intentions for the evening; "I want to make a lot of money tonight" is not as important as "I want to be of service to my guest" because that will set things up such that the money will come naturally. Mindfulness can start with focusing on communication. Whether you are at work or running errands in town, ask "How are you today?" and wait for a response

along with eye contact. Perhaps not when you are in the weeds at the bar, but start when it is slower. And not just the guests, but consider the dishwasher, the barback, and others who may not get noticed in life. Communication is a two way street so stop and listen to what people have to say. Of course, I can just hark back to my first bar manager who summed it up with "Don't be an ass-hole!" after hearing about a tiff I had with a server over ticket time when I was weeded. He was pleased when he had heard that I had apologized when things slowed down, but he made me think about getting to that point in the first place.

9. Mentor the barback with kindness. Remember that one day they may be your peer. It allows the bar manager more freedom to get other things done including mentoring you. Since I got my start as a barback and I vividly remember how well some bartenders treated me in addition to how horribly others did, I developed a sensitivity to developing proto-bartenders with kindness and teaching them the ropes. It always gave me a joy to hear the two barbacks on the weekend shifts arguing over who would work at my bar. But the most meaningful moment was working a New Year's Eve at the upstairs bar with a bar-tender who I had a great relationship from his barback days. We had both each other's back and respect in ways that I have to at-tribute to my time spent with him months before. He was not the once-barback now junior bartender, but my teammate and friend.

10. Represent your establishment wherever you go. Act appropriately. News travels.
Act like your potential future employers, employees, and guests are watching no matter where you are. Similarly, you represent your current establishment everywhere you go, so act with dig-nity and try not to do or say anything negative or hurtful. Re-member, you are a public figure. Treat others with kindness, for how you behave shows a window not only into your soul, but it projects the sense of hospitality one can expect in your bar or restaurant.

The Mindful Bartender

First published on the USBG blog in August 2016 that included excerpts taken from the Cocktail Virgin blog.

In reading Gary Regan's *Annual Manual for Bartenders: 2011* several years ago about the mindful bartender, I was struck by a quote taken from *This Must Be the Place*. That book was a biographical number penned by Morrill Cody about bartender Jimmie Charters' time in the Montparnasse area of Paris when it was a vibrant artist and literary enclave after World War I that fizzled out shortly after the onset of the Great Depression. During Jimmie's time behind a few of the bars there, he served literary giants like Ernest Hemingway, artists like Marcel Duchamp, and models like Kiki. The following quote moved me enough to find the book on Amazon and read it:

> *"Almost anyone can learn to mix drinks accurately and fast. That is the least of it. I have always believed success behind the bar comes from an ability to understand the man or woman I am serving, to enter into his joys or woes, make him feel the need of me as a person rather than a servant."*

Regan expounded on that quote by trying to figure out why a person is there at the bar and what they are trying to get out of the experience. From that, a mindful bartender can determine how much or how little interaction is desired and of what type. Regan describes how nobody goes to a bar just for a drink. You can drink at home, but people go out to celebrate, meet other people, find romance, conduct business, or read. People will go out for a drink if they hear that the place has quality cocktails, but they will not return if that is all they get. The most important goal of a bartender's job is to make sure that every guest leaves the bar happier than when they walked in. Gary frequently shares a quote from Maya Angelou that has a lot of applicability to bartending, "I've learned that people will forget what you said, people will forget what you did, but people will never forget how you made them feel."

Likewise, Jimmie spoke of trying to size up a customer to determine if they want to be alone or are really looking for companionship. Jimmie also made observations on the effects of alcohol on people, "Liquor always has one of three effects on people. Upon a few it brings a deep depression, because, I suppose, there is some sorrow there already. On the normal person, though, the effect is either to make him amorous or belligerent, and he or she can jump from one state to the other without difficulty."

This is an added dimension to the earlier point -- it is not just why a person is there at the bar, but how the experience can shape the side that comes out that night. Jimmie offered tales and tactics of how to diffuse fights, introduce people, and offer free drinks and other distractions to make the evening go smoothly. "Diplomacy," he explained, "is a first requisite, without which a man can never be a success in anything but a very formal bar." Moreover, keeping the customer satisfied is part of the game both with the bartender experience as well as with the fellow clientele. In dealing with drinkers, Jimmie learned to handle drunks from being drunk himself. His tactic was, "I have sympathy for them, and they respond to that treatment like no other. Criticism always makes them worse." Regan took it a step further by explaining certain phrasings that avoids the criticism aspect, such as "I wonder if you could think about lowering your voice just a little, please" instead of telling them bluntly to quiet down and stop annoying everyone.

Throughout the book are glimpses of life in Paris during that time -- everything from the art students and their gala events that were captured well in William Morrow's *Bohemian Paris of To-Day* to the surrealists including André Breton and Man Ray. While the book does delve into quite a bit of gossip of the day, the text returns to the art of the bar with some amusing anecdotes. One cute one was where a customer ordered a Port Flip, and after Jimmie had made that, he proudly presented it to the waiter in his best French "Porto Flip." A bit later, the person who ordered it got a bit peeved and wanted to know where his drink order was. Upon Jimmie asking the waiter, the waiter explained, "Porto flip? I thought you said *porte au flic* (take it to the cop)!" at which point Jimmie peered through the window at a police officer on the street corner enjoying his gift.

Overall, I highly recommend seeking out both *This Must Be the Place* and Gary Regan's treatises on mindful bartending whether in his books or by attending his Cocktails in the Country retreats.

Drinking Behind the Bar

First published on the USBG blog in September 2016.

The topic of drinking behind the bar has frequently come up and has been debated from a variety of angles. Indeed, I have worked or staged at places where drinking with each other is fine but not with the guests, where drinking with the guests and the other bartenders is fine, and where no drinking at all is preferred. These policies certainly shape how well drinks are made, the general atmosphere of the bar, how much and what type of hospitality can be given, and what sort of guests show up (or leave) at certain hours. I had not given the concept much thought recently until a clip of Sasha Petraske appeared on Facebook on the anniversary of his passing where he expressed his thoughts on the matter, but more on that in a bit.

I would break drinking at the bar down into three classes with their own benefits and consequences: drinking with the other bartenders, drinking with the guests, and drinking solo. With drinking with other bartenders, it can raise team cohesiveness, celebrate a good night, or thank a co-worker who is taking the cut for his night's efforts. With the guest, it can thank them for showing up and being good, loyal patrons; and with industry

guests, it can build camaraderie across town. With the solo drinker, it is surely time to recommend help or another profession. I am not talking about doing in that mis-order on occasion instead of sinking it, but intentionally pouring themselves a drink or four. I have seen some great bartenders go down that road and the only way we knew the details was that the barback would be told not to dump that pint glass mixed in with the others – the one that we would later learn contained vodka tonic or another path to destruction. Well, we knew that they were drinking just not how.

Instead of me just speaking from my experiences, I will bring up two modern and one century-old voices that spread a decent range of what is acceptable or desired at drinking establishments. Without further ado, here is the transcription of Sasha Petraske of Milk & Honey from a *Hey Bartender* clip:

> *"... almost all of my bartenders drink behind the bar; I encourage them to drink behind the bar. There is something really creepy and weird about people who remain totally sober while you get inebriated, and they socialize with you. This is where all of the social mores of toasting and making sure everyone is having something... because that thing in Casablanca where "I don't drink with my customers," well, that dude would have gone out of business in real life. Like someone who is in his bar but doesn't drink with his customers is an asshole. You need to have some good policy where people can drink behind the bar but don't get drunk."*

Taking a step back a century or so, Harry Johnson in his 1882 *Bartender's Manual* discussed drinking at work, but this passage would make more sense these days with the proprietor and the party/friends being switched for the bartender and his industry pals, respectively.

"It also creates a bad impression, if the landlord or proprietor sits in his place, and accepts drinks from his friends or customers. Sometimes the party, with whom he is sitting, drinks too much and becomes noisy. Therefore, as a rule, he should never engage in a social act of this kind. The guests will naturally judge the proprietor's character by the company he keeps. There is a proper time and place for drinking, and the place is always in the café or bar room. But it makes a bad impression upon the patrons of a café, where there are tables and chairs, to find the "boss" often sitting down with a party to drink champagne or any other wine. This action should be avoided entirely, if possible, for one reason: that when the proprietor is thus engaged, he must be neglecting, to some extent, his business. Furthermore, the other customers, who take only 10-cent or 15-cent drinks – men of moderate means – will feel slighted, and their feelings may possibly be hurt by seeing the proprietor too often engaged with these swell wine-drinking parties, and thus may come to the conclusion that he does not regard them or their patronage of any value."

The third voice that I want to call out is that of Pamela Wiznitzer, creative director at Seamstress and president of USBG National organization. In 2015, she spoke at Tales of the Cocktail during one of the S.E.D. Talks about why she does not drink while she works. She understood why people feel that they need to drink to get through the night because the job is, indeed, hard work. However, she finds alcohol to not be a stress reducer but a stress inducer. As a sober person, you're a contact and a resource, and this is your job and career. Moreover, there is a liability in incidents if you have been drinking, and fines can be a lot higher. Finally, she reminded us how horrible it is to visit a bar and have a wasted bartender.

In my experiences, I have enjoyed the places where I have been allowed to drink with my co-workers for it brought me closer to them and established a brother- and sisterhood. I never liked getting drunk behind the stick or having to cover for my co-worker who did so; splitting a build so that everyone got half a drink seemed like the perfect amount to take the edge off but not lose control. When a co-worker partook too much, being the one to make all the cocktails because the other could not hit a jigger with a speed pourer stream made the job extra tough. In addition, I never enjoyed letting people buy me a shot. I felt I had no control over my sobriety since someone else was dictating things. Moreover, I dislike people buying the bar a round or the bartenders a shot since that guest begins to feel like they own the place, and thus they become harder to manage.

At my current job, it is a bar in a restaurant where I will be running drinks and food if there is a slow moment. My teammates are not just the other bartenders but the whole staff. Therefore, I refuse to drink on the job for I feel that I need to have all my faculties to do the job the best I can. In addition, I need to be a role model for the other bartenders and staff. There may be an awkward moment or two when someone wants me to drink with them, but I explain that I am at work and this is my job. Unlike Sasha's idea of drinking together to bring the bartender and guest closer, I have the idea that I am the babysitter and the guide of the night to make their night the best that it can be. My good time will wait until later – whether at close or on my night off. Given moderation, there is no right answer. Figuring out how to stay within those bounds is the difficult part.

Bartender–Media Relations 101

First published on the USBG blog in October 2016.

Becoming more famous in your trade can come from word-of-mouth around town or from winning big competitions, but there are some easier ways -- namely, getting the press involved. Sometimes, the press will find you on their own but more likely the first contacts will be aided by your bar or restaurant's PR firm; however, getting contacted is not enough, *especially* if you hesitate.

Here are some pointers on how to improve your chances.

First, have a bio and photo prepared. Find a friend or co-worker with photography skills or hire a photographer to take a good headshot of you as well as a photo of you making a drink behind the bar. Low resolution will work well for web publicity but it will not do so well in magazines, so the more pixels the better! Whether it is an article, a bartender site like Shake-Stir, or a competition, most want a photo to go along with the name. Have one or a few on hand. The bio can be simple: your job position, the type of establishment you work at, and what sort of drinks you focus on. Some history of how you got there and your other accomplishments might help as well.

Second, utilize social media to establish a brand. People (including the press) will be able to find you and follow you. Moreover, in a way, you are creating your own press. Instagram is rather popular for drink photos, recipes, and bartending action shots, but do not neglect the old standbys of Facebook and Twitter. Video and podcasts are another way to get your voice out there, and the written word through blogging and article writing has been the pathway for several now famous bartenders. Get the message out there about what recipes you are creating, what your bar program is building, and what special events or theme nights you are scheming. If you have something to teach, consider starting an educational YouTube series (or see if there is an adult education class series that needs an instructor). Writers like to latch on to trends and promote events that happen. Consider tagging websites, magazines, and writers on social media to get their attention, or to start dialogues by assisting them in their searches (many writers will ask for help on stories on Facebook or Twitter).

There are also writers who ask their followers directly for content. I have had recipes and responses published by Gary Regan (newsletter and books), Tales of the Cocktail, Eater, and other outlets by just answering their calls for responses to their questions. So take some time to add key social media accounts and blogs to your feeds, and make sure you keep an eye out for the requests.

If your bar or restaurant has a PR firm, get to know them so that they feel comfortable contacting you about stories that come their way. Utilize them to for assistance in writing your bio if possible, and make sure that they have both your bio and photo(s) on hand so that they can easily disseminate these essentials without waiting for you to get back to them or their contacts. Often PR firms only deal with the bar manager or lead bartender, but getting to know them might sway them to include you if this is not the case.

When media does contact you, it is essential for you to be prompt -- meaning a couple of hours if possible. I remember one writer who contacted me about a recipe and I said that I could create something. When they replied that they needed a yes or no that night, instead of writing back immediately (I was out and away from my home bar), I got home, created the drink, took a photo, and wrote back a little before 11:30pm. To me that was "that night" but to that writer, they wrote someone else and went to bed, and I missed that opportunity. Writers do not have the same sleep schedules as bartenders, so keep that in mind. Deadlines are often short, and waiting 24 hours or so can miss getting your quote or recipe included in an article. Sometimes, the contact happens during your shift, and depending on your work place's policy, it might not be possible to write back (or even receive the message), but do try to write at the end of the shift even if it is to say that you will write them back the next day.

When dealing with the media, the more professional you are and the easier you are to work with, the more likely you are to be contacted again. Writers have a job to do, and if you are dependable and difficulty-free, they will remember that and utilize you more often. In addition, be as thorough as possible in your communications. Do not assume that the writers and editors have any bartending expertise, so make things obvious--especially in recipe directions.

Competitions are indeed a great way to get press, although it can take a lot of both stage presence and recipe development to start winning these events. Some competitions do a good job of promoting all of the contestants, whether with photos or recipe lists, while many only do the winner or the top two or three. There are also other ways besides competitions to get brands and their PR firms to work with you, especially if you can team up with them to develop their marketing for print or offsite events.

Finally, remember to be patient. Getting good at your craft takes years, as can getting noticed by the media. There are definitely ways to speed up both processes through educating yourself and creating your own press without the traditional media. Getting your voice out there through social media will help, as will trying to meet and interact with writers at events, on Twitter, and through other sites. Getting press and fame is not the be-all and end-all; try to find satisfaction and inner peace with the job you have chosen. Find the joy that will allow you to be in it for the long haul, for it can be a while before the press catches on, or if at all. Some of my favorite bartenders never get mentioned in articles. Their path to success was in making a warm, welcoming bar that guests return to over and over. There is no reason not to try to have both, but do not forget that our first obligation is to the guests and our establishments.

Staff Bonding of the Day

First published on the USBG blog in November 2016.

The owners of the restaurant I work at--for better or for worse--look to me to act as a role model and as a bridge between the bar staff and the rest of the front of the house. For the first many months after we opened, there was a decent divide between the two that was unfortunate since we pooled the house. The bar did not help run their drinks and they did not help us with washing and polishing the glassware, for example. While not optimal, things moved along for a while until we came up with ideas to bridge the gap.

One of the solutions was to have the Drink of the Day that one of the bartenders would come up with and explain in great detail to the servers. Some of the bartenders used this as testing grounds for new recipes that made my job easier to include them in the next menu change, so this was an added benefit. But even teaching servers about classics turned out to be incredibly useful since it gave them a better groundwork for drink basics and got them asking better questions. Classics afforded us the opportunity to explain drink families, cocktail and world history, and drink making theory. It paid dividends when the servers would sound more intelligent in their recommendations to their guests which, in turn, made the bar program shine since we were being utilized better. To include the servers even more, I would take requests for spirits and then narrow it down to whether they wanted to learn about a straight spirits drink or a citrus-driven one. It keeps me on my toes, but it allows me to suggest things that either

they or their guests prefer as of late. The whole process proved a great way to introduce the staff to more modern classics, and many of these have become staff favorites to recommend like the Division Bell and Fort Washington Flip.

Another great bonding mechanism and a good way to learn about my coworkers was to begin asking the Question of the Day, either at the slow part at the beginning of the service shift, or in the middle of a lagging moment. I found that it makes the less-senior colleagues, such as server assistants, feel important when you call them over and ask them for their input. Moreover, there is no playing favorites here; everyone gets asked.

Here are six of our most successful questions of the day:
• What non-aquatic bird is your favorite and why?
• What childhood viewed movie (seen 10 years old or before) that you revisited as an adult (18+) that is your new favorite from that era?
• Who is your favorite person at the circus and why?
• What is your favorite salad green?
• Which is your favorite imaginary or mythical creature and why?
• Which of the bottles back here would be your first grab in a bar fight?

I am reminded of the value of this exercise when I am too distracted to think up and ask a question, and someone inquires pleadingly if there will be a Question of the Day. Some of the questions are still being debated to this day, especially the melee weapon bottle question; Rick Dobbs of the Last Word had fun with it on Facebook after I told him about it when he visited Boston.

On Sunday nights, the business (and hence, the money)

is lower, but it has become one of the more fought over shifts. In one way, you can feel like you are at your guest-pampering best due to the amount of time you can spend with the guests, and it does not hurt that management and the kitchen have started sending out bonus dishes to make the night more pleasurable. But adding a theme has greatly helped. The summer before this one, we did a theme of Yacht Rock Sundays that made the two Sunday night servers with a great interest in that musical genre rather happy. We began wearing Hawaiian shirts (actually, due to those nights, I have not stopped as my wardrobe has expanded) and I conjured up a special drink menu each week of 8 drinks or so named after the songs. For the 2-3 new drinks each week, I solicited requests from the servers as well as the kitchen, and there was definitely an excitement to see whose drink name won out that week. Would it be Chef's epic duet of Kenny Loggins and Steve Perry's "Don't Fight It" envisioned as a Gin Swizzle? Or would it be one of the server's requests for a drink named the "Danger Zone?" Another popular Sunday was Cowboy Sunday with a soundtrack laden with Johnny Cash and Dolly Parton and with cowboy shirts and other accoutrements to add accent. Even without a dress-up aspect, a theme like Sinatra Sunday can change the way the restaurant feels--especially if your playlist is otherwise typically in a narrow range.

True, I have been part of bar staffs where drinking was the major form of staff bonding, but that definitely left out the servers. And our establishment is not the proper one to have those sorts of safety meetings that seem to work better at industry and party bars. Since none of the above acts include drinking (other than tasting the drink of the day), the management has generally been behind each of them. And they have been pleased with the greater ties between the various aspects of the front of the house and how well it has translated into a more pleasant experience for the guests.

Turn off the Music

First published on the USBG blog in December 2016.

On a Saturday afternoon in late Autumn 2016, I was busy juicing citrus for the night when Lila, one of the servers, arrived and mentioned that there was a big fire not too far away. I did not give it much thought until I saw a few emergency vehicles pass by the restaurant. I stopped juicing and peeked out the side door to see part of the smoke cloud. It was hard to gauge from that angle, so I went back to preparing for the evening as usual. It was not until I saw a pair of ladder trucks from two different towns that were not adjacent to our city pass by our restaurant that I realized the magnitude of what was going on, and we figured out through social media that the fire involved several houses and was only a few blocks away.

It also explained why I could not clock in for we were without internet connection due to the fire taking out the phone system, and this issue later prevented music streaming and our point of sale (POS) systems from working up to their full potential. Right before our pre-meal meeting with our chef, we heard a baby crying. I then realized that we would be playing a bigger role in this tragedy than business as usual. Indeed, some of the families that could not return home due to blocked off streets were taking shelter in our restaurant. We soon learned that the situation ratcheted up to a 10-alarm blaze, and later learned that it displaced around 125 people in our neighborhood.

While I was not bartending when the Boston Marathon explosions happened, I do remember hearing stories and reading articles about how service industry professionals dealt with their guests and kept a strong, calming influence over their respective establishments in the midst of the event and its aftershock. Between natural empathy that comes with being good at the job and the actor angle where they played the role of the strong, supportive, unworried one in the face of uncertainty, the restaurant industry provided shelter for the denizens of the city and the guests from far and wide needing a safe place to figure out what had just happened.

Although not on the same shocking level as an act of terrorism, the fire brought forth chaos between the smell of smoke, hazy sky, shut down streets, and loss of power and phone lines in different parts of the area. Furthermore, the steady stream of emergency and repair vehicles throughout the day and into the next was a constant reminder of the magnitude of what had happened.

As guests came in that night, many were indeed affected. The lack of music was at first strange, but it turned out for the best. Without music, it felt more like a tavern, and people talked to each other. Overall, there was a soothing level of chatter that filled the restaurant's roomspace, and there was no need to pick the right music to match the mood. As predicted, we did not get any guests who lost their apartments and condos for they had bigger concerns than coming in for dinner, but we had plenty of people who lived nearby and some that could not get home. We also had a lot of guests at the bar who were pleased to find out that we could still accept credit card payments; our POS system has the ability to queue up the authorizations and process them later with the risk, of course, of a bad card amounting to a loss to the restaurant. Other places were only cash only or decided to close for the night.

The management made sure during pre-meal to stress our function as a neighborhood liaison and to identify any guests that were more than just inconvenienced by the disaster. Even on a Saturday night, we made sure we took extra care to speak to our guests to find out how they were doing and how much their lives were altered. Definitely the bar guests reacted well to the extra warmth and concern, and many opened up looking for a bit of comfort and reassurance about the world.

Just before dinner on the following night, our internet service returned, but we were still on call to suss out who needed extra community warmth. The fragility of life and the uncertainty of our possessions and life directions were still on people's minds, and it was a great reminder that providing food and drink is only a small part of why our guests seek us out. Moreover, it should not take a disaster to remember to reach out to our guests further and make sure that their life's stresses are soothed as best we can.

The fire provided the opportunity to address people with more

warmth than usual, but there was no reason that should not be the case every shift. And that even on a busy Saturday night, it was a good reminder that plowing through the drink tickets is not necessarily the most important order of business even if it seems like it at the time. Sometimes the smile and warmth that goes along with the food and drink is even more important than the menu we are serving them.

History of Place

First published on the USBG blog in January 2017.

Learning history has been a very useful way to relate to guests. Indeed, cocktail knowledge is rather important to some guests as is being able to explain the tapestry of what American whiskey is. However, one of the best ways to relate to guests regardless of what they drink or even if they drink is learning the history of the bar's space. That space can be the building, the neighborhood, and events going on around it.

In terms of building, my previous bar, Russell House Tavern in Harvard Square in Cambridge, MA, relishes the fact that the building's first occupant in the mid 1800s was furniture dealer Thomas Russell, and the shop helped to tie Harvard Square as a center of business. However, with older guests, it was important to know that the spot was the Wursthaus from 1917 until 1996. Some would regale tales about the quality German beer brands that they served there when America was awash in flavorless macro-beer lagers. And I remember one couple who related that they were too poor as Harvard students to eat at the Wursthaus, but now that they were older and more successful, they could eat in the same space. My current bar, Loyal Nine in East Cambridge has a less regal history in terms of building location, but one that still is important nevertheless. The previous tenants were a successive pair of liquor stores, and neighborhood guests love telling stories about their decline into near-empty shelved and questionable establishments. One of my favorite comments about the space was from an old co-worker who commented, "I used to buy beer underage there," followed by his girlfriend's reply of "Yes, a lot of driving around town is a tour of where he bought beer underage."

The neighborhood's history is also important. This showed itself especially when I worked day shifts at Russell House Tavern, and it tapped into how people love to reminisce. Part of my knowledge stemmed from spending a large amount of time in the neighborhood when I moved here back in the 90s. However, when my regulars would talk about people or places that I did not know about, I turned to history books. Luckily, I could purchase the *Harvard Square: An Illustrated History Since 1950* book so I could look up that BBQ place around the corner that was gone before I got here so I could follow up with a guest the next time they came in. Web searches also helped, for the city's historical society has plenty of articles about establishments, figures, and trends. My current bar's neighborhood has a less notable history, but still one that can be tapped into in regards to what restaurants and stores were in the area throughout the years.

My current bar's neighborhood does have a lot of cultural history though being at the intersection of old Italian and Portuguese neighborhoods. Both have their respective festivals to learn about with the Italian ones being on the north side of Cambridge Street and the Portuguese ones being on the south side. While the Portuguese ones include parades with marching bands and church bell peels, the Italian festival every summer is a weekend long extravaganza that includes rides, carnie game booths, and food. Most of all, they have bands. This last festival, they had a few once-famous bands like the Spinners but they also had the current incarnation of the Village People. The Village People playing the neighborhood party was a big conversation piece, so I began to study up on Village People history including which were the original members that were still active, what years the hits were, and what the scandal with the U.S. Navy commercial was all about. That Saturday night, we made

the drink of the day a four rum Old Fashioned called In the Navy. Many of our guests that night had either gone to the festival before hand or were planning to catch the band afterwards, and the others at least knew about the goings on especially since Cambridge Street was blocked off starting a street away. The drink of the day gave a great talking piece to relate ideas about the neighborhood and interesting moments in music during the 1970s. That drink turned out to be the most successful drink of the day, and the recipe is as follows:

In the Navy

1/2 oz Smith & Cross Navy Strength Rum
1/2 oz Privateer Amber Rum
1/2 oz Old Ipswich Tavern Style Rum
1/2 oz Old Monk Rum
3/4 oz Demerara Syrup
1 heavy barspoon St. Elizabeth Allspice Dram
2 dash Angostura Bitters
Build in a rocks glass, add ice, stir to mix and chill, garnish with lemon and lime twists, and add straws. Recipe created by Fred Yarm and Jon Theris, at Loyal Nine in 2016.

The drink could be tied back to our neck of the woods being a major center of rum production before Prohibition, to the history of the song it was named after, or just as a hearty libation to be enjoyed. Bartender's choice. Or perhaps, it is better said the bartender's job to read the guest's choice of what they want to hear about and connect to.

The key to all of these interactions is that there is so much more to talk about besides the spirits on your back bar. And you will learn in exchange as people relate their stories and histories about the place and neighborhood. I remember New Year's Eve last year, an older gentleman took a break from visiting his elderly mother and stopped in for a beer. He taught me that our current space used to be two buildings with one of them having a sandwich shop on the first floor. A fire in one wiped out both buildings, and that is how our current space came to be built. The stories about the dangers of drug dealing on this strip during the 1980s were less useful but nevertheless colorful and entertaining. Overall, I definitely felt that the stories he had a chance to tell were better for his soul than the beer he had with us.

A Big Fish in a Small Pond

First published on the USBG blog in February 2017 with excerpts from my post on Reddit's bartenders forum.

Recently on Reddit, an user expressed concern that he was losing motivation and needed inspiration. He felt that he had reached the pinnacle of bartending in his town, and he wanted to excel to the level of those he looked up to in the big city. Most of us have had that feeling that we could do better or become better. Sometimes it comes from being in a more isolated drink community but other times it can just stem from being in a small bar program with no one around to mentor you. I came up with a list of a few pointers on how to improve the situation on Reddit, and I expounded on those points here.

1. Start teaching and expand the knowledge.
One of the best feelings is to bring up the people around you and under you by sharing your knowledge and enthusiasm. This can raise your bar community or bar program, and the aphorism "a rising tide lifts all boats" applies. Indeed, it may soon be possible to learn from those that you taught especially if they are motivated to learn on their own or if they ask you questions that make you think and research.

2. Travel.
Apply to be a Tales of the Cocktail apprentice or to attend Camp Runamok or the Bar Institute. You will meet and learn from people who know more.

When I first ventured out to Tales of the Cocktail, I certainly was not under the impression that I had hit my peak or had learned all that I could in my city. I was not even a professional bartender yet but a writer and home enthusiast. However, it brought me into contact with writers better than myself and with bartenders who could teach me things that were not as available to me in my city and my position. I have yet to be a Tales of the Cocktail apprentice, but Camp Runamok and Portland Cocktail Week (the predecessor of the Bar Institute) were great experiences in meeting a wide variety of bar professionals with many viewpoints, specialties, and techniques to share. And the learning kept up after those events through the connections I made.

3. Read.
The books are out there to guide you. Shoot for 2 per month if you can.

There is time to read if you look for it. Before you leave for work, during meals, when you get to work early and have time to kill, and on your days off are all times when you can read. I try to mix things up with books on history, spirits, beer, hospitality, recipes, technique, and theory. Sometimes the book titles come recommended by peers and other times it is Amazon suggesting similar titles or it is an article that mentions book titles. And other times, it comes from me web searching for guidance in a specific field. Regardless of where the respective authors are located, their teachings will be close at hand and wherever you go (assuming you remember to put the book in your bag).

4. Write.
Take yourself to the next level by becoming a scholar. Research and get your voice and name out there.

Both writing and giving talks have been some of the best ways to push myself into learning more about a topic. In many ways the process also harkens back to the first point of teaching and improving the level of your environment. But if part of the envy of those big name city bartenders is notoriety, then getting your name on a byline or book spine may help.

5. Stage or guest bartend at other places.
Change of environment and coworkers even temporarily will teach you. Or have others guest bartend or stage at your bar.

This is something that I wish I let myself follow more. At one point, I considered doing a stage a month, but I never pushed myself to follow through. However, doing guest shifts such as at a Tiki or blender drink night let me learn about how different bars are set up and allowed me to focus on a drink style that was not my normal specialty. The guest shifts and staging also help in learning about other philosophies and techniques. And on a short-staffed night at my current job, my owners allowed me to bring in a guest bartender to help me out for the evening. The bartender I selected was a sales rep who left bartending recently and missed it. While having an extra pair of hands back there was surely an asset, the true value was that he had wisdom from some of the finest spots in town where he had been behind the stick, and he was able to problem solve issues I was facing and share his knowledge about the trade. I think about this every shift when I insert a fish tub lid to keep my cubed ice separated from my crushed ice in the well.

6. Move.
I put this last after you've exhausted the others.

I do not have the luxury to just get up and move to a new state as freely as a young, single bartender might, but the option is there if need be. Move can be as simple as changing the bar or restaurant you work in or changing the city or state as well. There are so many ways of improving yourself within your position and location, but the world is a big one and so full of opportunities. And many of those opportunities will expose you to new challenges that can lead to self-improvement and learning. It may also lead you to understand that bartending is a combination of technique and hospitality, and some of the best recipe- and technique-driven establishments that get the press do it at the expense of some aspect of hospitality. Sometimes life is better when the simple things make your guests happy, and often there is a happy medium between the two.

Bartend as if You Were the Guest

First published on the USBG blog in March 2017.

One of the ways I learn to be a better bartender has been sitting at various bar stools and restaurant tables and observing how it feels to be a guest. I am not just talking about the good moments that you should figure out how to deliver to your own guests, but also the bad moments that you should figure out how to avoid. In a nutshell, I strive to bartend how I like to be treated as a patron.

Things I have thought about are how does it feel to be strong-armed into another round or how does it feel to be interrupted. For the former, I can recall a bartender that I knew socially who helped to rejuvenate an old establishment's program. I was one of his few guests that night and about two-thirds of the way through my first cocktail, he was already asking me if he could start on the next. When that happened as well on my next round that I was rushed into getting, I just asked for my check. I finished my drink, paid, and left never to return thinking, "dude, I'm not your cash-cow." On busy nights, there is definitely a need to turn over seats, but on slower nights, shortening your guests' visits makes the bar look more desolate and might impact their desire to return. Part of buying a drink is being able to rent the stool for your own third space needs whether it is to catch up on your phone or with your friend. A guest being rushed out (who is done ordering) when there is a line behind them will hopefully understand the reasons, but when there is not a line and in fact empty seats, it might seem like that bar stool has too high of a cost associated with it. All too often, I have seen bar-

tenders ask (or perhaps almost demand) if they can get a guest anything else – one in no appearance of being in a rush – and then hand them their bill; the bill is promptly paid and the guest abruptly leaves. This seems to fly in the face of hospitality and how I would want to be treated especially when I am visiting on a slow weekday night. In a way, it sort of delineates the difference between a guest and a customer.

For the latter in terms of interruptions, there are brunches and nights where I am catching up with my wife after not having spoken to her for several days due to differing schedules. How does it make me feel when a server or bartender interrupts me mid-sentence for something trivial? And how does it feel when I realize that I have lost my train of thought? How does this translate to two guests that meet up at your bar and need a moment to catch up? There is a point perhaps where you need to save them from themselves and refocus them on the fact that they met for food and drink, but understand that the drinking and dining part might be secondary in their evening's plans.

Some of these concepts even trickle down to drink service. When going out for beer, how does it feel getting an expensive brew with 2-3 inches or more of head? Or what about receiving an IPA with no head at all? Or in cocktail service, what does it feel like when a you receive a drink that has a sea of ice shards, a poorly presented garnish (if any), etc. at an otherwise respected cocktail joint? What is it like to be served by a drunk bartender or a bartender who is more interested in his friends or co-workers than you? In essence, serve drinks like you want to be served. Treat each request from mocktail to "make me something special, not too sweet... and with vodka" with the same respect as you would want your or your date's drink order taken.

Often, it is hard for a well-known bartender to get the same treatment as the commoner in many establishments. For example, there is one establishment in town that I like to go, but I recommend it with caution in lists of places to go for my guests; I explain that I get treated well there and the drinks are good, but I have often observed them treating guests rudely. However, there are always places and bartenders that do not know you in town who can give you their average handling, and if not, there are plenty of opportunities when traveling. On a recent trip, I went with my drinking buddy to three places after we broke off from the main group. The first was a recommended cocktail establishment, the second a whiskey bar, and the third a true dive bar. At the first, the three bartenders in suspenders where talking to their friends and I observed no drinks being made. After being ignored for a while at their dirty bar, we left. At the whiskey bar, we were given average treatment; after a Facebook photo that I posted, a friend contacted the owner who texted the bartender to give us a pour of something special. At the third place, Jack, the 70ish year old white-haired bartender, was the sweetest bartender I met all while still maintaining the room. He provided such warmth that I would return again if I were in that city (just as my drinking buddy did this time); drink-wise, all he had to offer us were cheap pours of Old Granddad Bonded. My friend commented that the second establishment's bartender was so great to us; I replied yes-and-no: unlike the second, the third was great because he did not need to be told by his boss to treat us special – he just did.

Unfortunately, a lot of this comes at odds to bars and restaurants being a business especially with interactions with the owners and management. And it also comes down to our tips. True, pouring a gigantic beer head means that beer costs go down, but is that what you truly want to

give to a guest or receive yourself? When I worked a lot of lunch shifts at my last job, we were taught a long term view of doing everything we could to get guests to return instead of thinking in the short term of how to maximize every encounter. There are definitely ways of enthusiastically selling to guests to increase their experience without seeming too aggressive. Whether it be dropping hints that there is a special down-cellar bottle or giving them a taste of another IPA to get them thinking about another round, there are ways of making the business side of things happy without stressing out your guests. In the end, try to be the guest's advocate and sense out what sort of experience and budget they are seeking; your read on their needs can help to ensure that your bar seats are more filled in the future.

So the next time you go out, don't just think about what to drink but use the opportunity to take notes on how to improve yourself in the trade. There are definitely some bartenders who I go visit partly just to watch how they interact with their guests to make them feel special all without necessarily sending out free food or drink.

Index by Ingredient:

Absinthe (Herbsaint, Pastis)
66b, 72a, 73a, 74a, 75b, 81b, 84a,
90a, 90c, 96c, 97d, 98b, 100e,
108d, 113c, 113d, 127b, 128b,
129b, 132a, 135b, 156d, 168b,
168c, 175d, 178a, 180b, 185a,
186d, 189c, 196a, 201b, 208d,
209d, 212b, 213d, 218c, 219a,
221d, 231d, 234c, 235a, 237d,
243b, 246b, 248a, 248d, 249c,
257a, 264a, 279c, 285d, 293b,
297a, 297b
D&T:27c, D&T:29b, D&T:48c,
D&T:49d, D&T:50b, D&T:51c,
D&T:59b, D&T:59c, D&T:60a,
D&T:62d, D&T:68c, D&T:72c,
D&T:81a, D&T:84c, D&T:89a,
D&T:89d, D&T:92b, D&T:95b,
D&T:99d, D&T:104a, D&T:105c,
D&T:109d, D&T:114b, D&T:115d,
D&T:116b, D&T:139a, D&T:141c,
D&T:146b, D&T:147a, D&T:152d,
D&T:155c, D&T:159a, D&T:161a,
D&T:164d, D&T:165d, D&T:168d

Amaro (Amer Picon, Bigalett)
177b, 187a, 187b, 217b, 247b
D&T:67d, D&T:92d, D&T:115b,
D&T:163b

Amaro (Aperol)
66c, 71b, 74d, 77d, 87a, 87b, 91b,
92a, 115a, 119c, 122e, 128d, 132d,
135d, 160b, 161a, 161c, 164c,
172a, 176e, 180d, 198a, 201a,
202c, 204d, 211a, 213a, 215d,
224a, 224c, 230a, 230b, 239d,
239e, 247d, 256a, 257d, 272a,
274a, 288a, 288d, 290c, 292d,
293a
D&T:23c, D&T:24d, D&T:25b,
D&T:27b, D&T:28b, D&T:40d,
D&T:43e, D&T:53c, D&T:57c,
D&T:70c, D&T:72a, D&T:84b,
D&T:97a, D&T:97c, D&T:105b,
D&T:106b, D&T:109b, D&T:119a,
D&T:120a, D&T:125c, D&T:125d,
D&T:131a, D&T:131b, D&T:139d,
D&T:140c, D&T:141b, D&T:143b,
D&T:148b, D&T:157b, D&T:163c,
D&T:166b, D&T:168c

Amaro (Averna)
77b, 77c, 85a, 89b, 111d, 121a,
135c, 137a, 137b, 170c, 172b,
174c, 206b, 225a, 232a, 241c,
256b, 265d, 272b, 288c, 296d,
299a
D&T:34a, D&T:34b, D&T:35d,
D&T:38c, D&T:46b, D&T:49b,
D&T:56a, D&T:78c, D&T:102b,
D&T:102c, D&T:104a, D&T:129c,
D&T:142a, D&T:142d, D&T:152d,
D&T:161b, D&T:162b

Amaro (Becherovka)
100c, 103d, 113b, 117e, 140b,
140d, 152a, 161e, 184c, 209a,
230b, 248e
D&T:23d, D&T:61b, D&T:68c,
D&T:73a, D&T:101a, D&T:105d,
D&T:107c, D&T:107d, D&T:111b,
D&T:112b. D&T:129b

Amaro (Campari, Gran Classico)
65d, 66d, 67b, 68c, 71a, 72b, 77d,
80d, 84c, 85d, 86a, 87c, 87d, 88b,

101a, 101b, 104a, 105c, 106d, 107b, 112c, 114a, 114b, 114d, 121b, 125b, 129b, 143d, 146c, 151b, 154c, 157a, 157b, 158a, 160a, 170a, 175b, 178e, 180d, 182a, 183b, 184a, 184d, 188c, 193c, 193d, 196c, 197c, 199b, 205a. 208d, 213b, 214a, 214b, 214c, 216a, 216c, 219b, 221b, 222b, 225d, 226a, 228c, 228d, 229d, 234b, 235b, 236b, 237d, 239b, 242b, 243a, 243b, 244d, 245b, 246a, 251a, 260d, 265b, 265d, 268d, 271d, 273a, 276c, 281c, 294a, 298c, 301a
D&T:24c, D&T:25b, D&T:25d, D&T:27b, D&T:28a, D&T:47b, D&T:50a, D&T:51a, D&T:52a, D&T:56d, D&T:63b, D&T:68a, D&T:97d, D&T:110c, D&T:129a, D&T:133b, D&T:141d, D&T:147b, D&T:147c, D&T:154a, D&T:156b, D&T:158b, D&T:158d, D&T:161b

Amaro (Cardamaro)

63c, 76a, 93b, 103a, 103b, 130b, 141d, 146a, 152c, 161c, 167a, 171b, 173b, 196e, 222b, 241a, 242a, 249a, 296d
D&T:83a, D&T:99a, D&T:137b, D&T:152d, D&T:159a

Amaro (Cynar)

64c, 66a, 68c, 74b, 78b, 79d, 84d, 85b, 87a, 87c, 89d, 90b, 93d, 94b, 99a, 106d, 106e, 109d, 110b, 111c, 113a, 117a, 117b, 122c, 128c, 136d, 137d, 138a, 141b, 150b, 154a, 155a, 156a, 156b, 164d, 165a, 172d, 181b, 181d, 184b, 192b, 193d, 196c, 199a, 199c, 204a, 215b, 217d, 222a, 225c, 229c, 231a, 234a, 247b, 255d, 260a, 269a, 274e, 276b, 279d, 280d, 290b

D&T:28b, D&T:30c, D&T:30d, D&T:32a, D&T:37a, D&T:40c, D&T:52d, D&T:60c, D&T:61a, D&T:62a, D&T:65d, D&T:67b, D&T:68b, D&T:68d, D&T:78d, D&T:90a, D&T:92c, D&T:97a, D&T:97b, D&T:100d, D&T:105a, D&T:115a, D&T:117b, D&T:125b, D&T:128d, D&T:136d, D&T:140c, D&T:144d, D&T:145d, D&T:147d, D&T:152a, D&T:159b, D&T:160a, D&T:161b, D&T:168c

Amaro (Fernet)

63a, 68a, 69c, 76b, 80c, 86b, 89c, 93d, 97b, 100a, 111a, 117d, 120b, 126a, 128a, 129a, 143a, 143b, 143c, 143d, 149b, 174a, 177b, 181a, 183b, 191a, 194c, 202c, 217a, 218a, 221a, 221d, 228b, 234a, 241a, 244c, 248b, 248d, 253c, 257b, 269d, 272c, 272e, 284b, 288a, 299b
D&T:28c, D&T:30b, D&T:36c, D&T:37a, D&T:37b, D&T:41a, D&T:43d, D&T:52b, D&T:58b, D&T:62b, D&T:68b, D&T:71b, D&T:73c, D&T:73d, D&T:79b, D&T:81d, D&T:86a, D&T:113a, D&T:128d, D&T:130b, D&T:133c, D&T:138b, D&T:140b, D&T:154b, D&T:158d, D&T:161c

Amaro (Montenegro)

67a, 68b, 80a, 119b, 124b, 135a, 136a, 137d, 148c, 160b, 161b, 162c, 169d, 180c, 181d, 185b, 204b, 204d, 209c, 214b, 214c, 218b, 220b, 220c, 221c, 234b, 257b, 257d, 258b, 267a, 269a, 297c, 297d
D&T:99a, D&T:99b

Amaro (Nonino)

73b, 73c, 81c, 153d, 198a, 205c,

340

220d, 231b, 233b, 234b, 263e, 285c, 286a
D&T:32c, D&T:44c, D&T:57e, D&T:64c, D&T:68d, D&T:70c, D&T:76c, D&T:97b, D&T:109b, D&T:165d

Amaro (Other)
63b, 83b, 85c, 89a, 90b, 91c, 97b, 100b, 101d, 105b, 109b, 111b, 120a, 122d, 124c, 124d, 132a, 133b, 136d, 137b, 138b, 141c, 144a, 145d, 150c, 151c, 154c, 159c, 162d, 167a, 170b, 171a, 174b, 176c, 186c, 189a, 190b, 194c, 200a, 202b, 205c, 207d, 215d, 218d, 224d, 225a, 227b, 228a, 233c, 237b, 237c, 239d, 241d, 245a, 246b, 253b, 253d, 255a, 258c, 259b, 260b, 272a, 278a, 278b, 279b, 280b, 281d, 283a, 288a, 291a, 298a
D&T:24b, D&T:31a, D&T:46d, D&T:49a, D&T:55b, D&T:63a, D&T:67d, D&T:77c, D&T:78b, D&T:78c, D&T:83d, D&T:110b, D&T:119a, D&T:123d, D&T:124d, D&T:136b, D&T:139d, D&T:152a, D&T:160c, D&T:168c

Amaro (Zucca)
63d, 64a, 108c, 127a, 133a, 162c, 201d, 226d, 245c, 252a, 258a, 258c, 275a, 292c, 299b
D&T:107a, D&T:115c, D&T:155d

Amer Picon (See Amaro)

Aperol (See Amaro)

Apple Brandy (and Calvados)
64c, 68a, 76a, 82b, 83c, 97a, 105b, 120b, 120c, 129c, 134b, 135c, 138d, 151a, 162d, 163a, 175c, 177d, 178a, 178b, 191c, 198b,

201b, 201c, 205d, 208d, 210b, 218b, 220b, 221a, 233b, 238b, 239a, 239c, 248e, 252c, 252d, 253a, 269a, 274c, 280a, 281d, 282b, 285c, 287b, 295b, 298c
D&T:23c, D&T:32b, D&T:34a, D&T:37c, D&T:41b, D&T:43d, D&T:45c, D&T:51c, D&T:64d, D&T:70d, D&T:73b, D&T:75c, D&T:77b, D&T:77e, D&T:84d, D&T:91a, D&T:94d, D&T:95b, D&T:97c, D&T:103b, D&T:109c, D&T:111a, D&T:111b, D&T:116c, D&T:117d, D&T:128a, D&T:134c, D&T:136a, D&T:139c, D&T:140d, D&T:146a, D&T:149c, D&T:159a, D&T:165c

Apple Cider (See Cider)

Apricot Liqueur
66a, 70a, 73c, 81b, 93a, 95d, 102a, 111b, 111c, 118b, 154d, 164d, 169a, 175b, 200d, 201d, 205b, 209a, 213c, 216b, 220d, 223a, 225c, 234c, 245d, 256a, 262a, 265c, 266b, 270a, 274d, 295c, 295d
D&T:26a, D&T:34b, D&T:37c, D&T:50a, D&T:56a, D&T:74b, D&T:78c, D&T:86c, D&T:100a, D&T:100b, D&T:103a, D&T:106a, D&T:108a, D&T:111b, D&T:113b, D&T:126a, D&T:131c, D&T:131d, D&T:139c, D&T:158b, D&T:161a, D&T:168b

Aquavit
82b, 98c, 210a, 271a

Legend:
• *123c* = Page 123, 3rd drink down
• *D&T:77b* = Drink & Tell (2012), Page 77, 2nd drink down

D&T:148c

Armagnac (See Cognac)

Aromatized Wine (Lillet, Cocchi Americano)
64a, 70a, 72a, 79c, 80d, 87d, 93a,
107a, 108b, 108c, 111a, 113b,
113c, 113d, 115b, 121c, 124d,
127e, 128b, 135b, 135c, 145b,
150c, 153a, 155a, 156b, 157c,
159b, 167a, 169d, 173d, 187a,
196d, 197c, 199d, 200c, 231b,
233a, 237b, 238a, 239a, 247d,
264a, 272e, 274e, 279a, 280c,
281c, 284b, 286b, 289c, 290a,
291a, 291b, 293a, 293c, 293d,
294a
D&T:29c, D&T:30c, D&T:32c,
D&T:35c, D&T:39b, D&T:41d,
D&T:46c, D&T:48c, D&T:56c,
D&T:65b, D&T:69a, D&T:75a,
D&T:75c, D&T:79a, D&T:88a,
D&T:88b, D&T:89c, D&T:95b,
D&T:105b, D&T:105d, D&T:112c.
D&T:130a, D&T:139d, D&T:143a,
D&T:146b, D&T:148a, D&T:150a,
D&T:153d, D&T:155a, D&T:155c,
D&T:158b, D&T:164c, D&T:165c,
D&T:168b

Aromatized Wine (Quinquina, Chinato)
65d, 75a, 75b, 82d, 83c, 84c, 84d,
93c, 105b, 116d, 133a, 136b,
152d, 153d, 159a, 161d, 187b,
193a, 196e, 197a, 200b, 205c,
206a, 210b, 232c, 236c, 245c,
262b, 263e, 271b, 272d, 273a,
279b, 282c
D&T:24a, D&T:28b, D&T:46c,
D&T:49b, D&T:59d, D&T:78a,
D&T:99c, D&T:102d, D&T:145a,
D&T:153c, D&T:155b, D&T:158d,
D&T:163b, D&T:166c

Averna (See Amaro)

Avèze (See Gentian Liqueur)

Batavia Arrack
74c, 81a, 88c, 93a, 104a, 119d,
125c, 177a, 179a, 185d, 191a,
217d, 231b, 287b, 292b
D&T:30a, D&T:35a, D&T:36d,
D&T:42b, D&T:70b, D&T:72b,
D&T:123c, D&T:137c, D&T:141c,
D&T:145c, D&T:149b, D&T:151b

Becherovka (See Amaro)

Beer
73b, 76c, 88b, 88c, 96b, 104a,
113a, 144d, 145c, 152c, 162b,
165c, 167d, 174c, 176b, 211a,
240a, 256c, 263a, 268d, 274b,
276b
D&T:23d, D&T:27b, D&T:37a,
D&T:37c, D&T:40a, D&T:41c,
D&T:53d, D&T:56b, D&T:57b,
D&T:58a, D&T:62a, D&T:63a,
D&T:73a, D&T:90b, D&T:107b,
D&T:108b, D&T:113d, D&T:115d,
D&T:120d, D&T:124b, D&T:130b,
D&T:136c, D&T:147a, D&T:150a,
D&T:158a, D&T:166d, D&T:168d

Benedictine
63a, 65b, 68a, 73d, 75a, 82b, 84a,
89c, 93b, 93c, 100a, 100d, 100e,
105c, 108d, 119d, 121d, 124a,
129a, 129c, 141a, 147b, 149d,
151a, 152d, 158b, 159a, 161d,
166a, 176a, 191c, 201b, 201c,
202d, 205d, 208a, 208c, 212b,
213c, 215a, 225b, 233a, 234c,
237c, 249a, 249b, 251b, 253a,
263e, 276b, 280a, 282b, 285d,
286b, 287c, 295b, 296a, 298b,
301b

D&T:27a, D&T:38b, D&T:38c, D&T:41d, D&T:47b, D&T:48c, D&T:54a, D&T:59c, D&T:66a, D&T:67d, D&T:70d, D&T:73b, D&T:76c, D&T:77d, D&T:77e, D&T:84d, D&T:85b, D&T:88b, D&T:89c, D&T:92b, D&T:93c, D&T:96c, D&T:100a, D&T:103b, D&T:126c, D&T:128a, D&T:140d, D&T:141a, D&T:144a, D&T:144b, D&T:145c, D&T:149a, D&T:158c, D&T:162a, D&T:166b

Blanc Vermouth (See Vermouth)

Bourbon (See Whiskey)

Brandy (See Cognac)

Cachaça
69d, 78a, 95d, 105a, 116c, 137b, 155b, 171b, 179b, 184d, 186a, 189c, 284c, 288b
D&T:41a, D&T:56c, D&T:70a, D&T:116a, D&T:120c, D&T:126c, D&T:127b, D&T:132b, D&T:139b, D&T:153d

Calvados (See Apple Brandy)

Campari (See Amaro)

Cardamaro (See Amaro)

Carrot Juice
196d, 292d

Champagne (See Wine, Sparkling)

Chartreuse (Green)
63d, 64b, 83a, 90a, 105a, 106a, 106b, 109a, 127b, 127e, 132b, 133d, 134a, 136d, 141b, 146b, 154b, 159b, 159c, 160c, 178c,

181c, 183d, 186a, 188d, 191a, 191c, 192a, 202a, 207a, 212c, 218a, 224b, 232d, 235a, 250c, 251b, 260b, 264d, 266a, 268c, 277c, 278b, 280b, 282c, 289c, 292b, 297b
D&T:23a, D&T:24c, D&T:29c, D&T:39a, D&T:43a, D&T:51b, D&T:51d, D&T:56d, D&T:57b, D&T:69a, D&T:71a, D&T:74b, D&T:75a, D&T:76d, D&T:78a, D&T:78d, D&T:83b, D&T:84c, D&T:92a, D&T:92d, D&T:94a, D&T:101d, D&T:102a, D&T:102e, D&T:104d, D&T:109a, D&T:109c, D&T:113d, D&T:115a, D&T:137c, D&T:142c, D&T:147c, D&T:148d, D&T:149c, D&T:151b, D&T:160a

Chartreuse (Yellow)
68b, 69b, 71c, 77a, 80c, 85b, 85c, 92b, 92d, 104d, 105d, 116b, 123a, 137d, 149a, 152c, 162a, 164b, 168c, 169b, 177a, 185b, 189b, 201b, 201c, 209a, 227a, 233b, 234d, 235a, 236a, 239a, 240c, 253a, 271a, 287d, 295b, 301b
D&T:25a, D&T:35c, D&T:40d, D&T:42a, D&T:46a, D&T:48d, D&T:49c, D&T:52d, D&T:57b, D&T:65c, D&T:67b, D&T:71a, D&T:81d, D&T:84a, D&T:85c, D&T:87a, D&T:93a, D&T:98b, D&T:100c, D&T:105b, D&T:110a, D&T:113c, D&T:117a, D&T:121d, D&T:125b, D&T:133c, D&T:137c, D&T:140a, D&T:145a, D&T:166a, D&T:166d, D&T:168a

Legend:
• *123c* = Page 123, 3rd drink down
• *D&T:77b* = Drink & Tell (2012), Page 77, 2nd drink down

343

Cherry Heering
92d, 100c, 117d, 120b, 122a,
129b, 165a, 201c, 215c, 221b,
222a, 252d, 253c, 254b, 265b,
269d, 273b, 276b, 284a
D&T:48a, D&T:59d, D&T:66b,
D&T:98a, D&T:103a, D&T:110d,
D&T:117c, D&T:126b, D&T:129c,
D&T:133a, D&T:134b, D&T:138a,
D&T:142d, D&T:143a, D&T:145b,
D&T:158a

Cider
D&T:70d, D&T:85b, D&T:118d

Cocchi Americano (See Aromatized Wine)

Coffee Liqueur (Syrup, Coffee)
65c, 76c, 84c, 94b, 96a, 97b, 124c,
128a, 140c, 163b, 183d, 192b,
227a, 240d, 241b, 242b, 250d,
254a
D&T:45d, D&T:46d, D&T:98a,
D&T:132d, D&T:142a, D&T:149a,
D&T:157a

Cognac (and Aged Grape Brandy)
66a, 76b, 77d, 84a, 86b, 92c, 93c,
116b, 120a, 121b, 128a, 132c,
133a, 139a, 144d, 145d, 147b,
148c, 155a, 158b, 159c, 168c,
169d, 172b, 173a, 173b, 175d,
186d, 192c, 197d, 208b, 210a,
210c, 213c, 214b, 220c, 226a,
234a, 237c, 239e, 242c, 245b,
249a, 251b, 252a, 253b, 263a,
263b, 272a, 272c, 282a
D&T:31a, D&T:32d, D&T:33b,
D&T:33d, D&T:38b, D&T:38d,
D&T:52b, D&T:52d, D&T:53b,
D&T:54c, D&T:55a, D&T:66b,
D&T:67b, D&T:72b, D&T:75b,
D&T:78a, D&T:79a, D&T:86d,

D&T:94c, D&T:100d, D&T:102a,
D&T:102b, D&T:104a, D&T:108c,
D&T:112d, D&T:121d, D&T:125a,
D&T:134d, D&T:136a, D&T:145d

Crème de Banane
79d, 83b, 90d, 136c, 141d, 165d,
190b, 213d, 225e, 271c

Crème de Cacao
75b, 76c, 78a, 81c, 82a, 84b, 97a,
109a, 112a, 116a, 116c, 116d,
135b, 143a, 146b, 158b, 170b,
183d, 190b, 197a, 214a, 216d,
221a, 229d, 232a, 248d, 249b,
250b, 250c, 255b, 271d, 298c,
299a
D&T:50a, D&T:53d, D&T:57a,
D&T:83d, D&T:93b, D&T:107a,
D&T:142b, D&T:154b, D&T:156b

Crème de Cassis
96c, 127a, 156d, 158a, 285e
D&T:84b, D&T:130b, D&T:153a,
D&T:154a

Crème de Menthe
155b

Crème de Mure/Fraise
77b, 160b, 192d, 227b
D&T:45d, D&T:83a

Crème de Peche
101b, 216c, 255a
D&T:44d

Crème de Violette (and Yvette)
115b, 173c, 224b, 230a, 241b,
247c
D&T:33c, D&T:59c, D&T:68a,
D&T:80b, D&T:106a, D&T:128b,
D&T:148c

Curaçao (Triple Sec and all

other Orange Liqueurs)
64a, 69c, 71d, 72c, 74c, 79b, 82c,
87e, 89a, 109b, 113c, 113d, 114a,
120d, 124d, 128b, 128d, 130a,
131a, 132c, 138a, 141c, 147b,
149a, 152b, 153c, 160a, 161a,
166a, 168a, 173a, 173d, 179b,
182b, 184b, 192c, 193c, 194d,
197b, 203b, 204c, 205a, 208d,
210b, 216d, 223b, 224c, 225b,
242c, 245b, 248b, 248c, 261a,
262a, 264a, 264d, 267b, 274e,
275a, 281c, 282c, 282d, 285b,
287c, 289a, 289b, 292a, 298a
D&T:30a, D&T:32d, D&T:35b,
D&T:36a, D&T:39a, D&T:40b,
D&T:40c, D&T:41a, D&T:42b,
D&T:52c, D&T:58b, D&T:59d,
D&T:62b, D&T:63b, D&T:65a,
D&T:65b, D&T:68b, D&T:69a,
D&T:70b, D&T:72b, D&T:75a,
D&T:77a, D&T:79a, D&T:85a,
D&T:86a, D&T:90a, D&T:92c,
D&T:95b, D&T:96b, D&T:101d,
D&T:102a, D&T:105c, D&T:106b,
D&T:110c, D&T:114a, D&T:116d,
D&T:121c, D&T:122b, D&T:124c,
D&T:126a, D&T:128a, D&T:132c,
D&T:133b, D&T:133d, D&T:139a,
D&T:140b, D&T:145d, D&T:151a,
D&T:152a, D&T:153d

Cynar (See Amaro)

Damson Gin (See Sloe Gin)

Dry Vermouth (See Vermouth)

Egg (White)
64d, 86b, 102a, 113d, 117b, 132b,
133d, 146a, 146c, 155b, 164c,
165a, 167b, 180a, 191d, 196d,
208d, 212a, 216c, 231d, 250a,
267a, 270a, 299b
D&T:26a, D&T:27c, D&T:30b,

D&T:38d, D&T:45b, D&T:49d,
D&T:51b, D&T:53b, D&T:59b,
D&T:60c, D&T:65a, D&T:79b,
D&T:80b, D&T:91b, D&T:99d,
D&T:101a, D&T:106a, D&T:113c,
D&T:114b, D&T:115d, D&T:116a,
D&T:124b, D&T:127b, D&T:132d,
D&T:141c, D&T:142a, D&T:150c,
D&T:153b, D&T:156c, D&T:160a,
D&T:162a, D&T:168d

Egg (Whole or Yolk)
96b, 103d, 121c, 128a, 142a, 142b,
143c, 144d, 157a, 175d, 193d,
250b, 250d, 272d, 273b, 287c,
301a, 301b
D&T:37a, D&T:41c, D&T:44b,
D&T:45a, D&T:45d, D&T:48a,
D&T:53d, D&T:61a, D&T:62a,
D&T:67b, D&T:69d, D&T:72d,
D&T:73a, D&T:76b, D&T:76c,
D&T:77e, D&T:85b, D&T:88d,
D&T:93c, D&T:96c, D&T:103b,
D&T:107b, D&T:116c, D&T:117d,
D&T:122a, D&T:126b, D&T:129c,
D&T:135a, D&T:136c, D&T:138b,
D&T:144a, D&T:147d, D&T:155d

Elderflower Liqueur (See St. Germain)

Fernet (See Amaro)

Galliano
71d, 95b, 116c, 124c, 204c, 250b,
269a, 296a
D&T:69b, D&T:94a, D&T:117d,
D&T:164a, D&T:164b

Legend:
• *123c* = Page 123, 3rd drink down
• *D&T:77b* = Drink & Tell (2012),
    Page 77, 2nd drink down

Genever

75a, 92d, 131a, 131b, 132a, 135b, 140b, 152b, 153a, 160b, 178c, 195a, 216d, 225d, 226d, 237d, 257d, 266c, 266d, 271b, 281d, 284d, 288a, 296c, 298b D&T:24b, D&T:25c, D&T:33a, D&T:52b, D&T:54a, D&T:56b, D&T:59a, D&T:67d, D&T:68c, D&T:69c, D&T:89c, D&T:102e, D&T:110c, D&T:114b, D&T:118a, D&T:121a, D&T:125c, D&T:129c, D&T:129d, D&T:138a, D&T:141b, D&T:165a, D&T:165b, D&T:166b, D&T:166d, D&T:168b

Gentian Liqueur (Suze, Avèze, and Salers)

69a, 73d, 80b, 80d, 91a, 96c, 99a, 104d, 105b, 112a, 125c, 164a, 168d, 169a, 176e, 185c, 192d, 194b, 200b, 200c, 203b, 207a, 208a, 215b, 224b, 232c, 233d, 237b, 248a, 258d, 264b, 264c, 274b, 279a, 280a, 280c, 292d, 299a

Gin

68c, 73a, 73b, 76a, 79c, 82c, 84c, 86a, 87d, 88d, 90d, 91c, 96d, 99a, 100b, 101b, 102b, 107b, 109c, 111c, 112c, 113b, 113c, 113d, 114b, 114c, 120d, 122b, 125a, 127e, 128c, 129b, 129d, 135a, 135d, 144b, 146c, 149c, 150a, 150c, 154d, 156a, 162b, 164b, 168d, 169b, 170b, 172a, 173c, 174a, 183b, 184b, 189b, 192c, 193c, 195b, 197b, 197c, 199d, 201a, 201c, 202c, 203b, 205d, 208c, 211a, 211b, 213d, 214c, 219a, 219b, 224b, 224c, 224d, 228b, 228c, 234e, 237b, 239b, 240a, 241b, 243a, 244c, 252d, 256a, 264c, 268c, 270a, 273c, 273d, 276b, 278b, 279e, 281c, 287b, 289a, 291b, 292d, 295d, 297b, 298a, 301a D&T:24b, D&T:24d, D&T:27c, D&T:29c, D&T:30c, D&T:32c, D&T:33a, D&T:35c, D&T:38a, D&T:40b, D&T:40c, D&T:40d, D&T:41d, D&T:43a, D&T:43b, D&T:43c, D&T:43e, D&T:44a, D&T:46c, D&T:50a, D&T:52a, D&T:56d, D&T:57c, D&T:59c, D&T:59d, D&T:60c, D&T:62c, D&T:65b, D&T:69d, D&T:72c, D&T:76a, D&T:76d, D&T:80a, D&T:80d, D&T:83b, D&T:83c, D&T:84a, D&T:86a, D&T:90a, D&T:92a, D&T:94d, D&T:96a, D&T:96b, D&T:100a, D&T:105d, D&T:107d, D&T:109b, D&T:110a, D&T:112a, D&T:113a, D&T:114a, D&T:115b, D&T:116d, D&T:117a, D&T:121c, D&T:121d, D&T:123b, D&T:124c, D&T:126b, D&T:128b, D&T:131d, D&T:133a, D&T:133b, D&T:139a, D&T:144c, D&T:145a, D&T:146b, D&T:148c, D&T:150c, D&T:151a, D&T:152a, D&T:152c, D&T:152d, D&T:153a, D&T:154a, D&T:155a, D&T:155d, D&T:157c, D&T:158a, D&T:158b, D&T:160a, D&T:162b

Ginger Ale and Ginger Beer

65a, 66b, 70b, 77b, 79d, 81b, 98a, 117a, 127d, 140c, 150b, 169c, 172c, 177a, 194a, 196b, 204b, 215a, 232b, 247e, 255c, 262b, 269d, 276d, 281a, 287b, 289d D&T:29a, D&T:55a, D&T:62c, D&T:62d, D&T:73c, D&T:93a, D&T:106a, D&T:106b, D&T:107c, D&T:121b, D&T:123b, D&T:126d, D&T:155c

Gran Classico (See Amaro)

Grand Marnier (See Curaçao)

Grappa
93b, 212a, 212c, 234d
D&T:28a, D&T:30b, D&T:77a,
D&T:92c, D&T:102d

Herbsaint (See Absinthe)

Kümmel
66d, 76b, 83a, 98d, 102b, 125d,
131b, 176c, 205b, 207c, 284c
D&T:85c

Lillet (See Aromatized Wine)

Madeira
97d, 122b, 170c, 171a, 195b,
197d, 210a, 218c, 226a, 239c,
243a, 250d, 273d, 275b, 285d,
298d
D&T:33c, D&T:57e, D&T:116c,
D&T:160c

Maraschino
69d, 72b, 80a, 80c, 88b, 101c,
102b, 105d, 108c, 114c, 114d,
116c, 122d, 126a, 128c, 129a,
134b, 138b, 150a, 164a, 164c,
172d, 173b, 183b, 194b, 196a,
226a, 229b, 230a, 233c, 235a,
236c, 244c, 244d, 247a, 248b,
258b, 259a, 266a, 269c, 275b,
279e, 284d, 285d, 287d, 288d,
295a
D&T:26b, D&T:36a, D&T:46b,
D&T:51a, D&T:56d, D&T:64c,
D&T:65d, D&T:78d, D&T:80a,
D&T:80c, D&T:81c, D&T:83a,
D&T:86b, D&T:91c, D&T:96a,
D&T:101b, D&T:102e, D&T:104b,
D&T:104c, D&T:111a, D&T:115b,
D&T:117b, D&T:118a, D&T:121b.
D&T:131a, D&T:145d, D&T:148b,
D&T:152a, D&T:161a, D&T:162b,
D&T:163c, D&T:164c, D&T:165a,
D&T:166d

Mezcal
63c, 64a, 64b, 64d, 68b, 68d, 69b,
70a, 75b, 78b, 80c, 81c, 82d, 83a,
90c, 91a, 104b, 104d, 106d, 110a,
112b, 116d, 124d, 127d, 128b,
129c, 133d, 137c, 141a, 142a,
144c, 145b, 151b, 152c, 153b,
153c, 160a, 163b, 176a, 176c,
178e, 182b, 185c, 191d, 193d,
197a, 198c, 203a, 204b, 209b,
209c, 214a, 215b, 223a, 223b,
223c, 223d, 224a, 228a, 228e,
229c, 229d, 232a, 232c, 236c,
237c, 240b, 240d, 245a, 248a,
253a, 253c, 255b, 258c, 258c,
259a, 259b, 263c, 264d, 265d,
266b, 266d, 269c, 269d, 274d,
277c, 281a, 284a, 286a, 288b,
288d, 293d, 297d, 298c, 299a
D&T:23c, D&T:25c, D&T:26b,
D&T:28c, D&T:29a, D&T:38c,
D&T:49b, D&T:49d, D&T:54d,
D&T:60a, D&T:64a, D&T:64c,
D&T:70b, D&T:75c, D&T:80c,
D&T:83d, D&T:88b, D&T:95a,
D&T:101d, D&T:106b, D&T:108d,
D&T:112c, D&T:115c, D&T:120b,
D&T:123d, D&T:134b, D&T:145d,
D&T:153b, D&T:157a, D&T:159b,
D&T:161c, D&T:161d, D&T:163b,
D&T:166a, D&T:168d, D&T:169a

Orange Liqueur (See Curaçao)

Pastis (See Absinthe)

Legend:
- *123c* = Page 123, 3rd drink down
- *D&T:77b* = Drink & Tell (2012),
  Page 77, 2nd drink down

Pear Brandy or Liqueur
137a, 139a, 149c, 164b, 167b,
172b, 173b, 197c, 206b, 266d
D&T:43e, D&T:75c, D&T:117a

Pimm's
79d, 87a, 126a, 127c, 133c, 142b,
145c, 169c, 188b, 196b, 199b,
234e, 236d, 246a, 257c, 274e,
289d
D&T:25a, D&T:36d, D&T:62c,
D&T:88a, D&T:88d, D&T:93c,
D&T:118d, D&T:124b, D&T:130b,
D&T:137a, D&T:138a, D&T:152b,
D&T:157c

Pineau des Chartentes
92a, 103d, 111d, 138c, 139a, 155a,
188a, 206b, 236a
D&T:120b

Pisco
64d, 71c, 71d, 133b, 153a, 179b,
185c, 192a, 196d, 208b, 215a,
225b, 234b, 237a, 258e, 271d,
293c, 295a
D&T:26a, D&T:30b, D&T:42a,
D&T:51a, D&T:52c, D&T:68b,
D&T:97a, D&T:106a

Port
63e, 103b, 249b, 296c
D&T:23b, D&T:25a, D&T:28d,
D&T:33b, D&T:42a, D&T:48d,
D&T:75b, D&T:117d, D&T:155b

Punt e Mes (See Vermouth)

R(h)um
65a, 65b, 65c, 67a, 69d, 70b, 71a,
72c, 74a, 74b, 74c, 76d, 77a, 77b,
79a, 79b, 81a, 81b, 84a, 84b, 85a,
85b, 87b, 87e, 89c, 89d, 91b, 92c,
94a, 94b, 95a, 95c, 96b, 97b, 97d,
100c, 101a, 102a, 103c, 104c,
109b, 109d, 115b, 116a, 116b,
117c, 118a, 119d, 120a, 121a,
121c, 122a, 122d, 123a, 123b,
124a, 125b, 125d, 130a, 130d,
132b, 135b, 138a, 138b, 138c,
140c, 140d, 141a, 141d, 143d,
144a, 144b, 144d, 147a, 147b,
148a, 148b, 149a, 150b, 152a,
152d, 153c, 154b, 154c, 156c,
156d, 157c, 157d, 160c, 160d,
162a, 164a, 164c, 165c, 166a,
167b, 167d, 168b, 170a, 171a,
173a, 175a, 177c, 178d, 180b,
180c, 180d, 182a, 183c, 183d,
184a, 185a, 186d, 188b, 188c,
190a, 191b, 192b, 192c, 193b,
194a, 194c, 196a, 196b, 197d,
199a, 200a, 200d, 201d, 202a,
202b, 202d, 204a, 204c, 205a,
206a, 207b, 207c, 207d, 210c,
213a, 215d, 216b, 217a, 217b,
217c, 219a, 220a, 220b, 225a,
225e, 226b, 226c, 229a, 231a,
231c, 232b, 232d, 236b, 236d,
237a, 239c, 241c, 242a, 244a,
244b, 244d, 245d, 246b, 249a,
249c, 249d, 250a, 250b, 250c,
251a, 254a, 255c, 255d, 256b,
257c, 258b, 261b, 261c, 262a,
263b, 264a, 266a, 267b, 268a,
269b, 271b, 271c, 273b, 275b,
276a, 276c, 276d, 277a, 277b,
278a, 279b, 279c, 280d, 282b,
282c, 282d, 283a, 285a, 287c,
287d, 289b, 289d, 290a, 290b,
290c, 292a, 294b, 295a, 296a,
297a, 331a
D&T:23a, D&T:27a, D&T:27b,
D&T:36b, D&T:36c, D&T:37b,
D&T:38d, D&T:39a, D&T:39b,
D&T:40a, D&T:41c, D&T:42b,
D&T:44b, D&T:45a, D&T:45d,
D&T:47b, D&T:48a, D&T:49b,
D&T:53a, D&T:53d, D&T:60b,

D&T:62b, D&T:63b, D&T:64a,
D&T:64b, D&T:65a, D&T:67a,
D&T:71b, D&T:72a, D&T:73d,
D&T:74a, D&T:74b, D&T:78c,
D&T:78d, D&T:79a, D&T:80b,
D&T:82b, D&T:84b, D&T:84c,
D&T:85a, D&T:86b, D&T:86d,
D&T:87a, D&T:87b, D&T:89d,
D&T:91a, D&T:91b, D&T:93b,
D&T:94b, D&T:94d, D&T:96c,
D&T:96d, D&T:99a, D&T:99d,
D&T:104c, D&T:105c, D&T:107b,
D&T:107c, D&T:108a, D&T:109d,
D&T:113b, D&T:116b, D&T:117b,
D&T:120d, D&T:122b, D&T:123b,
D&T:123c, D&T:125a, D&T:126a,
D&T:127a, D&T:128c, D&T:129b,
D&T:132c, D&T:132d, D&T:134a,
D&T:135a, D&T:135b, D&T:136b,
D&T:136c, D&T:136d, D&T:137c,
D&T:137d, D&T:140a, D&T:141c,
D&T:144a, D&T:144b, D&T:145b,
D&T:145c, D&T:147c, D&T:147d,
D&T:150b, D&T:156c, D&T:158c,
D&T:160b, D&T:164a, D&T:164c,
D&T:164d, D&T:166a, D&T:166c,
D&T:167a

Rye (See Whiskey)

Salers (See Gentian Liqueur)

Scotch (See Whiskey)

Sherry
63a, 65b, 65d, 68d, 69a, 73c, 77d,
79a, 79b, 79c, 82a, 83a, 85d, 88a,
90b, 90c, 92b, 93c, 94a, 94b, 97c,
98b, 98d, 100e, 104b, 104d, 105b,
106a, 106d, 108a, 108d, 109c,
110a, 112b, 114c, 118b, 121a,
122d, 123b, 126a, 126b, 128c,
130b, 134b, 136a, 136b, 137a,
137b, 137c, 141b, 141d, 145b,
148c, 152d, 153a, 154a, 154b,
154d, 158c, 161a, 164a, 172b,
172d, 174b, 177a, 183a, 185b,
185d, 191b, 192c, 192d, 193a,
194a, 195a, 197a, 199b, 200b,
200d, 201d, 202d, 203b, 208c,
209b, 209c, 210d, 214a, 216d,
218b, 221a, 221d, 224a, 224d,
225a, 226c, 227b, 228d, 229a,
229b, 229c, 232c, 233e, 236c,
238b, 242c, 244a, 245a, 247c,
248c, 249d, 251a, 252a, 252c,
252d, 254b, 258a, 258c, 258c,
260c, 260d, 261a, 261b, 263a,
263c, 263d, 265a, 266b, 267b,
270b, 271a, 271b, 277a, 278b,
279a, 282d, 284d, 285a, 285b,
285c, 286a, 288c, 290d, 291b,
292c, 295c, 296b, 297a, 297d
D&T:24b, D&T:24c, D&T:31a,
D&T:33a, D&T:33d, D&T:35b,
D&T:35d, D&T:36a, D&T:41b,
D&T:45a, D&T:47b, D&T:55a,
D&T:64a, D&T:65d, D&T:66a,
D&T:67a, D&T:67b, D&T:67d,
D&T:72d, D&T:75b, D&T:77a,
D&T:78b, D&T:81d, D&T:88b,
D&T:93c, D&T:94c, D&T:97a,
D&T:115c, D&T:121b, D&T:123d,
D&T:128c, D&T:132c, D&T:132d,
D&T:133d, D&T:146a, D&T:148d,
D&T:149a, D&T:155a, D&T:155d,
D&T:157a, D&T:161d, D&T:164a

Sloe Gin (and Damson Gin)
95d, 173c, 231d, 240d, 265c
D&T:44a, D&T:54a, D&T:80c,
D&T:96a, D&T:108c, D&T:133b,
D&T:137d, D&T:144c, D&T:150a,
D&T:156a

Soda Water, Tonic, and Soda
69d, 73d, 78b, 85b, 86a, 89d, 103c,
104b, 111c, 112b, 113d, 119a,
128a, 128d, 134a, 139b, 149b,
157a, 159b, 161a, 165a, 167a,
176e, 180b, 186c, 193b, 212a,
216a, 228e, 231d, 239d, 242d,
246a, 247d, 250a, 252b, 255d,
272b, 272e, 273b, 273c, 275a,
278a, 281b, 281c, 284b, 290d,
293b
D&T:29b, D&T:38d, D&T:49d,
D&T:53b, D&T:59b, D&T:60c,
D&T:79b, D&T:80b, D&T:80c,
D&T:83b, D&T:84c, D&T:91b,
D&T:98b, D&T:99a, D&T:99d,
D&T:105b, D&T:113a, D&T:116a,
D&T:127a, D&T:150c, D&T:154a,
D&T:156c, D&T:164d

St. Germain (and St. Elder)
64d, 112c, 119c, 121d, 124b, 125d,
150a, 166b, 169c, 170d, 186a,
199d, 202b, 211a, 215b, 215d,
218a, 218c, 235b, 236d, 240c,
246b, 248a, 268d, 273c, 279d,
279e, 287b, 290c
D&T:24d, D&T:29a, D&T:29c,
D&T:30d, D&T:36d, D&T:43b,
D&T:45c, D&T:52a, D&T:54d,
D&T:55b, D&T:58a, D&T:64b,
D&T:68c, D&T:69b, D&T:69c,
D&T:70a, D&T:80d, D&T:84a,
D&T:86d, D&T:89a, D&T:90b,
D&T:101b, D&T:105a, D&T:108d,
D&T:110a, D&T:112a, D&T:118b,
D&T:119b, D&T:120a, D&T:121a,
D&T:124a, D&T:133a, D&T:133c,
D&T:139c, D&T:141b, D&T:143b,
D&T:147a, D&T:147b, D&T:149b,
D&T:150c, D&T:161b, D&T:168a

Suze (See Gentian Liqueur)

Swedish Punsch
82a, 90c, 98b, 99b, 102a, 107a,
127c, 138d, 185a, 223c, 239b,
274d, 280c
D&T:43a, D&T:112c, D&T:113b,
D&T:132a, D&T:151a, D&T:156a

Sweet Vermouth (See Vermouth)

Tequila
97a, 98a, 103b, 106b, 106c, 107a,
108b, 108d, 112a, 122e, 128d,
130c, 132d, 136b, 136c, 138d,
158c, 159d, 163b, 164d, 167c,
168a, 172d, 184c, 188a, 188d,
192d, 194d, 197a, 198c, 206b,
208a, 213b, 215b, 223b, 227a,
228d, 229b, 233a, 234d, 240d,
242b, 253c, 255a, 259b, 263d,
264d, 268b, 270b, 274d, 285e,
286b, 290b, 292c, 293b
D&T:23d, D&T:25d, D&T:26b,
D&T:28d, D&T:29b, D&T:32a,
D&T:46d, D&T:50b, D&T:53c,
D&T:54d, D&T:55b, D&T:58a,
D&T:68a, D&T:69a, D&T:69b,
D&T:81b, D&T:82a, D&T:84d,
D&T:92d, D&T:93a, D&T:94a,
D&T:101b, D&T:102c, D&T:105a,
D&T:107a, D&T:108b, D&T:109a,
D&T:110b, D&T:112c, D&T:116a,
D&T:120a, D&T:122b, D&T:124d,
D&T:130a, D&T:142b, D&T:143b,
D&T:146a, D&T:147b, D&T:153c,
D&T:155b, D&T:156a, D&T:168d

Triple Sec (see Curaçao)

Vermouth (Amber)
D&T:49a

Vermouth (Blanc)
64d, 69a, 72a, 73a, 76a, 91a, 109c,
110b, 144b, 146b, 148a, 157b,

167c, 205d, 241b, 252b, 258a, 276c, 279d
D&T:28a, D&T:68a, D&T:78a, D&T:86a, D&T:104d, D&T:110b, D&T:164a, D&T:164c, D&T:165b

Vermouth (Dry)
71d, 80a, 90a, 101b, 103b, 105c, 116a, 121b, 125a, 135a, 138a, 148a, 149d, 159a, 163b, 181b, 182a, 184b, 196a, 201c, 204d, 212b, 216a, 216b, 220d, 225d, 233e, 234d, 236a, 245d, 247a, 247e, 251a, 251b, 252b, 265c, 269b, 271d, 275a, 276c, 284d, 292b, 298d
D&T:30a, D&T:30d, D&T:36a, D&T:45c, D&T:48c, D&T:52c, D&T:57c, D&T:59c, D&T:63b, D&T:64d, D&T:72c, D&T:82a, D&T:83c, D&T:85c, D&T:89a, D&T:100a, D&T:104b, D&T:104d, D&T:108c, D&T:112a, D&T:115b, D&T:125c, D&T:125d, D&T:126c, D&T:128b, D&T:131c, D&T:132a, D&T:133d, D&T:137a, D&T:148c, D&T:152c, D&T:165a, D&T:169a

Vermouth (Punt e Mes)
65b, 65c, 71b, 74d, 88b, 92b, 93d, 99b, 100c, 101c, 105d, 106c, 108a, 113a, 118a, 124b, 126b, 128a, 129b, 129d, 130c, 141d, 154a, 154c, 162d, 166b, 173d, 174b, 175b, 176d, 177b, 181d, 199a, 200a, 202d, 203a, 212b, 216c, 228b, 233d, 237d, 238b, 241a, 242b, 245b, 247c, 252a, 256b, 258a, 260b, 266b, 269c, 282b, 287c, 288d, 290a, 296d, 297c, 298b
D&T:25b, D&T:26b, D&T:27a, D&T:41a, D&T:43c, D&T:45d, D&T:46b, D&T:47a, D&T:52b, D&T:54d, D&T:57a, D&T:57d,

D&T:58b, D&T:64a, D&T:76c, D&T:77d, D&T:80a, D&T:83a, D&T:89d, D&T:96c, D&T:104b, D&T:108d, D&T:109c, D&T:115e, D&T:118c, D&T:124c, D&T:131a, D&T:132bm D&T:134d, D&T:138a, D&T:140b, D&T:144d, D&T:150b, D&T:166b

Vermouth (Rosé)
291b
D&T:32a, D&T:117c, D&T:162a

Vermouth (Sweet)
64b, 66d, 71a, 74b, 80d, 82d, 84d, 85c, 87e, 88d, 91c, 93b, 93d, 102b, 108a, 109b, 114b, 119a, 119b, 120c, 122e, 124c, 125c, 126a, 126b, 127a, 129c, 130d, 134a, 135a, 136a, 137c, 140a, 148c, 160d, 161b, 161e, 168b, 170d, 174b, 178c, 183b, 187b, 191c, 192a, 194b, 194c, 194d, 196c, 198a, 201d, 207d, 209d, 210b, 210c, 211b, 221d, 226d, 228a, 233e, 234b, 234c, 239d, 241c, 241d, 242d, 244a, 244d, 248d, 253d, 258d, 260a, 264b, 264c, 272b, 280a, 281b, 287a, 288a, 292b, 295d, 301a
D&T:25b, D&T:25d, D&T:30b, D&T:30c, D&T:34a, D&T:37c, D&T:44d, D&T:56d, D&T:67a, D&T:68b, D&T:69c, D&T:81c, D&T:84d, D&T:88c, D&T:92b, D&T:98a, D&T:99c, D&T:105a, D&T:110d, D&T:111a, D&T:125c D&T:125d, D&T:131b, D&T:134b, D&T:137b, D&T:147d, D&T:148b,

D&T:149c, D&T:155c, D&T:157b,
D&T:158c, D&T:159a, D&T:163b,
D&T:163c

Vodka
82c, 115a, 119c, 137d, 213c, 256a
D&T:63a, D&T:123a, D&T:124a

Walnut Liqueur
79c, 120c, 138c, 140a, 169a, 176a,
183a, 193a, 217d, 233d, 241c,
245c, 254b, 256c, 260a, 296d,
297c
D&T:41b, D&T:72d, D&T:77b,
D&T:96c, D&T:141a

Whisk(e)y (Bourbon)
66d, 80b, 85c, 85d, 89b, 92b, 94b,
95a, 98d, 99b, 105c, 114d, 124b,
133c, 136d, 139b, 146a, 151d,
153d, 157b, 161b, 161c, 161e,
165b, 169a, 169c, 170d, 172c,
174c, 175b, 180a, 181a, 183c,
186b, 196c, 196e, 205b, 205c,
207a, 209a, 210d, 220c, 221b,
221c, 222a, 225a, 225c, 228c,
229d, 230a, 248b, 253d, 257b,
260a, 265b, 269b, 272d, 287a,
288c, 289c
D&T:23c, D&T:24c, D&T:35b,
D&T:39b, D&T:44c, D&T:44d,
D&T:45a, D&T:45b, D&T:67c,
D&T:68d, D&T:70c, D&T:72d,
D&T:77c, D&T:89b, D&T:97d,
D&T:98a, D&T:98b, D&T:101c,
D&T:103b, D&T:107b, D&T:115e,
D&T:118b, D&T:131c, D&T:156b,
D&T:160d, D&T:161a, D&T:164b

Whisk(e)y (Rye)
63a, 69c, 73c, 74d, 80a, 80c, 83b,
84d, 87a, 95b, 96c, 100a, 101c,
106e, 110b, 111d, 117d, 129a,
130b, 133b, 138c, 141c, 142b,
149b, 151a, 151c, 156d, 159c,

161d, 162c, 166b, 177b, 181c,
181d, 186c, 187a, 187b, 192b,
194b, 198a, 198b, 204d, 209b,
209d, 226b, 227b, 230b, 233c,
233d, 234a, 238b, 240c, 241d,
243b, 244d, 245c, 247b, 250d,
256c, 257a, 262b, 265c, 268d,
272a, 273a, 282d, 285b, 290d,
291a, 295c, 297c, 301b
D&T:23b, D&T:24a, D&T:25b,
D&T:27a, D&T:28b, D&T:46a,
D&T:46b, D&T:47a, D&T:48d,
D&T:49a, D&T:51b, D&T:56a,
D&T:57a, D&T:57d, D&T:57e,
D&T:59b, D&T:61d, D&T:62b,
D&T:71a, D&T:77d, D&T:81a,
D&T:85b, D&T:85c, D&T:85d,
D&T:86c, D&T:88a, D&T:88c,
D&T:89a, D&T:97c, D&T:103a,
D&T:104b, D&T:118c, D&T:122a,
D&T:125b, D&T:125d, D&T:126d,
D&T:131a, D&T:131b, D&T:132a,
D&T:133c, D&T:137a, D&T:142a,
D&T:142d, D&T:149a, D&T:157b,
D&T:161b, D&T:163a, D&T:163c,
D&T:165d, D&T:167a, D&T:168c

Whisk(e)y (Scotch)
63b, 63e, 64c, 66c, 67b, 68a, 76c,
85a, 87c, 88a, 94b, 96a, 97c, 98b,
105d, 111b, 117e, 120c, 122e,
140a, 145a, 154a, 156b, 165d,
173d, 178a, 183a, 186c, 212b,
215c, 217d, 220d, 231c, 233b,
235a, 238a, 247a, 249b, 260b,
263e, 266c, 267a, 279b, 283b,
296b, 299b
D&T:30d, D&T:31b, D&T:32b,
D&T:35a, D&T:41c, D&T:43c,
D&T:48b, D&T:49b, D&T:54b,
D&T:58b, D&T:61b, D&T:61c,
D&T:62a, D&T:66a, D&T:70a,
D&T:78d, D&T:83a, D&T:92b,
D&T:97b, D&T:110d, D&T:115d,
D&T:119b, D&T:121b, D&T:140b,

D&T:140c, D&T:140d, D&T:141a, D&T:144d, D&T:147c, D&T:148b, D&T:150a, D&T:160b, D&T:166a

Whisk(e)y (Other)
72a, 83c, 90a, 96a, 103a, 113a, 121d, 134a, 146b, 176b, 185b, 190b, 247c, 258d, 293a
D&T:65c, D&T:81c, D&T:81d, D&T:91b, D&T:91c, D&T:100b, D&T:117c, D&T:119a, D&T:137b, D&T:143a, D&T:158d, D&T:160c

Wine (Red, White, Rosé)
72b, 75a, 103a, 119b
D&T:30c

Wine (Sparkling)
68b, 69a, 77a, 77c, 116b, 117b, 135d, 145a, 157c, 158a, 159d, 162a, 168a, 182b, 186b, 193c, 201a, 222b, 234e, 235b, 248e, 258e, 268c, 274a, 290c, 293c
D&T:32d, D&T:33c, D&T:38b, D&T:48b, D&T:49c, D&T:51c, D&T:61c, D&T:71a, D&T:75a, D&T:76d, D&T:99b, D&T:99c, D&T:100c, D&T:104d, D&T:116d, D&T:120a, D&T:121a, D&T:129a, D&T:134d, D&T:139d, D&T:144c, D&T:148a, D&T:162a, D&T:164b, D&T:168a

Zucca (See Amaro)

Index by Establishment:

Legend:
- *123c* = Page 123, 3rd drink down
- *D&T:77b* = Drink & Tell (2012), Page 77, 2nd drink down

223c, 228b, 229b, 266b, 272c, 282d, 285c, 288d, 290b
D&T:23a, D&T:37b, D&T:47a, D&T:61b, D&T:62b, D&T:74a, D&T:81c, D&T:102b, D&T:116d, D&T:133d, D&T:140a, D&T:148b, D&T:148d, D&T:155c, D&T:161d, D&T:163c

Citizen Restaurant (Worcester)
139b
D&T:41a, D&T:83c, D&T:113b, D&T:156a

Clio
95d, 121b, 194d, 244a
D&T:24d, D&T:67a, D&T:79a, D&T:94c, D&T:96d, D&T:102a, D&T:103a, D&T:110c, D&T:138a, D&T:142d, D&T:153d, D&T:157b, D&T:160a, D&T:167a

Coppa
D&T:35d , D&T:57b, D&T:109c,

Craigie on Main
73b, 82b, 87a, 96b, 130b, 130d, 133a, 135d, 146a, 154a, 158c, 206b, 209a, 231b, 232a, 256b, 263e, 277b, 290c
D&T:25b, D&T:25d, D&T:29b, D&T:30c, D&T:39b, D&T:45d, D&T:47b, D&T:49a, D&T:49b, D&T:51c, D&T:64a, D&T:64c, D&T:71a, D&T:75a, D&T:76c, D&T:83a, D&T:88d, D&T:93c, D&T:94a, D&T:96b, D&T:96c, D&T:97a, D&T:102e, D&T:105a, D&T:106b, D&T:107d, D&T:115b, D&T:115c, D&T:119b, D&T:125c, D&T:128a, D&T:129a, D&T:129c, D&T:137d, D&T:155d, D&T:166a, D&T:168c

Dante

D&T:30d

Deep Ellum
86a, 88d, 93d, 95a, 97b, 148a, 163b, 194c, 198c, 223a, 223d, 237b, 263a, 292b, 294b, 296b
D&T:43a, D&T:45b, D&T:51b, D&T:64d, D&T:73c, D&T:78d, D&T:80d, D&T:88c, D&T:89b, D&T:105b, D&T:108c, D&T:109a, D&T:110d, D&T:111a, D&T:112c, D&T:125b, D&T:138b, D&T:139b, D&T:144c, D&T:157c, D&T:159a, D&T:163b, D&T:164c, D&T:165b

Drink
112a, 116d, 122c, 144d, 147a, 148b, 165c, 181c, 187a, 191a, 199c, 200c, 225d, 240c, 245d, 248b, 248c, 253b, 258a, 260d, 296a
D&T:25c, D&T:26b, D&T:27a, D&T:27b, D&T:29a, D&T:30a, D&T:33a, D&T:38a, D&T:38c, D&T:46b, D&T:49d, D&T:53b, D&T:59b, D&T:60c, D&T:61a, D&T:62a, D&T:62d, D&T:65a, D&T:65d, D&T:66a, D&T:68a, D&T:70a, D&T:70b, D&T:70c, D&T:72c, D&T:77d, D&T:78a, D&T:81d, D&T:85c, D&T:86b, D&T:86c, D&T:86d, D&T:89a, D&T:89d, D&T:90a, D&T:91b, D&T:91c, D&T:93b, D&T:95a, D&T:97c, D&T:100d, D&T:104c, D&T:105c, D&T:112a, D&T:112d, D&T:114a, D&T:117b, D&T:123c, D&T:123d, D&T:129b, D&T:130a, D&T:132d, D&T:136c, D&T:140d,

Legend:
- *123c* = Page 123, 3rd drink down
- *D&T:77b* = Drink & Tell (2012), Page 77, 2nd drink down

355

D&T:35a, D&T:40a, D&T:43b,
D&T:48d, D&T:49c, D&T:54b,
D&T:54c, D&T:56a, D&T:61d,
D&T:64b, D&T:71b, D&T:77e,
D&T:92a, D&T:94d, D&T:100c,
D&T:101b, D&T:106b, D&T:108a,
D&T:108d, D&T:124a, D&T:125b,
D&T:126d, D&T:133a, D&T:144a,
D&T:144b, D&T:149b, D&T:166b

Hawthorne
71d, 90d, 95c, 100b, 103b, 110a,
137c, 141c, 142b, 146c, 165d,
189a, 196e, 199d, 207b, 215a,
219b, 220a, 220d, 244b, 250b,
250c, 253b, 286a, 298a
D&T:31a, D&T:52d, D&T:56dm
D&T:65c, D&T:71a, D&T:75b,
D&T:121b, D&T:137c, D&T:148b

Highball Lounge
69d, 80b, 112b, 151b, 152a, 157d,
249a

Highland Kitchen
80d
D&T:28d, D&T:40c, D&T:46a,
D&T:46c, D&T:58a, D&T:134c

Hojoko
97d, 123b

Hungry Mother
63e, 64b
D&T:23b, D&T:23c, D&T:23d,
D&T:24a, D&T:24b, D&T:24c,
D&T:73d

Independent
100c, 132d, 163a, 185c, 242a,
268c, 298b
D&T:28c, D&T:34a, D&T:109b,
D&T:118c, D&T:125d, D&T:155b,
D&T:160c, D&T:166c

Island Creek Oyster Bar
87b, 159b, 230b, 236d, 270b, 296c
D&T:25a, D&T:99b, D&T:99c,
D&T:145a, D&T:146a, D&T:148a,
D&T:165d

J.M. Curley
87d, 92d, 164d, 174c, 175c, 180a
D&T:158d

Kirkland Tap & Trotter
97a, 114c, 236a, 253d, 256a, 256c,
258b, 265a, 266c, 272e, 276a,
279c

La Brasa
147b

Lincoln
81c

Lineage
121d, 142b, 160c, 184b
D&T:32b, D&T:35b, D&T:41c,
D&T:48a, D&T:57d, D&T:65b,
D&T:67d, D&T:72a, D&T:74b,
D&T:80a, D&T:83b, D&T:106a,
D&T:115a, D&T:116d, D&T:126b,
D&T:133b, D&T:154b, D&T:162b,
D&T:165a

Little Donkey
76d, 238b

Local 149
65d, 72a, 88b, 113a, 140d, 153d,
154b, 202d, 220c, 258d, 268b,
269c, 274a
D&T:97b, D&T:130b

> **Legend:**
> • *123c* = Page 123, 3rd drink down
> • *D&T:77b* = Drink & Tell (2012),
>   Page 77, 2nd drink down

Lone Star Taco Bar
D&T:53c

Loyal Nine
77c, 89c, 102a, 103c, 113d, 118a,
119d, 120d, 124d, 125c, 127e,
128b, 129b, 138d, 149d, 151a,
162c, 164b, 166a, 167c, 169b,
169c, 170c, 171a, 175b, 176e,
185a, 186d, 188a, 191c, 197c,
197d, 205a, 216b, 218c, 224c,
225b, 226a, 234c, 242d, 252b,
261c, 274d, 275a, 275b, 276c,
277c, 280d, 282b, 285d, 289d,
293b, 298d, 331a

Merrill & Co.
82a, 181a, 272b, 285b

Mooo
266d

Myers & Chang
89d, 178c

No. 9 Park
71a, 83b, 84a, 84c, 90a, 90c, 98b,
122b, 125a, 127b, 128d, 133d,
135b, 144b, 151c, 156d, 172a,
175d, 176d, 182b, 183c, 184c,
192d, 193c, 193d, 210c, 226b,
241b, 241d, 250b, 253a, 261b,
263d, 264a, 265c, 271a, 273b,
281c, 284b, 289b
D&T:33b, D&T:56d, D&T:57c,
D&T:59c, D&T:75c, D&T:77b,
D&T:77c, D&T:78c, D&T:90a,
D&T:92b, D&T:98b, D&T:101d,
D&T:107b, D&T:110a, D&T:115d,
D&T:115e, D&T:121b, D&T:122a,
D&T:123a, D&T:124b, D&T:124c,
D&T:139a, D&T:140b, D&T:142b,
D&T:145c, D&T:147d, D&T:150c,
D&T:151b, D&T:164d, D&T:168d

Park Cambridge
81a, 119b, 211a, 282c
D&T:158a

Pomodoro
92a, 98c, 138c, 208b, 238a
D&T:32a, D&T:102d

Puritan & Co.
127a, 285c

Regal Beagle
102b

Rendezvous
95b, 96c, 117b, 129d, 149c, 156b,
193b, 219b, 234d, 239a, 243b
D&T:30a, D&T:33c, D&T:42a,
D&T:43d, D&T:45c, D&T:46d,
D&T:52b, D&T:63b, D&T:66b,
D&T:70d, D&T:95b, D&T:118d,
D&T:132a, D&T:134a, D&T:134d,
D&T:136b, D&T:136d, D&T:153c,
D&T:164b

Rialto
D&T:103a

Ribelle
151b

Russell House Tavern
64c, 70b, 74d, 75b, 104c, 107a,
109a, 111a, 114a, 115a, 128a,
129c, 136b, 137a, 140c, 141a,
145a, 149b, 152b, 159d, 160a,
161d, 161e, 168b, 168c, 170b,
191b, 204d, 205c, 217a, 217c,
217d, 218b, 228c, 235a, 239b,
240a, 244c, 257a, 260a, 264c,
276d, 280a
D&T:36d, D&T:50b, D&T:55b,
D&T:63a, D&T:84b, D&T:96a,
D&T:100b, D&T:104a, D&T:137b,

D&T:140c, D&T:150a, D&T:161b

Saloon
103a, 138a, 234e, 267a

Sarma
67a, 210a, 222b, 241a, 297d

Scholars
96a, 257c, 259a, 273a
D&T:69a

Shojo
181d

Short & Main
183b

Sichuan Garden II (Baldwin Bar and Baldwin & Sons Trading Company)
66b, 67b, 72d, 73d, 77b, 78a, 101a, 105c, 107b, 111c, 117a, 119a, 127d, 141d, 146c, 154c, 155b, 157a, 161b, 162b, 165a, 177b, 178d, 178e, 188c, 189c, 202a, 216a, 217b, 221b, 221d, 226d, 227b, 228a, 237d, 241c, 245c, 247b, 247d, 248d, 249d, 250a, 260c, 265b, 269b, 270a, 271b, 271c, 273c, 279b, 281b, 288b, 288c, 290a, 294a, 296d, 297c

Silvertone
80a, 82d, 165b, 166b, 262b, 293a, 297b
D&T:51d, D&T:141b

Sinclair
98a, 115b, 130c, 201a

Spoke
65b, 68b, 75a, 85b, 128b, 153a, 186c, 213a, 251a, 258e

State Park
171b, 215b

Steel & Rye
134a, 157c, 182a, 198b, 203b, 206a, 250d, 272a

Stoddard's
71c, 89a, 91b, 99b, 106b, 144a, 173a, 178a, 215c, 216d, 229a, 234a, 262a, 280c
D&T:31b, D&T:40b, D&T:44a, D&T:80b, D&T:84c, D&T:113a, D&T:119a, D&T:125a

Straight Law
69a, 101d, 252a

Sunday Salon
194a, 195a
D&T:37a, D&T:38d, D&T:40d, D&T:52a, D&T:55a, D&T:60b, D&T:109d, D&T:127a, D&T:160b

Sycamore
157b, 287d

Tavern Road
90b, 116c, 122d, 129a, 144c, 224a, 233e, 249b, 249c, 276b
D&T:40b

Temple Bar
80c
D&T:105d, D&T:146b, D&T:161b, D&T:161c

Think Tank
192a

Legend:
- *123c* = Page 123, 3rd drink down
- *D&T:77b* = Drink & Tell (2012), Page 77, 2nd drink down